STANDING
ON THE
Promises

STANDING
ON THE
Promises

365 DAILY ASSURANCES
OF GOD'S LOVE, CARE, AND GUIDANCE

Our Daily Bread
Publishing™

Standing on the Promises: 365 Daily Assurances of God's Love, Care, and Guidance
© 2021 by Our Daily Bread Ministries

The devotional readings collected in this book were first published over a span of years in the *Our Daily Bread* devotional booklets that are distributed around the world in more than fifty languages.

Requests for permission to quote from this book should be directed to: Permissions Department, Our Daily Bread Publishing, PO Box 3566, Grand Rapids, MI 49501, or contact us by email at permissionsdept@odb.org.

Scripture quotations, unless otherwise indicated, are taken from the Holy Bible, New International Version®, NIV®. Copyright © 1973, 1978, 1984, 2011 by Biblica, Inc.™ Used by permission of Zondervan. All rights reserved worldwide. www.zondervan.com.

Scripture quotations marked ESV are taken from the ESV® Bible (The Holy Bible, English Standard Version®), copyright © 2001 by Crossway, a publishing ministry of Good News Publishers. Used by permission. All rights reserved.

Scripture quotations marked KJV are taken from the Authorized Version, or King James Version, of the Bible.

Scripture quotations marked NASB are from the New American Standard Bible®, copyright © 1960, 1971, 1977, 1995, 2020 by The Lockman Foundation. Used by permission. All rights reserved. www.Lockman.org.

Scripture quotations marked NKJV are from the New King James Version®. Copyright © 1982 by Thomas Nelson. Used by permission. All rights reserved.

Scripture quotations marked NLT are taken from the Holy Bible, New Living Translation, copyright © 1996, 2004, 2015 by Tyndale House Foundation. Used by permission of Tyndale House Publishers, Inc., Carol Stream, Illinois 60188. All rights reserved.

Scripture quotations marked PHILLIPS are from The New Testament in Modern English, copyright © 1958, 1959, 1960 J. B. Phillips and 1947, 1952, 1955, 1957 The Macmillan Company, New York. Used by permission. All rights reserved.

Any use of italic in Bible quotations has been added by Our Daily Bread Publishing.

ISBN: 978-1-64070-103-8

Library of Congress Cataloging-in-Publication Data Available

Printed in China
22 23 24 25 26 27 28 / 8 7 6 5 4 3 2

INTRODUCTION

Her hands trembling and her face aglow, she clutched the piece of paper with both hands as she looked lovingly into his eyes. Among the words she softly spoke to him were these: "I promise to love you under all circumstances, the good times and the hard times—whatever it may be—for the rest of my days."

A sacred promise made as the two exchanged their marriage vows.

It was a privilege to be standing so close to the young couple as I presided over their wedding. I could see the genuineness of their promises to each other in their eyes and tender smiles.

But there was One who was far closer to them than me, Someone who was truly *with* these two believers in Jesus—God. He alone is the Perfect One who can be counted on to keep all His promises like this treasured one: "Never will I leave you; never will I forsake you" (Hebrews 13:5).

In my own marriage of nearly forty years, my bride and I have strived to cling to that promise and many others. Our marriage verses are Proverbs 3:5–6, which includes this promise about God: "In all your ways submit to him, and he will make your paths straight."

Unlike us, who sometimes break even the most solemn of vows, God alone can be counted on to always keep His promises. In His perfect, uncompromising character and love, He can't go back on a promise He's made. We can trust Him with all our hearts.

In *Standing on the Promises*, Dave Branon has compiled *Our Daily Bread* devotional articles from classic and contemporary authors, offering you a treasury of promises made by the One who stands close to you. May you find encouragement and refreshment as you ponder each promise God has made to you.

TOM FELTEN
Executive Editor
Our Daily Bread

God Promises

A Harvest—in His Timing

PLANTING TIME
GALATIANS 6:6–10

Do not be deceived: God cannot be mocked.
A man reaps what he sows.

Galatians 6:7

Somewhere in the world right now a farmer is dropping seeds into the ground. Soon those seeds will begin to change the place where they were planted. The carefully prepared soil that appears barren today will become a field ready for harvest.

In the same way, New Year's resolutions can be seeds to alter the landscape of life for others and ourselves. This prayer of Saint Francis of Assisi is a powerful model of this longing to bring positive change in a hurting world:

Lord, make me an instrument of Your peace. Where there is hatred, let me sow love; where there is injury, pardon; where there is doubt, faith; where there is despair, hope; where there is darkness, light; and where there is sadness, joy.

A farmer who sows wheat is never surprised when wheat grows from the ground where it was planted. That's the universal law of sowing and reaping. Paul used it to illustrate a corresponding spiritual principle: "Do not be deceived: God cannot be mocked. A man reaps what he sows" (Galatians 6:7). Our sinful nature says, "Satisfy yourself," while the Spirit urges us to please God (v. 8).

This day—this year—is planting time. God has promised: "At the proper time we will reap a harvest if we do not give up" (v. 9).

David McCasland

God Promises
To Respond to Us

HE WILL REPLY
PSALM 91

He will call on me, and I will answer him.
Psalm 91:15

I was elated when I came upon the Twitter page of my favorite Korean movie star, so I decided to drop her a note. I crafted the best message I could and waited for a reply. I knew it was unlikely I would receive a response. A celebrity like her would receive an enormous amount of fan mail every day. Still, I hoped she would reply. But I was disappointed.

Thankfully, we know that God will respond to us. He is the "Most High," the "Almighty" (Psalm 91:1). His position is exalted and His power is limitless, yet He is accessible to us. God invites: "Call upon Me, and I will answer" (v. 15 NKJV).

An ancient legend tells of a monarch who hired weavers to make tapestries and garments for him. The king gave the silk and the patterns to the weavers with the strict instructions to seek his aid immediately if they had any difficulties. One young weaver was happy and successful while the others were always experiencing trouble. When the boy was asked why he was so successful, he said, "Didn't you notice how often I called for the king?" They replied, "Yes, but he's very busy, and we thought you were wrong in disturbing him so frequently." The boy answered, "I just took him at his word, and he was always happy to help me!"

Our God is like that king—only so much greater. He is loving and kind enough to care about our smallest concern and faintest whisper.

Poh Fang Chia

God Promises
To Reward Those Who Seek Him

HOW TO KNOW THERE'S A GOD
HEBREWS 11:1–7

*Anyone who comes to him must believe that he exists
and that he rewards those who earnestly seek him.*

Hebrews 11:6

An atheist said to a Quaker, "Have you ever seen God? Have you ever felt God? Have you ever smelled God? And you say you have a God!"

After a long pause, the Quaker replied, "Hast thou ever seen thy brains? Hast thou ever felt thy brains? Hast thou ever smelled thy brains? And thou sayest thou hast brains!"

There are relatively few atheists—people who have seriously thought about life and concluded that there is no God. There are more agnostics—thinking people who say, "I don't know." The vast majority of individuals, however, affirm—at least intellectually—that God exists.

Hebrews 11:6 tells us that recognizing God's existence is the first step to knowing Him personally. Then we must seek Him and believe that He will reward our quest to know Him.

Our search will ultimately lead us to consider Jesus. He declared, "I and the Father are one" (John 10:30). He also said that the person who desires to obey God will recognize that He, Jesus, spoke the truth (7:17).

You or someone you know may be at step one: recognizing that God exists. Remember, the Lord rewards those who earnestly seek to know Him. And a personal relationship with Him comes only through faith in Christ.

Dennis DeHaan

God Promises
To Heal and Mend

GOD IS HERE
LUKE 4:16–21

He heals the brokenhearted and binds up their wounds.

Psalm 147:3

Leslie and her two daughters were about to be evicted from their home. Although Leslie believed that God could help, so far He hadn't given a clue as to how. She wondered, *Where is God?* As she drove to the courthouse, she prayed for God's intervention. Then she heard a song on the radio proclaiming, "God is here! Let the brokenhearted rejoice." Could this be the assurance from God that she was longing to hear?

Inside the courtroom, Leslie stood before the judge, heard his decision, and signed the legal documents. But God still had not given her an answer.

As Leslie was walking to her car, a truck pulled up beside her. "Ma'am," said the driver, "I heard your testimony inside the courtroom, and I believe God wants me to help you." And he did. Gary helped Leslie get in contact with a woman from a local church who was able to work with the parties involved to reverse the process so that she and her girls could stay in their home.

When people ask, "Where is God?" the answer is, "Right here." One way God is at work is through Christians like Gary who are continuing the work Jesus started—healing the brokenhearted and binding up their wounds (Psalm 147:3).

Julie Ackerman Link

God Promises
Fresh Blessings Each Day

NEW EVERY MORNING
LAMENTATIONS 3:19-26

[God's] compassions never fail. They are new every morning.
Lamentations 3:22–23

My brother Paul grew up battling severe epilepsy, and when he entered his teenage years it became even worse. Nighttime became excruciating for him and my parents, as he experienced continuous seizures for often more than six hours at a time. Doctors couldn't find a treatment that would alleviate the symptoms while also keeping him conscious for at least part of the day. My parents cried out in prayer: "God, oh God, help us!"

Although their emotions were battered and their bodies exhausted, Paul and my parents received enough strength from God for each new day. In addition, my parents found comfort in the words of the Bible, including the book of Lamentations. Here Jeremiah voiced his grief over the destruction of Jerusalem by the Babylonians, remembering "the bitterness and the gall" (3:19). Yet Jeremiah didn't lose hope. He called to mind the mercies of God, that His compassions "are new every morning" (v. 23). So too did my parents.

Whatever you're facing, know that God is faithful every morning. He renews our strength day by day and gives us hope. And sometimes, as with my family, He brings relief. After several years, a new medication became available that stopped Paul's continuous nighttime seizures, giving my family restorative sleep and hope for the future.

When our souls are downcast within us (v. 20), may we call to mind the promises of God that His mercies are new every morning.

Amy Boucher Pye

God Promises
To Care for the Oppressed

SETTING PRISONERS FREE
PSALM 146

He upholds the cause of the oppressed and gives food to the hungry.
The LORD sets prisoners free.

Psalm 146:7

When my wife and I visited the National Museum of the Mighty Eighth Air Force near Savannah, Georgia, we were especially moved by the prisoner-of-war exhibit, with its re-creation of a German prisoner-of-war camp's barracks. Marlene's dad, Jim, served in the Eighth Air Force, the "Mighty Eighth," as they flew missions over Europe during World War II. During the war, the Eighth Air Force suffered over 47,000 injuries and more than 26,000 deaths. Jim was one of those shot down and held as a prisoner of war. As we walked through the exhibit, we recalled Jim telling about the absolute joy he and his fellow prisoners felt the day they were set free.

God's care for the oppressed and liberation of the imprisoned is detailed in Psalm 146. The psalmist describes the one who "upholds the cause of the oppressed and gives food to the hungry," who "sets prisoners free" (v. 7). All of this is cause for celebration and praise. But the greatest freedom of all is freedom from our guilt and shame. No wonder Jesus said, "So if the Son sets you free, you will be free indeed" (John 8:36).

Through Christ's sacrifice, we are set free from the prison of sin to know His joy and love and the freedom that only forgiveness can bring.

Bill Crowder

God Promises

To Restore Weary Souls

CAST-DOWN SHEEP
PSALM 23

He restores my soul.
Psalm 23:3 (NKJV)

In his classic book *A Shepherd Looks at Psalm 23*, W. Phillip Keller gives a striking picture of the care and gentleness of a shepherd. In verse 3 when David says, "He restores my soul" (NKJV) he uses language every shepherd would understand.

Sheep are built in such a way that if they fall over on their side and then onto their back, it is very difficult for them to get up again. They flail their legs in the air, bleat, and cry. After a few hours on their backs, gas begins to collect in their stomachs, the stomach hardens, the air passage is cut off, and the sheep will eventually suffocate. This is referred to as a "cast down" position.

When a shepherd restores a cast-down sheep, he reassures it, massages its legs to restore circulation, gently turns the sheep over, lifts it up, and holds it so it can regain its equilibrium.

What a picture of what God wants to do for us! When we are on our backs, flailing because of guilt, grief, or grudges, our loving Shepherd reassures us with His grace, lifts us up, and holds us until we've gained our spiritual equilibrium.

If you've been cast down for any reason, God is the only one who can help you get on your feet again. He will restore your confidence, joy, and strength.

Marvin Williams

God Promises
That Our Troubles Are Temporary

WHAT'S YOUR FOCUS?
2 CORINTHIANS 4:7–18

We fix our eyes not on what is seen, but on what is unseen.

2 Corinthians 4:18

A company that boasted its antiaging cream could "banish" wrinkles was asked to prove it in court. Findings showed that the cream did tighten skin, but only temporarily. The wrinkles were soon obvious again. Millions of people swallow such wild claims because they've believed the myths behind them: that the aging process is unacceptable and that undoing it is possible. The focus is on visible effects—all temporary—which is discouraging for those who trust in them.

In 2 Corinthians 4:16, Paul emphasized that physical decline is inevitable. He said, "Outwardly we are wasting away." But Paul didn't lose heart. Here's why: "Inwardly we are being renewed day by day." Because of this daily inner renewal, our focus doesn't need to be on the visible things, which are temporary, but instead on the invisible things, which are eternal.

When eternity is our primary focus, we are more able to recognize the temporary nature of our troubles. Paul called these "light and momentary" compared to the greater weight of eternal gain and glory they are working for us (v. 17). That's not just another wild claim. It's a promise of God's Word, guaranteed by His power. This we can believe!

Joanie Yoder

God Promises
To Give Us Strength

HANG IN THERE
ISAIAH 41:8–13

I will strengthen you and help you;
I will uphold you with my righteous right hand.
Isaiah 41:10

When my father-in-law turned seventy-eight, we had a family gathering to honor him. Someone asked him, "What's the most important thing you've learned in your life so far?" His answer? "Hang in there."

Hang in there. It might be tempting to dismiss those words as simplistic. But my father-in-law wasn't promoting blind optimism or positive thinking. He's endured tough things in his nearly eight decades. His determination to press on wasn't grounded in some vague hope that things might get better, but in Christ's work in his life.

"Hanging in there"—the Bible calls it "perseverance"—isn't possible through mere willpower. We persevere because God promised, over and over, that He's with us, that He'll give us strength, and that He'll accomplish His purposes in our lives. That's the message He spoke to the Israelites through Isaiah: "So do not fear, for I am with you; do not be dismayed, for I am your God. I will strengthen you and help you; I will uphold you with my righteous right hand" (Isaiah 41:10).

What does it take to "hang in there"? According to Isaiah, the foundation for hope is God's character. Knowing God's goodness allows us to release our grip on fear so we can cling to the Father and His promise that He will provide what we need each day: strength, help, and God's comforting, empowering, and upholding presence.

Adam Holz

God Promises
To Guarantee His Word

NO COSIGNER REQUIRED
HEBREWS 6:13-20

*People swear by someone greater than themselves,
and the oath confirms what is said.*

Hebrews 6:16

When a person without a strong history of paying his or her bills on time wants to obtain a loan to purchase a home or car, lenders are often reluctant to take the financial risk. Without a track record, that person's promise to repay what he borrows is insufficient for the bank. The would-be borrower usually resorts to finding someone who does have a history of making good on their debts, asking that person to put his or her name on the loan too. The cosigner's promise assures the lender the loan will be repaid.

When someone makes a promise to us—whether for financial, marital, or other reasons—we expect him or her to keep it. We also want to know that God will keep His promises. When He promised Abraham that He would bless him and give him "many descendants" (Hebrews 6:14; see Genesis 22:17), Abraham took God at His word. As the Creator of all that exists, there is no one greater than He; only God could guarantee His own promise.

Abraham had to wait for the birth of his son (Hebrews 6:15) (and never saw how innumerable his offspring would grow to be), but God proved faithful to His promise. When He promises to be with us always (13:5), to hold us securely (John 10:29), and to comfort us (2 Corinthians 1:3–4), we too can trust Him to be true to His word.

Kirsten Holmberg

God Promises
To Give Us Wisdom

"THE BEAUTY OF LIFE"
JAMES 3:13–17

If any of you lacks wisdom, you should ask God.

James 1:5

Wisdom is the beauty of holiness. James says wisdom is reasonable; flexible; forgiving; peaceful; caring; given to friendly visits, small acts of courtesy, and kind words. It is humble, transparent, simple, gentle, and gracious to the core (James 3:17).

Where can wisdom be found? It comes from our heavenly Father (1:5). "Wisdom," wrote Charles Spurgeon, "is a beauty of life that can only be produced by God's workmanship in us."

It's good to ask from time to time: "Am I growing in wisdom?" After all, life is relentlessly dynamic. We're either growing sweeter and wiser as the days go by, or we're growing into foolish or even sour-faced curmudgeons. Into what are we growing?

It's never too late to begin growing in wisdom. God loves us with an ardent, intense affection that can deliver us from our foolishness if we yield ourselves to Him. His love can make the most difficult personality into a miracle of astonishing beauty. It may hurt a little and it may take a while, but God relentlessly seeks our transformation. When we ask, His wisdom will begin to rise in us and pour itself out to others.

We have this promise: "If any of you lacks wisdom, you should ask God, who gives generously to all without finding fault, and it will be given to you" (1:5).

David Roper

God Promises
To Work Things Out for His Good

ON PURPOSE
GENESIS 50:15–21

We know that in all things God works for the good of those
who love him, who have been called according to his purpose.

Romans 8:28

When a cowboy applied for an insurance policy, the agent asked, "Have you ever had any accidents?" After a moment's reflection, the applicant responded, "Nope, but a bronc did kick in two of my ribs last summer, and a couple of years ago a rattlesnake bit me on the ankle."

"Wouldn't you call those accidents?" replied the puzzled agent. "Naw," the cowboy said, "they did it on purpose!"

That story reminds me of the biblical truth that there are no accidents in the lives of God's children. In today's Scripture, we read how Joseph interpreted a difficult experience that had seemed like a great calamity. He had been thrown into a pit and then sold as a slave. This was a great test of his faith, and from the human standpoint it appeared to be a tragic case of injustice, not a providential means of blessing. But Joseph later learned that "God intended it for good" (Genesis 50:20).

Are you passing through the deep waters of trial and disappointment? Does everything seem to be going against you? These apparent misfortunes are not accidents. The Lord allows such things for a blessed purpose. So patiently trust Him. If you know the Lord, someday you will praise Him for it all!

Richard DeHaan

God Promises
To Forget Our Sins

TAKING OUT THE TRASH
PSALM 103

*As far as the east is from the west, so far has
[God] removed our transgressions from us.*

Psalm 103:12

My wife usually has to remind me to take out the garbage on trash pick-up days. It's not one of my favorite jobs, but I muster up the determination to get it done and then just do it. Afterward it's a nice feeling to have it out of the house, and I forget about it till the following week.

Just as we need trucks to pick up the garbage that accumulates in our homes, we need to let Jesus remove the "trash" that inevitably accumulates in our hearts. When we forget to take out the trash, it's not a pretty picture. Jesus wants us to dump it regularly at the foot of the cross. In fact, He has promised to remove it and forget it.

But wait a minute! Could we be rummaging through the cans, trying to find that thing we weren't quite ready to part with? A sinful habit we don't want to give up, a fantasy we want to cling to, a revenge that we still want to ignite? Why do we want to hang on to the garbage?

Taking out the trash begins with confession and then counting on Jesus to get rid of it. "If we confess our sins, he is faithful and just and will forgive us our sins and purify us from all unrighteousness" (1 John 1:9).

Today is garbage day. Take it out and then leave it there!

Joe Stowell

God Promises

That We Know the End of the Story

THE GREAT MYSTERY
LUKE 16:19–31

*We are confident, I say, and would prefer to be
away from the body and at home with the Lord.*

2 Corinthians 5:8

Many people love mysteries. It's exciting to put ourselves in the shoes of a detective and try to figure out "whodunit" as we turn the pages of a mystery novel. But there's a cliffhanger that we'll never resolve—until we experience it ourselves.

Those of us who have watched in sadness as someone close to us has died may wonder about their new existence. Our hearts ache to know what they are doing or where they are. If they had trusted Jesus Christ as Savior, we know they are in heaven. But for now a veil separates us from our loved ones, and we cannot see behind it.

We do have a few clues about this mystery, though. We know that our departed loved ones are enjoying God's presence (2 Corinthians 5:8). We also know that they are recognizable and conscious of their surroundings— just like the rich man and the beggar Jesus spoke of in Luke 16:22–23. And we know that they haven't yet received the perfect body that will be theirs when Christ returns (1 Thessalonians 4:13–17).

Beyond that, we are left with this truth: God, in His matchless love and power, is planning a glorious reunion. Then our eternal rejoicing will begin. The last page of this great mystery has a happy ending.

Dave Branon

God Promises

To Blot Out Our Sin

AS WHITE AS SNOW
ISAIAH 1:1–14, 12–18

Though your sins are like scarlet, they shall be as white as snow.

Isaiah 1:18

I was driving my son home from school one day when snow began to fall. The cottony fluff came down steadily and quickly. Eventually, we slowed to a stop, boxed in by traffic. From inside our vehicle, we watched a transformation take place. Dark patches of soil turned white. Snow softened the sharp outlines of buildings; it coated the cars around us and accumulated on every tree in sight.

That snowfall reminded me of a spiritual truth: Just as that snow covered everything in sight, God's grace covers our sin. But grace doesn't just cover sin; grace erases sin. Through the prophet Isaiah, God appealed to the Israelites, saying, "Come now, let us settle the matter. Though your sins are like scarlet, they shall be as white as snow" (Isaiah 1:18). When God made this promise, His children had a painful problem with sin. God compared them to a physical body plagued with "wounds and welts and open sores, not cleansed or bandaged or soothed with olive oil" (v. 6).

As bad as their sin was, God was willing to extend His grace to them. As His children today, we have the same assurance. Sin may stain our lives, but when we repent and confess it, we have "the forgiveness of sins, in accordance with the riches of God's grace" (Ephesians 1:7).

Jennifer Benson Schuldt

God Promises

To Hear Our Cries for Help

ONLY TRUST
1 KINGS 17:8–16

*So there was food every day for Elijah
and for the woman and her family.*

1 Kings 17:15

Three hundred children were dressed and seated for breakfast, and a prayer of thanks was offered for the food. But there was no food! Situations like this were not unusual for orphanage director and missionary George Mueller (1805–1898). Here was yet another opportunity to see how God would provide. Within minutes of Mueller's prayer, a baker who couldn't sleep the night before showed up at the door. Sensing that the orphanage could use the bread, he had made three batches. Not long afterward, the town milkman appeared. His cart had broken down in front of the orphanage. Not wanting the milk to spoil, he offered it to Mueller.

It's normal to experience bouts of worry, anxiety, and self-pity when we lack resources essential to our well-being—food, shelter, health, finances, friendships. First Kings 17:8–16 reminds us that God's help can come through unexpected sources like a needy widow. "I don't have any bread—only a handful of flour in a jar and a little olive oil in a jug" (v. 12). Earlier it was a raven that provided for Elijah (vv. 4–6). Concerns for our needs to be met can send us searching in many directions. A clear vision of God as the Provider who has promised to supply our needs can be liberating. Before we seek solutions, let's be careful to seek Him first. Doing so can save us time, energy, and frustration.

Arthur Jackson

God Promises
To Be There for Us in Heaven

AWAKENED BY A CLOSE FRIEND
JOHN 14:1–7

*I will come back and take you to be with me
that you also may be where I am.*

John 14:3

A few years ago I had some tests to screen for cancer, and I was nervous about the outcome. My anxiety was magnified as I thought about the fact that while the medical personnel were well-trained and extremely competent, they were also strangers who had no relationship with me.

After awakening from the anesthesia, however, I heard the beautiful sound of my wife's voice: "It's great, Honey. They didn't find anything." I looked up at her smiling face and was comforted. I needed the assurance of someone who loved me.

A similar assurance lies ahead for all who have trusted Jesus. Believers can be comforted in knowing that when they wake up in heaven, One who loves them greatly—Jesus—will be there.

The Book of Common Prayer expresses this Christian hope: "After my awakening, [my Redeemer] will raise me up; and in my body I shall see God. I myself shall see, and eyes behold Him who is my friend and not a stranger."

Do you have trouble facing mortality? Jesus promised to be there when we slip from this world into the next. He said, "You also may be where I am [in heaven]" (John 14:3). What a comfort for believers to know that after death we will be awakened by a close Friend.

Dennis Fisher

God Promises
An Abundant Life

COME TO ME
JOHN 6:30–40

I am the bread of life. Whoever comes to me will never go hungry.

John 6:35

When Jesus lived on this earth, He invited people to come to Him, and He still does today (John 6:35). But what do He and His Father in heaven have that we need?

Salvation. Jesus is the only way to have forgiveness of sin and the promise of heaven. "Everyone who believes may have eternal life in him" (John 3:15).

Purpose. We are to give all of our heart, soul, mind, and strength to following Jesus. "Whoever desires to come after Me, let him deny himself, and take up his cross, and follow Me" (Mark 8:34 NKJV).

Comfort. In trial or sorrow, the "God of all comfort . . . comforts us in all our troubles" (2 Corinthians 1:3–4).

Wisdom. We need wisdom beyond our own for making decisions. "If any of you lacks wisdom, you should ask God, . . . and it will be given to you" (James 1:5).

Strength. When we're weary, "the LORD gives strength to his people" (Psalm 29:11).

Abundant life. The fullest life is found in a relationship with Jesus. "I have come that they may have life, and have it to the full" (John 10:10).

Jesus said, "Whoever comes to me I will never drive away" (John 6:37). Come!

Anne Cetas

God Promises
To Carry Our Burdens

PIGS DON'T PRAY
PSALM 68:4–10

*Praise be to the Lord, to God our Savior,
who daily bears our burdens.*

Psalm 68:19

A Christian farmer went to the city on business and stopped at a small restaurant for lunch. When his food was served, he bowed his head and gave God thanks, just as he always did at home. A young fellow at the next table noticed that the farmer was praying. Thinking that he was a little backward and not in touch with "city ways," he asked loudly to embarrass him, "Say, farmer, does everyone do that out in the country where you live?" The earnest Christian turned to him and replied kindly, "No, son, the pigs don't."

The more I observe people, the more I notice that it is the exception rather than the rule to see people bow and give thanks to God in public. We seem to have become a very self-indulgent and ungrateful society.

In Psalm 68, David reviewed the many ways God had cared for His people Israel. After surveying Jehovah's faithfulness, he exclaimed, "Praise be to the Lord, to God our Savior, who daily bears our burdens. Our God is a God who saves!" (vv. 19–20). From a heart overflowing with love for the Lord, David gave thanks often. Should we not respond in like manner for every blessing God has so freely given? Shouldn't we express to Him our gratitude at all times?

Let's remember to say thanks to God for our daily supply of blessings—even in a crowded restaurant. Let's not be like the pigs.

Paul Van Gorder

God Promises
To Grant Wisdom

WHEN LIFE IS TOO BIG
1 KINGS 3:4–14

*LORD my God, you have made your servant king in
place of my father David. But I am only a little child
and do not know how to carry out my duties.*

1 Kings 3:7

As a young man, Jimmy Carter was a junior officer in the US Navy. He was deeply impacted by Admiral Hyman Rickover, the mastermind of the US nuclear submarine fleet.

Shortly after Carter's inauguration as president in 1977, he invited Rickover to the White House for lunch, where the admiral presented Carter with a plaque that read, "O, God, Thy sea is so great, and my boat is so small." That prayer is a useful perspective on the size and complexity of life and our inability to manage it on our own.

Solomon, too, knew that life could be overwhelming. When he succeeded his father, David, as king of Israel, he confessed his weakness to God, saying, "LORD my God, you have made your servant king in place of my father David. But I am only a little child and do not know how to carry out my duties" (1 Kings 3:7). As a result, he asked for the wisdom to lead in a way that would please God and help others (v. 9).

Is life feeling too big for you? There may not be easy answers to the challenges you are facing, but God promises that, if you ask for wisdom, He will grant it (James 1:5). You don't have to face the overwhelming challenges of life alone.

Bill Crowder

God Promises
To Keep Us Always in Mind

ENGRAVED ON HIS HANDS
ISAIAH 49:14–18

See, I have engraved you on the palms of my hands.
Isaiah 49:16

During Charles Spurgeon's many years of preaching at his London church during the 1800s, he loved to speak about the riches of Isaiah 49:16. That verse says God engraves us on the palms of His hands. Spurgeon said, "Such a text as this is to be preached hundreds of times!" This thought is so precious that we can run over it in our minds again and again.

Spurgeon makes the wonderful connection between this promise of the Lord to His people, the Israelites, and God's Son, Jesus, on the cross as He died for us. Spurgeon asked, "What are these wounds in Your hands? . . . The engraver's tool was the nail, backed by the hammer. He must be fastened to the Cross, that His people might be truly engraved on the palms of His hands." As the Lord promised to engrave His people on His palms, so Jesus stretched out His arms on the cross, receiving the nails in His hands so we could be free of our sins.

If and when we're tempted to think that God has forgotten us, we only need to look at our palms and remember God's promise. He has put indelible marks on His hands for us. He loves us that much!

Amy Boucher Pye

God Promises

That His Word Is Eternal

IT'S REMARKABLE!
PSALM 119:89–96

Your word, LORD, is eternal; it stands firm in the heavens.
Psalm 119:89

The discovery of the Dead Sea Scrolls in 1947 has been called the greatest archaeological find of the twentieth century. The ancient manuscripts hidden in the caves near Qumran in Israel are the oldest known copies of key Old Testament books. The San Diego Natural History Museum hosted an exhibition featuring twenty-four of these scrolls. One often-repeated theme in the exhibit was that during the past two thousand years the text of the Hebrew Bible (the Christian Old Testament) has remained virtually unchanged.

Followers of Christ who believe that the Bible is the eternal, unchanging Word of God find more than coincidence in this remarkable preservation. The psalmist wrote: "Your word, LORD, is eternal; it stands firm in the heavens. Your faithfulness continues through all generations" (119:89–90). Jesus said: "My words will never pass away" (Matthew 24:35).

The Bible is more than a historical relic. It is the living, powerful Word of God (Hebrews 4:12), in which we encounter the Lord and discover how to live for Him and honor Him. "I will never forget your precepts," the psalmist concluded, "for by them you have preserved my life" (119:93).

What a privilege we have each day to seek God in His remarkable Word!

David McCasland

God Promises

His Loving Care No Matter What

WHO KNOWS?

ECCLESIASTES 6:12; 7:13–14

When times are good, be happy; but when times are bad, consider this: God has made the one as well as the other.

Ecclesiastes 7:14

According to Chinese legend, when Sai Weng lost one of his prized horses, his neighbor expressed sorrow for his loss. But Sai Weng was unconcerned. He said, "Who knows if it may be a good thing for me?" Surprisingly, one day the lost horse returned home with another horse. As the neighbor congratulated him, Sai Weng said, "Who knows if it may be a bad thing for me?" As it turned out, his son broke his leg when he rode on the new horse. This seemed like a misfortune, until the army arrived at the village to recruit all able-bodied men to fight in the war. Because of the son's injury, he wasn't recruited, which ultimately could have spared him from death.

This is the story behind a Chinese proverb that teaches us this truth: A difficulty can be a blessing in disguise, and vice versa. This ancient wisdom has a close parallel in Ecclesiastes 6:12, where the inspired author observes: "Who knows what is good for a person in life?" Indeed, none of us knows what the future holds. An adversity might have positive benefits, and prosperity might have ill effects.

Each day offers new opportunities, joys, struggles, and suffering. As God's beloved children, we can rest in His sovereignty and trust Him through the good and bad times alike. God has "made the one as well as the other" (7:14). He's with us in all the events in our lives, and He promises His loving care.

Poh Fang Chia

God Promises
Faithful Love

LISTENING BEYOND THE STARS
ISAIAH 55:1–7

Seek the LORD while he may be found.
Isaiah 55:6

Imagine life without cell phones, Wi-Fi, GPS, Bluetooth devices, or microwave ovens. That's the way it is in the little village of Green Bank, West Virginia, known as "the quietest town in America." It's the location of the Green Bank Observatory, the world's largest steerable radio telescope. The telescope needs "quiet" to "listen" to naturally occurring radio waves emitted by the movement of pulsars and galaxies in deep space. It has a surface area larger than a football field and stands in the center of the National Radio Quiet Zone, a 13,000-square-mile area established to prevent electronic interference to the telescope's extreme sensitivity.

This intentional quiet enables scientists to hear "the music of the spheres." It also reminds me of our need to quiet ourselves enough to listen to the One who created the universe. God communicated to a wayward and distracted people through the prophet Isaiah, "Give ear and come to me; listen, that you may live. I will make an everlasting covenant with you" (Isaiah 55:3). God promises His faithful love to all who will seek Him and turn to Him for forgiveness.

We listen intentionally to God by turning from our distractions to meet Him in Scripture and in prayer. God isn't distant. He longs for us to make time for Him so He can be the priority of our daily lives.

James Banks

God Promises
To Be Our Rock

OUR BEST DEFENSE
PSALM 31:1–8

Be my rock of refuge, a strong fortress to save me.
Psalm 31:2

In late January 1956, during the tense days of the Montgomery Boycott, civil rights leader Dr. Martin Luther King Jr. could not sleep. A threatening phone call had terrified him. So he prayed, "I am here taking a stand for what I believe is right. But Lord, I must confess that I'm weak now, I'm faltering. I'm losing my courage. Now, I am afraid. . . . The people are looking to me for leadership, and if I stand before them without strength and courage, they too will falter. I am at the end of my powers. . . . I can't face it alone."

Dr. King later wrote, "At that moment I experienced the presence of the Divine as I never experienced Him before. It seemed as though I could hear the quiet assurance of an inner voice saying, 'Stand up for righteousness, stand up for truth; and God will be at your side forever.' Almost at once my fears began to go. My uncertainty disappeared. I was ready to face anything."

The rest is history. Dr. King wanted to see people of all colors freed of the tyranny of racism and prejudice.

If we face opposition when we're trying to do what's right, we too must cry out to the Lord. He alone is our "rock of refuge, a strong fortress" (Psalm 31:2). He is our reliable source of strength and protection.

David Egner

God Promises
Never to Change

OUR CHANGING WORLD
PSALM 102:25–27

I the LORD do not change.
Malachi 3:6

Change is one thing we can be sure of in this life. Our relationships change as we move to new places, experience illness, and ultimately face death. Even the cells in our bodies are always in the process of change. When cells wear out, most are replaced by new ones. This is especially noticeable with our skin—we shed and regrow outer skin cells about every twenty-seven days.

Yes, change is the one certainty in our world. Henry Lyte's melancholy line in his hymn "Abide with Me" is true: "Change and decay in all around I see." But the hymn immediately adds, "O Thou who changest not, abide with me!"

By faith in Jesus Christ we can have a relationship with the unchanging God, who says of himself in Malachi 3:6, "I the LORD do not change." We can depend on God to be the same forever, as the psalmist says (Psalm 102:27). Hebrews 13:8 adds this reassuring testimony: "Jesus Christ is the same yesterday and today and forever." He is our firm foundation, who can give us confidence and security in this changing world.

Although we are caught up in the swirling tide of time, we can rest our souls on the everlasting arms, which will never let us go.

Vernon Grounds

God Promises

The Blessing of Forgiveness

FIRE IN THE DESERT
EXODUS 3:1–10

*I am sending you to Pharaoh to bring
my people the Israelites out of Egypt.*

Exodus 3:10

While riding in the Chihuahuan Desert in the southwestern part of the US in the late 1800s, Jim White spotted a strange cloud of smoke spiraling skyward. Suspecting a wildfire, the young cowboy rode toward the source, only to discover that the "smoke" was a vast swarm of bats spilling from a hole in the ground. White had come across what is now called Carlsbad Caverns, an immense and spectacular system of caves in New Mexico.

As Moses was tending sheep in a Middle Eastern desert, he too saw an odd sight that grabbed his attention—a flaming bush that didn't burn up (Exodus 3:2). When God himself spoke from the bush, Moses realized he had come to something far grander than it had first appeared. The Lord told Moses, "I am the God of your father, the God of Abraham" (v. 6). God was about to lead an enslaved people to freedom and show them their true identity as His children (v. 10).

More than six hundred years earlier, God had made this promise to Abraham: "All peoples on earth will be blessed through you" (Genesis 12:3). The flight of the Israelites from Egypt was but one step in that blessing—God's plan to rescue His creation through the Messiah, Abraham's descendant.

Today we can enjoy the benefits of that blessing, for God offers this rescue to everyone. Jesus came to die for the sins of the whole world. By faith in Him, we too become children of the living God.

Tim Gustafson

God Promises

To Be with His People

THROUGH THE WATERS
ISAIAH 43:1–7

When you pass through the waters, I will be with you.

Isaiah 43:2

The movie *The Free State of Jones* tells the US Civil War story of Newton Knight and some Confederate deserters and slaves who aided the Union Army and then resisted slaveholders after the war. Many herald Knight as the hero, but two slaves first saved his life after his desertion. They carried him deep into a secluded swampland and tended a leg wound he suffered while fleeing Confederate forces. If they had abandoned him, he would have died.

The people of Judah were wounded and desperate, facing enemies and feeling helpless. Israel had been overtaken by Assyria, and Isaiah prophesied that one day they (Judah) would also be overcome by an enemy—Babylonia. Judah needed a God who would help, who would rescue and not forsake them. Imagine, then, the surging hope when the people heard God's assurance: "Do not be afraid, for I am with you" (Isaiah 43:5). Whatever calamity they faced or trouble they would endure, He would be with them. He would "pass through the waters" with them, leading them to safety (v. 2). He would "walk through the fire" with them, helping them through the scorching flames (v. 2).

Throughout Scripture, God promises to be with His people to care for us, guide us, and never abandon us—whether in life or death. Even when you will find yourself in difficult places, God is with you. Trust Him! He will help you pass through the waters.

Winn Collier

God Promises
To Answer Prayer

SIMPLY ASK
2 KINGS 5:9-17

Before they call I will answer.
Isaiah 65:24

Her doctor said her detached retinas couldn't be repaired. But after living without sight for fifteen years—learning Braille, and using a cane and service dog—a Montana woman's life changed when her husband asked another eye doctor a simple question: Could she be helped? The answer was yes. As the doctor discovered, the woman had a common eye condition, cataracts, which were removed from her right eye. When the eye patch came off the next day, her vision was 20/20. A second surgery for her left eye met with equal success.

A simple question also changed the life of Naaman, a powerful military man with leprosy. But Naaman raged arrogantly at the prophet Elisha's instructions to "wash yourself seven times in the Jordan, and your flesh will be restored" (2 Kings 5:10). Naaman's servants, however, asked the military leader a simple question: "If the prophet had told you to do some great thing, would you not have done it?" (v. 13). Persuaded, Naaman washed "and his flesh was restored and became clean" (v. 14).

In our lives, sometimes we struggle with a problem because we won't ask God: Will you help? Should I go? Will you lead? He doesn't require complicated questions from us to help. "Before they call I will answer," God promised His people (Isaiah 65:24). So today, simply ask Him.

Patricia Raybon

God Promises

To Wipe Away All Tears

BOWL OF TEARS
PSALM 55:4-19

As for me, I call to God, and the LORD saves me.
Psalm 55:16

In Boston, Massachusetts, a plaque titled "Crossing the Bowl of Tears" honors people who braved the Atlantic to escape death during the catastrophic Irish potato famine of the late 1840s. More than a million people died in the famine, while another million or more abandoned home to cross the ocean, which John Boyle O'Reilly poetically called "a bowl of tears." Driven by hunger and heartache, these travelers sought some measure of hope during desperate times.

In Psalm 55, David shares how he pursued hope. While we're uncertain about the specifics of the threat he faced, the weight of his experience was enough to break him emotionally (vv. 4–5). His instinctive reaction was to pray, "Oh, that I had the wings of a dove! I would fly away and be at rest" (v. 6).

Like David, we may want to flee to safety in the midst of painful circumstances. After considering his plight, however, David chose to run to his God instead of running from his heartache, singing, "As for me, I call to God, and the LORD saves me" (v. 16).

When trouble comes, remember that the God of all comfort is able to carry you through your darkest moments and deepest fears. He promises that one day He himself will wipe away every tear from our eyes (Revelation 21:4). Strengthened by this assurance, we can confidently trust Him with our tears now.

Bill Crowder

God Promises

Assurance of Life That Is Eternal

WE CAN KNOW FOR SURE!
1 JOHN 5:10–15

*I write these things to you . . . that you
may know that you have eternal life.*

1 John 5:13

As I sat on a train headed for an important appointment, I began to wonder if I was on the right train. I had never traveled that route before and had failed to ask for help. Finally, overcome by uncertainty and doubt, I exited at the next station—only to be told I had indeed been on the right train!

That incident reminded me how doubt can rob us of peace and confidence. At one time I had struggled with the assurance of my salvation, but God helped me deal with my doubt. Later, after sharing the story of my conversion and my assurance that I was going to heaven, someone asked, "How can you be sure you are saved and going to heaven?" I confidently but humbly pointed to the verse that God had used to help me: "I write these things to you who believe in the name of the Son of God so that you may know that you have eternal life" (1 John 5:13).

God promises that through faith in His Son, Jesus, we already have eternal life: "God has given us eternal life, and this life is in his Son" (v. 11). This assurance sharpens our faith, lifts us up when we are downhearted, and gives us courage in times of doubt.

Lawrence Darmani

God Promises
To Be Our Refuge and Strength

HE IS THERE
PSALM 139:1–12

The LORD your God goes with you;
he will never leave you nor forsake you.

Deuteronomy 31:6

Tanya's fiancé, David was lying in the intensive care unit after a delicate procedure to repair a brain aneurysm. David's eyes focused on Tanya, who had hardly left his side in several days. In wonder, he said, "Every time I look up, you're here. I love that. Every time I think of you, I open my eyes and you are there."

That young man's appreciation for the woman he loves reminds me of the way we should feel about God's presence in our lives.

He is always there. The Lord's presence gives us comfort and security. He has promised, "Never will I leave you; never will I forsake you" (Hebrews 13:5). Who knows us more completely? Who loves us more fully? Who cares for us so well?

In Psalm 139, we read what King David thought of God's precious presence. He wrote, "You have searched me, LORD, and you know me. You know when I sit and when I rise; . . . you are familiar with all my ways. . . . If I go up to the heavens, you are there" (vv. 1–3, 8).

No matter what happens to us, we have this assurance: "God is our refuge and strength, an ever-present help in trouble" (Psalm 46:1). Open your eyes and your heart. He is there.

Cindy Hess Kasper

God Promises
That We Won't Travel Life Alone

YOUR JOURNEY
JOHN 14:15–21

I will not leave you as orphans; I will come to you.
John 14:18

I grew up in the rebellious 1960s and turned my back on religion. I had attended church all my life but didn't come to faith until my early twenties after a terrible accident. Since that time, I have spent my adult years telling others of Jesus's love for us. It has been a journey.

Certainly "a journey" describes life in this broken world. On the way we encounter mountains and valleys, rivers and plains, crowded highways and lonely roads—highs and lows, joys and sorrows, conflict and loss, heartache and solitude. We can't see the road ahead, so we must take it as it comes, not as we wish it would be.

The follower of Christ, however, never faces this journey alone. The Scriptures remind us of the constant presence of God. There is nowhere we can go that He is not there (Psalm 139:7–12). Jesus, after promising to send the Holy Spirit, told His disciples, "I will not leave you as orphans; I will come to you" (John 14:18).

The challenges and opportunities we face on our journey can be met confidently, for God has promised us His never-failing presence.

Bill Crowder

God Promises

To Honor His Covenants

PROMISES STILL KEPT
GENESIS 15:5–21

*When the sun had set and darkness had fallen, a smoking firepot
with a blazing torch appeared and passed between the pieces.*
Genesis 15:17

In the ancient Near East a treaty between a superior (a lord or king) and an inferior (his subjects) was called a suzerain treaty. The ratification ceremony required animals to be sacrificed and cut in half. The animal parts were then arranged in two rows on the ground, forming an aisle between them. As the suzerain walked between the halves, he was publicly declaring he would keep the covenant and would become like the slain animals if he failed to keep his word.

When Abram asked God how he could be sure His promises would come to pass, God used the culturally significant symbolism of the suzerain treaty to affirm His promises (Genesis 15). When the burning torch passed through the pieces of the sacrifice, Abram understood that God was declaring it was His job to keep the covenant.

God's covenant with Abram and His assurance of its completion extend to followers of Christ. That is why Paul repeatedly refers to believers as sons of Abraham in his New Testament writings (Romans 4:11–18; Galatians 3:29). Once we accept Jesus Christ as Savior, God becomes the keeper in our covenant of faith (see John 10:28–29).

Because God is the keeper of our salvation, with renewed confidence we trust Him with our lives.

Randy Kilgore

God Promises

His Nearness

QUESTIONS FOR GOD
JUDGES 6:11-16, 24

Go with the strength you have . . . . I will be with you.
Judges 6:14, 16 NLT

What would you do if the Lord showed up in the middle of your workday with a message? This happened to Gideon, one of the ancient Israelites. "The angel of the LORD appeared to him and said, 'Mighty hero, the LORD is with you!'" Gideon could have responded with a wordless nod and gulp, but instead he said, "If the LORD is with us, why has all this happened to us?" (Judges 6:12–13 NLT). Gideon wanted to know why it seemed as if God had abandoned His people.

God didn't answer that question. After Gideon had endured seven years of enemy attacks, starvation, and hiding in caves, God didn't explain why He never intervened. God could have revealed Israel's past sin as the reason, but instead He gave Gideon hope for the future. God said, "Go with the strength you have, . . . I will be with you. And you will destroy the Midianites" (vv. 14, 16 NLT).

Do you ever wonder why God has allowed suffering in your life? Instead of answering that specific question, God may satisfy you with His nearness today and remind you that you can rely on His strength when you feel weak. When Gideon finally believed that God was with him and would help him, he built an altar and called it "The LORD Is Peace" (v. 24).

There is peace in knowing that whatever we do and wherever we go, we go with God, who promised never to leave or forsake His followers.

Jennifer Benson Schuldt

God Promises
That We Will See Jesus

FROM GRIEF TO JOY
JOHN 16:16-22

Very truly I tell you, you will weep and mourn while the world rejoices. You will grieve, but your grief will turn to joy.
John 16:20

Kelly's pregnancy brought complications, and doctors were concerned. During her long labor, they decided to whisk her away for a Cesarean section. But despite the ordeal, Kelly quickly forgot her pain when she held her newborn son. Joy had replaced anguish.

Scripture affirms this truth: "A woman giving birth to a child has pain because her time has come; but when her baby is born she forgets the anguish because of her joy that a child is born into the world" (John 16:21). Jesus used this illustration with His disciples to emphasize that though they would grieve because He would be leaving soon, that grief would turn to joy when they saw Him again (vv. 20–22).

Jesus was referring to His death and resurrection—and what followed. After His resurrection, to the disciples' joy, Jesus spent another forty days walking with and teaching them before ascending and leaving them once again (Acts 1:3). Yet Jesus did not leave them grief-stricken. The Holy Spirit would fill them with joy (John 16:7–15; Acts 13:52).

Though we have never seen Jesus face-to-face, as believers we have the assurance that one day we will. In that day, the anguish we face on this earth will be forgotten. But until then, the Lord has not left us without joy—He has given us His Spirit (Romans 15:13; 1 Peter 1:8–9).

Alyson Kieda

God Promises
Great Things

PROMISES TO LEAN ON!
2 PETER 1:1–7

He has given us his very great and precious promises, so that through them you may participate in the divine nature, having escaped the corruption in the world caused by evil desires.

2 Peter 1:4

All of us have probably made a promise at one time or another that we could not keep. But this is never true of God. He always stands behind His word, and what He says can be depended on. Because of the scope and perfection of His promises, the apostle Peter calls them "very great and precious" (2 Peter 1:4). Here are a few on which we may lean:

1. *Help in time of need.* "God has said, 'Never will I leave you; never will I forsake you.' So we say with confidence: 'The Lord is my helper'" (Hebrews 13:5, 6).

2. *Strength in our weakness.* "Do not fear, for . . . I will strengthen you and help you; I will uphold you with my righteous right hand" (Isaiah 41:10).

3. *Cheer in despondency.* "Take courage! It is I. Don't be afraid" (Matthew 14:27).

4. *Guidance in perplexity.* "For this God is our God for ever and ever; he will be our guide even to the end" (Psalm 48:14).

5. *Comfort in trouble.* "As a mother comforts her child, so will I comfort you" (Isaiah 66:13).

6. *Joy in sorrow.* The Lord says, "Those who sow with tears will reap with songs of joy" (Psalm 126:5).

7. *Power in service.* "You will receive power when the Holy Spirit comes on you, and you will be my witnesses in Jerusalem" (Acts 1:8).

Are you God's child? Then trust His word and claim His "great and precious promises" (2 Peter 1:4). They're the kind you can lean on!

Henry Bosch

God Promises

That His Creations Proves His Trustworthiness

OF TREES AND STARS
GENESIS 15:1-6

"Look up at the sky and count the stars—if indeed you can count them."
Then he said to him, "So shall your offspring be."
Genesis 15:5

"In my front yard are six huge oak trees that must be over one hundred years old," a friend from Texas told me. "I look at them and realize that the leaves must have barrels of fresh water each day to stay green.

"God causes their roots to exert a working pressure of more than three thousand pounds per square foot just to move the water up to the leaves— not considering the resistance of the wood. That is just another of God's 'miracles' that occur every day unnoticed."

God didn't ask Abraham to look at trees but directed his attention to the stars. As Abraham contemplated the vast numbers of stars, God said, "So shall your descendants be." I believe that was more than a promise of large numbers. To me it implies that if God could create and maintain all those stars, He would have no trouble fulfilling His promise that Abraham would have a son in his old age. And Abraham got the picture, for we read that he "believed the LORD" (Genesis 15:6).

Let's consider the wonders of creation that exist all around us. Doing so is a good way to strengthen our faith in the promises of the Creator.

Dennis DeHaan

God Promises
To Support Us

HE HOLDS OUR HAND
ISAIAH 41:8–13

I will strengthen you and help you;
I will uphold you with my righteous right hand.
Isaiah 41:10

The little girl who navigated the stairway one Sunday at church was cute, spunky, and independent. One by one the child—who appeared to be not much over two years old—took the steps down to the lower level. Descending the stairs was her mission and she accomplished it. I smiled to myself as I pondered the daring independence of this courageous toddler. The child wasn't afraid, because she knew her caring mother's watchful eye was always on her and her loving hand was extended to help her. This aptly pictures the Lord's readiness to help His children as they make their way through life with its varied uncertainties.

Today's Scripture includes two "hand" references. After cautioning His ancient people not to fear or be dismayed, the Lord told them, "I will uphold you with my righteous right hand" (Isaiah 41:10). Many anxious and fearful children have been steadied by the strength of a parent. Here God's power comes into view. In the second "hand" reference, once again it's the Lord who acted to secure the safety of His own. "For I am the LORD your God who takes hold of your right hand" (v. 13). While life situations and times have changed, the Lord hasn't. We need not despair (v. 10) because the Lord still assures us with the promise of His support and with the words we desperately need to hear: "Do not fear" (vv. 10, 13).

Arthur Jackson

God Promises
Spiritual Food

DAILY BREAD
LEVITICUS 24:1–9

I am the living bread that came down from heaven.
Whoever eats this bread will live forever.
John 6:51

Bread has come to be regarded as something less than what it was in Bible times. We don't usually think of it as a symbol of life's necessities. In Jesus's day, however, bread represented nourishment in all its many forms.

This helps us understand why the Lord told Israel to put bread in the Holy Place of the tabernacle—His "house of symbols." There in that first room, twelve loaves were to be displayed on a golden table "before the LORD" (Leviticus 24:6). Those loaves reminded Israel that God always provides for His own when they come to Him on His terms. The bread reflected God's promise to provide for all who hunger and thirst for righteousness (Matthew 5:6; 6:31–34).

For the believer in Christ, bread may represent the Bible, Jesus, Christian fellowship, or any of the provisions God has made for our spiritual needs. He cares for us and He's ready to feed us, but His offer is not unconditional. He promised to provide daily "bread" for those who in obedience have separated themselves to live and to eat from the hand of God.

The Lord cares for all who willingly and humbly receive their physical and spiritual food from Him.

Mart DeHaan

God Promises
Strength to the Weary

POWER UP!
ISAIAH 40:25-31

He gives strength to the weary and increases the power of the weak.
Isaiah 40:29

While it is still dark, a solitary car drives through the gate to the factory. A lone figure makes his way to a back door, unlocks it, and steps inside. A light goes on, then another. Large machines are fired up, temperature control equipment is engaged, banks of machinery soon begin to hum. By the time 7 a.m. rolls around, the millwright has the plant all powered up and ready for a new day's production.

As followers of Jesus Christ, we can experience a similar "powering up." It should happen every morning. We aren't prepared for a day of spiritual and personal productivity until we've spent time "warming up." A chapter of Scripture, some well-spent moments of devotional reading, meditation, and prayer set the proper spiritual climate for the rest of the day.

We need God's power even more when we go through periods of emptiness, depression, or testing. Feeling shut down, we cry out to God. Isaiah declared that the Lord "gives strength to the weary and increases the power of the weak" (40:29).

We need the strength of the Lord not only for severe trials but also for everyday living—and He has promised it. When we turn to God, we can "soar on wings like eagles" (v. 31). Go to Him daily to power up.

David Egner

God Promises

To Honor the Upright

BROKEN THINGS
PSALM 31:9–24

I have become like broken pottery.

Psalm 31:12

Broken lives in this world are useful to God. Few men and women can fulfill their hopes and plans without some interruption and disappointment along the way.

But man's disappointments are often God's appointments, and the things we believe are tragedies may be the very opportunities through which God chooses to exhibit His love and grace. We have but to follow these lives to the end to see that people who have been broken become better and more effective Christians than if they had carried out all their own plans and purposes.

Are you being broken today? Has the dearest thing in your life been torn away? Then remember that if you could see the purpose of it all from God's standpoint, you would praise the Lord.

The best things that come to us are not those that accrue from having our way, but by letting God have His way. Though the way of testing and trial and sorrow often seems hard and cruel, it is the way of God's love. In the end it will be the best way for us.

Remember, we have the Lord's promise: "No good thing does he withhold from those whose walk is blameless" (Psalm 84:11).

M. R. DeHaan

God Promises
To Remember Sins No More

DOES GOD FORGET?
HEBREWS 8

I will forgive their wickedness and will remember their sins no more.
Hebrews 8:12

God longs to forgive sinners! But in the minds of many people, this thought seems too good to be true. Countless sermons have been preached to convince guilt-ridden individuals that it is true. Many of these sermons emphasize that God not only forgives the sinner but also forgets the sin. I've often said it myself, never doubting its soundness.

Then one Sunday I heard a sermon that revolutionized my thinking. The speaker caught my attention when he said, "The idea that God forgets my sins isn't very reassuring to me. After all, what if He suddenly remembered? In any case, only imperfection can forget, and God is perfect."

As I was questioning the biblical basis for such statements, the pastor read Hebrews 8:12, "I will forgive their wickedness and will remember their sins no more." Then he said, "God doesn't say He'll forget our sins—He says He'll remember them no more! His promise not to remember them ever again is stronger than saying He'll forget them. Now that reassures me!"

Do you worry that there are certain sins you'll be punished for someday? Because Christ died for all our sins (1 Corinthians 15:3), God promises to forgive us and never bring up our sin again (Psalm 103:12).

Joanie Yoder

God Promises
His Strength and Protection

GOD'S STRONG ARM
EXODUS 6:1-8

I will redeem you with an outstretched arm.

Exodus 6:6

My friend Joann had a strong desire to become a concert pianist and to travel and perform as either a soloist or as a piano accompanist. While majoring in piano performance in college, she developed tendinitis in her right arm, and it became too weak to perform the solo recital that was required. She graduated with a degree in music history and literature instead.

She knew Jesus as her Savior, but she had been rebelling against Him for several years. Then through further difficult circumstances, she sensed the Lord reaching out to her, and she turned back to Him. Eventually her arm grew stronger, and her dream of traveling and performing came about. She says, "Now I could play to God's glory instead of my own. His outstretched arm restored my spiritual life and the strength in my arm to enable me to serve Him with the gift He gave me."

The Lord promised Moses that His outstretched arm would rescue the Israelites from bondage in Egypt (Exodus 6:6). He kept that promise even though His often-rebellious people doubted (14:30–31). God's mighty arm is outstretched for us as well. No matter the outcome of our situation, He can be trusted to bring about His will for each of His children. We can depend on God's strong arm.

Anne Cetas

God Promises

A Needed Replacement

NEED A NEW HEART?
EZEKIEL 36:24–27

*I will give you a new heart and put a new spirit in you; I will
remove from you your heart of stone and give you a heart of flesh.*

Ezekiel 36:26

The news was grim.

My father had been having chest pains, so his doctor ordered a test to
peer into his heart. The result? Blockage found in three arteries.

Triple-bypass surgery was scheduled for February 14. My dad, though
anxious, saw that date as a hopeful sign: "I'm getting a new heart for Val-
entine's Day!" And he did! The surgery went perfectly, restoring life-giving
blood flow to his struggling heart—his "new" heart.

My father's surgery reminded me that God offers us a new life as well.
Because sin clogs our spiritual "arteries"—our capacity to connect with
God—we need spiritual "surgery" to clear them.

That's what God promised His people in Ezekiel 36:26. He assured
the Israelites, "I will give you a new heart. . . . I will remove from you your
heart of stone and give you a heart of flesh." He also promised, "I will
cleanse you from all your impurities" (v. 25) and "put my Spirit in you"
(v. 27). To a people who had lost hope, God promised a fresh start as the
One who could renew their lives.

That promise was ultimately fulfilled through Jesus's death and resurrection. When we trust in Him, we receive a new spiritual heart, one that's
cleansed of our sin and despair. Filled with Christ's Spirit, our new heart
beats with the spiritual lifeblood of God, that "we too may live a new life"
(Romans 6:4).

Adam Holz

God Promises
New Life in Christ

INNOCENCE FOUND
2 CORINTHIANS 5:14–21

See what great love the Father has lavished on us.
1 John 3:1

"I'm not who I once was. I'm a new person."

Those simple words from my son, spoken to students at a school assembly, describe the change God made in his life. Once addicted to heroin, Geoffrey previously saw himself through his sins and mistakes. But now he sees himself as a child of God.

The Bible encourages us with this promise: "If anyone is in Christ, the new creation has come: The old has gone, the new is here!" (2 Corinthians 5:17). No matter who we've been or what we've done in our past, when we trust Jesus for our salvation and receive the forgiveness offered through His cross, we become someone new. Since the garden of Eden, the guilt of our sins has separated us from God, but He has "reconciled us to himself through Christ," "not counting" our sins against us (vv. 18–19). We are His dearly loved children (1 John 3:1–2), washed clean and made new in the likeness of His Son.

Jesus is innocence found. He liberates us from sin and its dominating power, and He restores us to a new relationship with God—where we are free to no longer live for ourselves but "for him who died for [us] and was raised again" (2 Corinthians 5:15). Christ's transforming love gave Geoffrey a new identity and a new purpose—to point others to the Savior. And He does the same for us!

James Banks

God Promises

To Take You from the Darkness

WORDS OF LIGHT
JOHN 8:12–20

I am the light of the world.

John 8:12

Jesus, an itinerant rabbi from the town of Nazareth, asserted that He was the light of the world. That was an incredible claim from a man in first-century Galilee, an obscure region in the Roman Empire. It could not boast of any impressive culture and had no famous philosophers, noted authors, or gifted sculptors. And we have no record that Jesus had any formal education.

More than that, Jesus lived before the invention of the printing press, radio, television, and internet. How could He expect His ideas to be circulated around the globe? The words He spoke were committed to the memories of His followers. Then the Light of the world was snuffed out by the darkness—or so it seemed.

Centuries later we still listen with amazement to Jesus's words, which His Father has miraculously preserved. His words lead us out of darkness into the light of God's truth; they fulfill His promise: "Whoever follows me will never walk in darkness, but will have the light of life" (John 8:12).

I encourage you to read the words of Jesus in the Gospels. Ponder them. Let them grip your mind and change your life. You'll exclaim as His contemporaries did: "No one ever spoke the way this man does" (John 7:46).

Vernon Grounds

God Promises
Sufficient Grace

DO THE HARD WORK
1 TIMOTHY 6:6–19

*Fight the good fight of the faith. Take hold of the
eternal life to which you were called.*
1 Timothy 6:12

After living more than eighty years, I know that any claim that offers an effortless way to develop a lean, well-conditioned body is a hoax. So is any sermon title that promises an easy way to become like Christ.

Author Brennan Manning tells of an alcoholic who asked his minister to pray over him to be delivered from his drinking problem. He thought this would be a quick and easy way to overcome his addiction. Recognizing his motive in asking for prayer, the minister replied, "I've got a better idea. Go to Alcoholics Anonymous." He counseled the man to follow the program diligently and read his Bible daily. "In other words," the minister concluded, "do the hard work."

Do the hard work—that's what Paul was saying to Timothy when he told him how he should order his life so he could teach believers how they should live. Notice the action verbs: "Pursue righteousness, godliness, faith, love, endurance and gentleness. Fight the good fight of the faith. Take hold of the eternal life to which you were called" (1 Timothy 6:11–12).

Just as there is no easy path to being delivered from alcoholism, so too, there is no effort-free route to Christlikeness. If we really want to become like Jesus, we must keep on doing the hard work.

Herb Vander Lugt

God Promises
Great Treasures

FAITH AND RICHES
EPHESIANS 1

*I pray that the eyes of your heart may be enlightened
in order that you may know the hope to which he has
called you, the riches of his glorious inheritance.*

Ephesians 1:18

Do you want to be rich? Do you think your faith will bring you riches?
What kind of riches are you looking for?

There's good news and bad news if wealth is what you want. The good
news is that God's Word does promise riches to the believer. The "bad"
news is that it doesn't have anything to do with money.

Here are some examples of the riches that can be ours as believers in
Jesus Christ:

- An understanding of God the Father and the Son, "in whom are
  hidden all the treasures of wisdom and knowledge" (Colossians 2:2–3).
- Christ, "the hope of glory," living in us (Colossians 1:27).
- Mighty strength in our inner being, "through his Spirit"
  (Ephesians 3:16).
- Having all our needs met by God (Philippians 4:19).
- The "wisdom and knowledge of God" (Romans 11:33).
- "Redemption through his blood, the forgiveness of sins," which
  comes from God's grace (Ephesians 1:7).

Yes, God's Word promises us great riches—treasures that we cannot
even attempt to purchase with any amount of money. It is these riches that
we must seek, enjoy, and use to glorify their source—our heavenly Father.

Dave Branon

God Promises
Guidance for the Path

A SEASON FOR EVERYTHING
ECCLESIASTES 3:1–13

*There is a time for everything, and a season
for every activity under the heavens.*

Ecclesiastes 3:1

If you're like me, you've struggled with having to say no to taking on a new responsibility—especially if it's for a good cause and directly related to helping others. We may have sound reasons for carefully selecting our priorities. Yet sometimes, by not agreeing to do more, we may feel guilty or we may think that somehow we have failed in our walk of faith.

But according to Ecclesiastes 3:1–8, wisdom recognizes that everything in life has its own season—in human activities as in the realm of nature. "There is a time for everything, and a season for every activity under the heavens" (3:1).

Perhaps you are getting married or becoming a parent for the first time. Maybe you are leaving school and entering the workforce, or moving from full-time work to retirement. As we move from season to season, our priorities change. We may need to put aside what we did in the past and funnel our energy into something else.

When life brings changes in our circumstances and obligations, we must responsibly and wisely discern what kind of commitments we should make, seeking in whatever we do to "do it all for the glory of God" (1 Corinthians 10:31). Proverbs 3:6 promises that as we acknowledge Him in all our ways, He will guide us in the way we should go.

Poh Fang Chia

God Promises
That He Sees Us Faultless in Jesus

ALL SPRUCED UP
JUDE VV. 20–25

[Jesus] is able to keep you from stumbling and to present you before his glorious presence without fault.

Jude v. 24

Getting our children to look good for church was always a challenge. Ten minutes after arriving at church all spruced up, our little Matthew would look like he didn't have parents. I'd see him running down the hall with his shirt half untucked, glasses cockeyed, shoes scuffed up, and cookie crumbs decorating his clothes. Left to himself, he was a mess.

I wonder if that is how we look sometimes. After Christ has clothed us in His righteousness, we tend to wander off and live in ways that make us look like we don't belong to God. That's why Jude's promise that Jesus is "able to keep you from stumbling and to present you . . . without fault" gives me hope (Jude v. 24).

How can we keep from looking like we don't have a heavenly Father? As we become more yielded to His Spirit and His ways, He will keep us from stumbling. Think of how increasingly righteous our lives would become if we would take time in His Word to be cleansed with "the washing with water through the word" (Ephesians 5:26).

What a blessing that Jesus promises to take our stumbling, disheveled lives and present us faultless to the Father! May we increasingly look like children of the King as we reflect His loving care and attention.

Joe Stowell

God Promises

Grace, Strength, and Joy

WELLS OF SALVATION
ISAIAH 12

With joy you will draw water from the wells of salvation.

Isaiah 12:3

When people drill holes deep into the earth, it is normally for pulling up core samples of rock, accessing oil, or finding water.

In Isaiah 12, we learn that God wanted His people, who were living in a spiritual desert as well as a geographical desert, to discover His "wells of salvation." The prophet Isaiah compared God's salvation to a well from which the most refreshing of all waters can be drawn. After many years of turning their back on God, the nation of Judah was destined for exile as God allowed foreign invaders to conquer the nation, scattering the people. Yet the prophet Isaiah said a remnant would eventually return to their homeland as a sign that God was with them (Isaiah 11:11–12).

Isaiah 12 is a hymn, praising God for His faithfulness in keeping His promises, especially the promise of salvation. Isaiah encouraged the people that deep in God's "wells of salvation" they would experience the cool water of God's grace, strength, and joy (vv. 1–3). This would refresh and strengthen their hearts and cause praise and gratitude to God (vv. 4–6).

God wants each of us to discover through confession and repentance the deep, cool waters of joy found in the everlasting well of His salvation.

Marvin Williams

God Promises
To Fill Us

THE ULTIMATE SATISFACTION
ISAIAH 55:1–7

Come, all you who are thirsty, come to the waters;
and you who have no money, come, buy and eat!
Isaiah 55:1

As we distributed snacks for children at a Bible school program, we noticed a little boy who devoured his snack. Then he also ate the leftovers of the children at his table. Even after I gave him a bag of popcorn, he still wasn't satisfied. As leaders, we were concerned as to why this little boy was so hungry.

It occurred to me that we can be like that boy when it comes to our emotions. We look for ways to satisfy our deepest longings, but we never find what fully satisfies us.

The prophet Isaiah invites those who are hungry and thirsty to "come, buy and eat" (Isaiah 55:1). But then he asks, "Why spend money on what is not bread, and your labor on what does not satisfy?" (v. 2). Isaiah is talking about more than just physical hunger here. God can satisfy our spiritual and emotional hunger through the promise of His presence. The "everlasting covenant" in verse 3 is a reminder of a promise God made to David in 2 Samuel 7:8–16. Through David's family line, a Savior would come to reconnect people to God. Later, in John 6:35 and 7:37, Jesus extended the same invitation Isaiah gave, thus identifying himself as the Savior foretold by Isaiah and other prophets.

Hungry? God invites you to come and be filled in His presence.

Linda Washington

God Promises
Salvation!

WHAT'S INSIDE
2 CORINTHIANS 4:7–18

*But we have this treasure in jars of clay to show that
this all-surpassing power is from God and not from us.*
2 Corinthians 4:7

"Do you want to see what's inside?" my friend asked. I had just complimented her on the old-fashioned rag doll her daughter held in her small arms. Instantly curious, I replied that yes, I very much wanted to see what was inside. She turned the doll face down and pulled open a discreet zipper sewn into its back. From within the cloth body, Emily gently removed a treasure: the rag doll she had held and loved throughout the years of her own childhood more than two decades prior. The "outer" doll was merely a shell without this inner core to give it strength and form.

Paul describes the truth of Jesus's life, death, and resurrection as a treasure, carried about in the frail humanity of God's people. That treasure enables those who trust in Him to bear up under unthinkable adversity and continue in their service. When they do, His light—His life—shines brightly through the "cracks" of their humanness. Paul encourages us all not to "lose heart" (2 Corinthians 4:16) because God strengthens us to do His work.

Like the "inner" doll, the gospel treasure within us lends both purpose and fortitude to our lives. When God's strength shines through us, it invites others to ask, "What's inside?" We can then unzip our hearts and reveal the life-giving promise of salvation in Christ.

Kirsten Holmberg

FEBRUARY 24

To Continually Be with Us

HIS PRESENCE
EXODUS 3:7–12

*The LORD replied, "My Presence will go with you,
and I will give you rest."*
Exodus 33:14

The anxious father and his teenage son sat before the psychic. "How far is your son traveling?" the psychic asked. "To the big city," the man replied, "and he will be gone for a long time." Handing the father a talisman (a kind of good-luck charm), he said, "This will protect him wherever he goes."

I was that boy. However, that psychic and that talisman could do nothing for me. While in that city, I put my faith in Jesus. I threw away the talisman and clung to Christ. Having Jesus in my life guaranteed God's presence.

Thirty years later, my father said to me as we rushed my brother to the hospital, "Let us first pray; the Spirit of God goes with you and will be with you all the way!" We had learned that God's presence and power is our only security.

Moses learned a similar lesson. He had a challenging task from God—to lead the people out of bondage in Egypt and into the promised land (Exodus 3:10). But God assured him, "I will be with you" (v. 12).

Our journey too is not without challenges, but we're assured of God's presence. As Jesus told His disciples, "I am with you always, to the very end of the age" (Matthew 28:20).

Lawrence Darmani

God Promises

To Travel with Us Along the Way

A ROAD NOT TRAVELED
ISAIAH 42:10–17

I will lead the blind by ways they have not known,
along unfamiliar paths I will guide them.
Isaiah 42:16

People ask me if I have a five-year plan. How can I plan five years "down the road" on a road I've never traveled?

I think back to the 1960s when I was a minister to students at Stanford University. I'd been a physical education major in college and had a lot of fun, but I left no record of being a scholar. I felt wholly inadequate in my new position. Most days I wandered around the campus, a blind man groping in the darkness, asking God to show me what to do. One day a student "out of the blue" asked me to lead a Bible study in his fraternity. It was a beginning.

God doesn't stand at a juncture and point the way: He's a guide, not a signpost. He walks with us, leading us down paths we never envisioned. All we have to do is walk alongside Him.

The path won't be easy; there'll be "rough places" along the way. But God has promised that He will "turn the darkness into light" and "will not forsake" us (Isaiah 42:16). He'll be with us all the way.

Paul said that God is "able to do immeasurably more than all we ask or imagine" (Ephesians 3:20). We can scheme and envision, but our Lord's imagination far transcends our plans. We must hold them loosely and see what God has in mind.

David Roper

God Promises
To Hear Our Cries

OUR SAFE PLACE
PSALM 91

*I will say of the LORD, "He is my refuge and
my fortress, my God, in whom I trust."*

Psalm 91:2

My very first job was at a fast-food restaurant. One Saturday evening, a guy kept hanging around, asking when I got out of work. It made me feel uneasy. As the hour grew later, he ordered fries, then a drink so the manager wouldn't kick him out. Though I didn't live far, I was scared to walk home alone through a couple of dark parking lots and a stretch through a sandy field. Finally, at midnight, I went in the office to make a phone call.

And the person who answered—my dad—without a second thought got out of a warm bed and five minutes later was there to take me home.

The kind of certainty I had that my dad would come to help me that night reminds me of the assurance we read about in Psalm 91. Our Father in heaven is always with us, protecting and caring for us when we are confused or afraid or in need. He declares: "When they call on me, I will answer" (Psalm 91:15 NLT). He is not just a place we can run to for safety. He is our shelter (v. 1). He is the Rock we can cling to for refuge (v. 2).

In times of fear, danger, or uncertainty, we can trust God's promise that when we call on Him, He will hear and be with us in our trouble (vv. 14–15). God is our safe place.

Cindy Hess Kasper

God Promises

Instruction and Counsel

ALWAYS IN HIS CARE
PSALM 32:1–11

I will instruct you and teach you in the way you should go;
I will counsel you with my loving eye on you.

Psalm 32:8

On the day our youngest daughter was flying from Munich to Barcelona, I visited my favorite flight tracking website to follow her progress. After I entered her flight number, my computer screen showed that her flight had crossed Austria and was skirting the northern part of Italy. From there the plane would fly over the Mediterranean, south of the French Riviera toward Spain, and was scheduled to arrive on time. It seemed that the only thing I didn't know was what the flight attendants were serving for lunch!

Why did I care about my daughter's location and circumstances? Because I love her. I care about who she is, what she's doing, and where she's going in life.

In Psalm 32, David celebrated the marvel of God's forgiveness, guidance, and concern for us. Unlike a human father, God knows every detail of our lives and the deepest needs of our hearts. The Lord's promise to us is, "I will instruct you and teach you in the way you should go; I will counsel you with my loving eye on you" (v. 8).

Whatever our circumstances today, we can rely on God's presence and care because "the LORD's unfailing love surrounds the one who trusts in him" (v. 10).

David McCasland

God Promises

The Comfort of Jesus

YOU'VE GOT A FRIEND
PSALM 23

I no longer call you servants, because a servant does not know his master's business. Instead, I have called you friends, for everything that I learned from my Father I have made known to you.

John 15:15

One of the ironic consequences of the sweeping growth of social media is that we often find ourselves more personally isolated. One online article warns: "Those who oppose leading one's life primarily or exclusively online claim that virtual friends are not adequate substitutes for real-world friends, and . . . individuals who substitute virtual friends for physical friends become even lonelier and more depressive than before."

Technology aside, all of us battle with seasons of loneliness, wondering if anyone knows, understands, or cares about the burdens we carry or the struggles we face. But followers of Christ have an assurance that brings comfort to our weary hearts. The comforting presence of the Savior is promised in words that are undeniable, for the psalmist David wrote, "Even though I walk through the darkest valley, I will fear no evil, for you are with me; your rod and your staff, they comfort me" (Psalm 23:4).

Whether isolated by our own choices, by the cultural trends that surround us, or by the painful losses of life, all who know Christ can rest in the presence of the Shepherd of our hearts. What a friend we have in Jesus!

Bill Crowder

God Promises
To Wipe Away Our Guilt

GUILT AND FORGIVENESS
ROMANS 2:12–16

*They show that the requirements of
the law are written on their hearts.*

Romans 2:15

In his book *Human Universals*, anthropologist Donald Brown lists more than four hundred behaviors that he considers common across humanity. He includes such things as toys, jokes, dances, and proverbs, wariness of snakes, and tying things with string! Likewise, he believes all cultures have concepts of right and wrong, where generosity is praised, promises are valued, and things like meanness and murder are understood to be wrong. We all have a sense of conscience, wherever we're from.

The apostle Paul made a similar point many centuries ago. While God gave the Jewish people the Ten Commandments to clarify right from wrong, Paul noted that since gentiles could do right by obeying their conscience, God's laws were evidently written on their hearts (Romans 2:14–15). But that didn't mean people always did what was right. The gentiles rebelled against their conscience (1:32), the Jews broke the Law (2:17–24), leaving both guilty. But through faith in Jesus, God removes the death penalty from all our rule-breaking (3:23–26; 6:23).

Since God created all humans with a sense of right and wrong, each of us will likely feel some guilt over a bad thing we've done or a good thing we failed to do. When we confess those sins, God wipes away the guilt like a whiteboard wiped clean. All we have to do is ask Him—whoever we are, wherever we're from.

Sheridan Voysey

God Promises

A Meeting in the Sky with Jesus

ANTICIPATION
1 Thessalonians 4:13–18

I will come back and take you to be with me.

John 14:3

At the beginning of March, my friend began a countdown. Marked on the calendar in her office were the twenty days left until the first day of spring. One morning when I saw her, she volunteered, "Only twelve more days!" A few days later, "Only six!" Her enthusiasm started to rub off on me, and I began to keep track as well. "Just two more days, Jerrie!" "I know!" she beamed.

As believers, we have something to look forward to that is even more exciting than the anticipation of budding flowers and lots of sunshine after a long winter. God has made many promises in His Word, and each one has been or will be fulfilled. But the certainty that Christ will return is one of the greatest promises of all. "For the Lord himself will come down from heaven, with a loud command, with the voice of the archangel and the trumpet call of God. . . . After that, we who are still alive and are left will be caught up together with them in the clouds to meet the Lord in the air. And so we will be with the Lord forever" (1 Thessalonians 4:16–17).

Although no one can know the exact day, we have God's promise that Jesus will come back (Acts 1:7–11). As we celebrate the spring and coming Easter season, let's encourage each other in anticipation of that day!

Cindy Hess Kasper

God Promises
To Meet Our Needs

HOPE'S SURE FOUNDATION
HEBREWS 11:1–6

---

*My God will meet all your needs according to
the riches of his glory in Christ Jesus.*
Philippians 4:19

Lessons on faith can come from unexpected places—like the one I learned from my 110-pound, black Labrador retriever, Bear. His large metal water bowl was located in a corner of the kitchen. Whenever it was empty, he wouldn't bark or paw at it. Instead, he would lie down quietly beside it and wait. Sometimes he would have to wait several minutes, but Bear had learned to trust that I would eventually walk into the room, see him there, and provide what he needed. His simple faith in me reminded me of my need to place more trust in God.

The Bible tells us that "faith is confidence in what we hope for and assurance about what we do not see" (Hebrews 11:1). The foundation of this confidence and assurance is God himself, who "rewards those who earnestly seek him" (v. 6). God is faithful to keep His promises to all who believe and come to Him through Jesus.

Sometimes having faith in "what we do not see" isn't easy. But we can rest in God's goodness and His loving character, trusting that His wisdom is perfect in all things—even when we have to wait. He is always faithful to do what He says. He promised to save our eternal souls and meet our deepest needs, now and forever.

James Banks

God Promises
To Do What He Said He Would Do

STANDING ON THE PROMISES
JOHN 15:5-8

Ask whatever you wish, and it will be done for you.
John 15:7

When my friend and his sister were both children, he assured her an umbrella had enough lift to hold her up if she would only "believe." So "by faith" she jumped off a barn roof and knocked herself out, suffering a minor concussion.

What God has promised, He will do. But we must be sure we stand on God's actual word when we claim a promise, for only then do we have the assurance that God will do or give what He's promised. Faith has no power in itself. It only counts when it's based on a clear and unambiguous promise from God. Anything else is just wishful thinking.

Here's a case in point: God has promised, "Ask whatever you wish, and it will be done for you. This is to my Father's glory, that you bear much fruit" (John 15:7–8). These verses are not a promise that God will answer every prayer we utter, but rather a promise that He will respond to every longing for personal righteousness, what Paul calls "the fruit of the Spirit" (Galatians 5:22–23). If we hunger and thirst for holiness and ask God for it, He will begin to satisfy us. It will take time; for spiritual growth, like human growth, is gradual. Don't give up. Keep asking God to make you holy. In His time and at His pace "it will be done for you." God doesn't make promises He doesn't keep.

David Roper

God Promises
To Keep Us from Falling

A SAFE PAIR
PSALM 138

Though I walk in the midst of trouble, you preserve my life.

Psalm 138:7

Edwin van der Sar, goalkeeper for the Manchester United soccer team, had a "safe" pair of hands. He kept the ball from entering his team's goal for 1,311 minutes, a world record in one season! That means that for almost fifteen games of ninety minutes each, no one was able to score even one goal against his team while he was guarding the goalposts. That's an amazing record of safe hands.

The psalmist David found comfort in the safest pair of hands—God's hands. He wrote of God's protection in Psalm 138, "You stretch out your hand . . . and with your right hand you save me" (v. 7). Like David, we can look to God's safe hands to keep us from spiritual danger and defeat.

Another assurance from God's Word for followers of Christ is Jude vv. 24–25: "To him who is able to keep you from stumbling and to present you before his glorious presence without fault and with great joy—to the only God our Savior be glory, majesty, power and authority, through Jesus Christ our Lord, before all ages, now and forevermore! Amen." That doesn't mean we'll never stumble. But it does mean we won't stumble so badly that God cannot pick us up.

God's safe pair of hands can never fail—ever!

C. P. Hia

God Promises
To Be Our Strong Tower

TRUE SHELTER
JOSHUA 20:1–9

The name of the LORD is a fortified tower;
the righteous run to it and are safe.
Proverbs 18:10

In March 2014 a tribal conflict broke out in my hometown area of Ghana, forcing my father's household, along with other refugees, to take cover in the region's capital city. Throughout history, people who have felt unsafe in their homelands have traveled to other places searching for safety and something better.

As I visited and talked with people from my hometown, I thought of the cities of refuge in Joshua 20:1–9. These were cities designated as places of safety for those fleeing from "relatives seeking revenge" in the case of an accidental killing (v. 3 NLT). They offered peace and protection.

People today still seek places of refuge, although for a variety of reasons. But as needed as these sanctuaries are, supplying shelter and food, they cannot completely meet the needs of refugees and fugitives. That rest is found only in God. Those who walk with God find true shelter and the safest protection in Him. When ancient Israel was sent into exile, the Lord said, "I have been a sanctuary [safe haven] for them in the countries where they have gone" (Ezekiel 11:16).

With the psalmist, we can say confidently to the Lord, "You are my hiding place; you will protect me from trouble and surround me with songs of deliverance" (32:7).

Lawrence Darmani

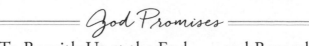

God Promises

To Be with Us at the End . . . and Beyond

LIFE AND DEATH
GENESIS 50:22–26

I am about to die. But God will surely come to your aid.
Genesis 50:24

I will never forget sitting at the bedside of my friend's brother when he died; the scene could be seen as "the ordinary visited by the extraordinary." Three of us were talking quietly when we realized that Richard's breathing was becoming more labored. We gathered around him, watching, waiting, and praying. When he took his last breath, it felt like a holy moment; the presence of God enveloped us in the midst of our tears over a wonderful man dying in his forties.

Many of the heroes of our faith experienced God's faithfulness when they died. For instance, Jacob announced he would soon be "gathered to [his] people" (Genesis 49:29–33). Jacob's son Joseph also announced his impending death: "I am about to die," he said to his brothers while instructing them how to hold firm in their faith. He seems to be at peace, yet eager that his brothers trust the Lord (50:24).

None of us know when or how we will breathe our last breath, but we can ask God to help us realize that He will be with us. We can believe the promise that Jesus will prepare a place for us in His Father's house (John 14:2–3).

Amy Boucher Pye

God Promises
Hope and Provision

A DOUBLE PROMISE
ISAIAH 25:1–9

*In perfect faithfulness you have done
wonderful things, things planned long ago.*
Isaiah 25:1

Since she suffered cancer several years ago, Ruth has been unable to eat, drink, or even swallow properly. She has also lost a lot of her physical strength, and numerous operations and treatments have left her a shadow of what she used to be.

Yet Ruth is still able to praise God; her faith remains strong, and her joy is infectious. She relies on God daily and holds on to the hope that she will recover fully one day. She prays for healing and is confident that God will answer—sooner or later. What an awesome faith!

Ruth explained that what keeps her faith strong is the secure knowledge that God will not only fulfill His promises in His time but will also sustain her until that happens. This was the same hope that God's people had as they waited for Him to complete His plans (Isaiah 25:1), deliver them from their enemies (v. 2), wipe away their tears, remove their disgrace, and "swallow up death forever" (v. 8).

In the meantime, God gave His people refuge and shelter (v. 4) as they waited. He comforted them in their ordeals, gave them strength to endure, and gave them assurance that He was there with them.

This is the double promise we have—the hope of deliverance one day, plus the provision of His comfort, strength, and shelter throughout our lives.

Leslie Koh

God Promises
Peace and Comfort

SAFE IN HIS ARMS
ISAIAH 66:5–13

As a mother comforts her child, so will I comfort you.
Isaiah 66:13

I sat next to my daughter's bed in a recovery room after she had undergone surgery. When her eyes fluttered open, she realized she was uncomfortable and started to cry. I tried to reassure her by stroking her arm, but she only became more upset. With help from a nurse, I moved her from the bed and onto my lap. I brushed tears from her cheeks and reminded her that she would eventually feel better.

Through Isaiah, God told the Israelites, "As a mother comforts her child, so will I comfort you" (Isaiah 66:13). God promised to give His children peace and to carry them the way a mother totes a child around on her side. This tender message was for the people who had a reverence for God—those who "tremble at his word" (v. 5).

God's ability and desire to comfort His people appears again in Paul's letter to the Corinthian believers. Paul said the Lord is the one "who comforts us in all our troubles" (2 Corinthians 1:3–4). God is gentle and sympathetic with us when we are in trouble.

One day all suffering will end. Our tears will dry up permanently (Revelation 21:4), and we will be safe in God's arms forever. Until then, we can depend on God's love to support us when we suffer.

Jennifer Benson Schuldt

God Promises

A Changed Heart and Spirit

TRANSFORMED HEARTS
EZEKIEL 36:22–31

Above all else, guard your heart, for everything you do flows from it.
Proverbs 4:23

During the early 1970s in Ghana, a poster titled "The Heart of Man" appeared on walls and public notice boards. In one picture, all kinds of reptiles— symbols of the vile and despicable—filled the heart-shaped painting with the head of a very unhappy man on top of it. In another image, the heart shape was clean and serene with the head of a contented man. The caption beneath the images read: "What is the condition of your heart?"

In Matthew 15:18–19, Jesus explained what pollutes a person. "The things that come out of a person's mouth come from the heart, and these defile them. For out of the heart come evil thoughts—murder, adultery, sexual immorality, theft, false testimony, slander." That is the condition of a heart separated from God—the situation ancient Israelites found themselves in when their sins forced them into exile (Ezekiel 36:23).

God's promise in Ezekiel 36:26 is beautiful: "I will give you a new heart, and I will put a new spirit in you. I will take out your stony, stubborn heart and give you a tender, responsive heart" (NLT; see also 11:19). God will take away our stubborn hearts that have been corrupted by all kinds of evil and give us a clean heart that is responsive to Him. Praise God for such a wonderful gift!

Lawrence Darmani

God Promises

That Jesus Will Return

BECAUSE I LOVE HIM
REVELATION 22:12–21

"Yes, I am coming soon." Amen. Come, Lord Jesus.
Revelation 22:20

The day before my husband was to return home from a business trip, my son said, "Mom! I want Daddy to come home." I asked him why, expecting him to say something about the presents his daddy usually brings back or that he missed playing ball with him. But with solemn seriousness he answered, "I want him to come back because I love him!"

His answer made me think about our Lord and His promise to come back. "I am coming soon," Jesus says (Revelation 22:20). I long for His return, but why do I want Him to come back? Is it because I will be in His presence, away from sickness and death? Is it because I am tired of living in a difficult world? Or is it because when you've loved Him so much of your life, when He has shared your tears and your laughter, when He has been more real than anybody else, you want to be with Him forever?

I'm glad my son misses his daddy when he's away. It would be terrible if he didn't care at all about his return or if he thought it would interfere with his plans. How do we feel about our Lord's return? Let us long for that day passionately, and earnestly say, "Lord, come back! We love you."

Keila Ochoa

God Promises

An Eternal Home for Us

A PLACE TO GO
NEHEMIAH 1:4-11

*My Father's house has many rooms; if that were not so, would
I have told that I am going there to prepare you a place for you?*
John 14:2

A thousand strands of time, events, and people weave into a tapestry we call *place*. More than just a house, place is where meaning, belonging, and safety come together under the covering of our best efforts at unconditional love. Place beckons us with memories buried deep in our souls. Even when our place isn't perfect, its hold on us is dramatic, magnetic.

The Bible speaks frequently of *place*. We see an example in Nehemiah's longing for a restored Jerusalem (Nehemiah 1:3–4; 2:2). It's no surprise, then, that Jesus would speak of place when He wants to comfort us. "Let not your heart be troubled," He began. Then He added: "I go to prepare a place for you" (John 14:1–2 NKJV).

For those who have fond memories of earthly places, this promise links us to something we can easily understand and look forward to. And for those whose earthly places have been anything but comforting and safe, Jesus promises that one day they will hear the sweet song place sings, for they will inhabit it with Him.

Whatever the struggle, whatever the faltering on your faith journey, remember this: There's a place in heaven already waiting, planned just for you. Jesus wouldn't have said so if it weren't true.

Randy Kilgore

God Promises
His Care

FLYING MACHINE
PSALM 6

*I am worn out with my groaning. All night I flood my bed
with weeping and drench my couch with tears.*

Psalm 6:6

Recording artist James Taylor exploded onto the music scene in early 1970 with the song "Fire and Rain." In it, he talked about the disappointments of life, describing them as "sweet dreams and flying machines in pieces on the ground." That was a reference to Taylor's original band Flying Machine, whose attempt at breaking into the recording industry had failed badly, causing him to wonder if his dreams of a musical career would ever come true. The reality of crushed expectations had taken their toll, leaving Taylor with a sense of loss and hopelessness.

The psalmist David also experienced hopeless despair, as he struggled with his own failures, the attacks of others, and the disappointments of life. In Psalm 6:6 he said, "I am worn out with my groaning. All night I flood my bed with weeping and drench my couch with my tears." The depth of his sorrow and loss drove him to heartache—but in that grief he turned to the God of all comfort. David's own crushed and broken "flying machines" gave way to the assurance of God's care, prompting him to say, "The LORD has heard my cry for mercy; the LORD accepts my prayer" (v. 9).

In our own seasons of disappointment, we too can find comfort in God, who cares for our broken hearts.

Bill Crowder

God Promises

To Support the Church with His Power

KEEP CALM AND CARRY ON
EZRA 5:7–17

We are the servants of the God of heaven and earth.

Ezra 5:11

"Keep calm and call mom." "Keep calm and eat bacon." "Keep calm and put the kettle on." These sayings are variations of the phrase: "Keep Calm and Carry On." This message was created in Great Britain in 1939 as the government sought ways to encourage the citizenry if the country were to be attacked. While it was never used as designed, the idea resurfaced around the turn of the century and caught on as a clever slogan.

Having returned to the land of Israel after a time of captivity, the Israelites had to overcome their own fear and enemy interference as they began to rebuild the temple (Ezra 3:3). Once they finished the foundation, their opponents "bribed officials to work against them and frustrate their plans" (4:5). Israel's enemies also wrote accusing letters to government officials and successfully delayed the project (vv. 6, 24). Despite this, King Darius eventually issued a decree that allowed them to complete the temple (6:12–14).

When we are engaged in God's work and we encounter setbacks, we can calmly carry on because, like the Israelites, "We are the servants of the God of heaven and earth" (5:11). Obstacles and delays may discourage us, but we can rest in Jesus's promise: "I will build my church, and all the powers of hell will not conquer it" (Matthew 16:18 NLT). It is God's power that enables His work, not our own.

Jennifer Benson Schuldt

God Promises
To Carry Our Burdens for Us

A SANCTUARY
MATTHEW 11:25–30

*Come to me, all you who are weary
and burdened, and I will give you rest.*
Matthew 11:28

Upon entering a church in Klang, Malaysia, I was intrigued by the sign welcoming us into the building. It declared the place to be "A Sanctuary for the Heavy Laden."

Few things better reflect the heart of Christ than for His church to be a place where burdens are lifted and the weary find rest. This was vital in Jesus's ministry, for He said, "Come to me, all you who are weary and burdened, and I will give you rest" (Matthew 11:28).

Jesus promised to take our burdens and exchange them for His light load. "Take my yoke upon you and learn from me, for I am gentle and humble in heart, and you will find rest for your souls. For my yoke is easy and my burden is light" (vv. 29–30).

This promise is backed by His great strength. Whatever burdens we may carry, in Christ we find the strong shoulders of the Son of God, who promises to take our heavy burdens and exchange them for His light load.

Christ, who loves us with an everlasting love, understands our struggles and can be trusted to provide us with a rest we can never find on our own. His strength is enough for our weakness, making Him our "sanctuary for the heavy laden."

Bill Crowder

═══════ *God Promises* ═══════

A Renewed, Renovated Body in Heaven

NEW BIRTH
PSALM 139:7–16

You created my inmost being;
you knit me together in my mother's womb.

Psalm 139:13

What is there about babies that makes us smile? Many people will stop everything at the sight or sound of a baby and will flock to gaze at the little one. I noticed this when I visited my dad at a nursing home. Though most of the residents were wheelchair-bound and suffered from dementia, the visit of a family with a baby almost unfailingly brought a spark of joy to their eyes that—tentatively at first but then undoubtedly—became a smile. It was amazing to watch.

Perhaps babies bring a smile because of the wonder of a new life—so precious, tiny, and full of promise. Seeing a baby can remind us of our awesome God and the great love He has for us. He loved us so much that He gave us life and formed us in our mother's womb. "You created my inmost being," the psalmist says; "you knit me together in my mother's womb" (Psalm 139:13).

Not only does He give us physical life but He also offers us spiritual rebirth through Jesus (John 3:3–8). God promises believers new bodies and life eternal when Jesus returns (1 Corinthians 15:50–52).

Physical life and spiritual rebirth—gifts to celebrate from our Father's hand.

Alyson Kieda

God Promises
To Reward our Perseverance

CONFIDENCE IN GOD
HEBREWS 10:22-29

Do not throw away your confidence; it will be richly rewarded.
Hebrews 10:35

There is an old adage that says, "Don't bite off more than you can chew." It's wise not to take on more responsibilities than we can handle. At some time, however, we will likely feel overwhelmed by the size and difficulty of a task we have agreed to do.

This can happen even in our walk of faith in Christ when our commitment to God seems too much to bear. But the Lord has an encouraging word for us when our confidence wavers.

The writer of Hebrews urged his readers to recall the courage they demonstrated during the early days of their faith (10:32–33). Despite public insults and persecution, they aided believers in prison, and they joyfully accepted the confiscation of their own property (vv. 33–34). With that in mind, he says, "So do not throw away your confidence; it will be richly rewarded. You need to persevere so that when you have done the will of God, you will receive what he has promised" (vv. 35–36).

Our confidence is not in ourselves but in Jesus and His promise to return at just the right time (v. 37).

David McCasland

MARCH 17

God Promises

If You Reach Out to God, He Will Help You

DADDY!

2 KINGS 19:10–19

Give ear, LORD, and hear; open your eyes, LORD, and see.

2 Kings 19:16

Twenty-month-old James was leading his family confidently through the hallways of their large church. His daddy kept an eye on him the whole time as James toddled his way through the crowd of "giants." Suddenly the little boy panicked because he could not see his dad. He stopped, looked around, and started to cry, "Daddy, Daddy!" His dad quickly caught up with him and little James reached up his hand, which Daddy strongly clasped. Immediately James was at peace.

Second Kings tells the story of King Hezekiah, who reached up to God for help (19:15). Sennacherib, the king of Assyria, had made threats against Hezekiah and the people of Judah, saying, "Do not let the god you depend on deceive you. . . . Surely you have heard what the kings of Assyria have done to all the countries, destroying them completely. And will you be delivered?" (vv. 10–11). King Hezekiah went to the Lord and prayed for deliverance so "that all the kingdoms of the earth may know that you alone, LORD, are God" (vv. 14–19). In answer to his prayer, the angel of the Lord struck down the enemy, and Sennacherib withdrew (vv. 20–36).

If you're in a situation where you need God's help, reach up your hand to Him in prayer. He has promised His comfort and help (2 Corinthians 1:3–4; Hebrews 4:16).

Anne Cetas

God Promises
Himself as a Companion

NEVER ALONE
HEBREWS 13:1–8

*Keep your lives free from the love of money and be
content with what you have, because God has said,
"Never will I leave you; never will I forsake you."*
Hebrews 13:5

Having played intercollegiate soccer, I've never lost my love for "The Beautiful Game." I especially enjoy watching the English Premier League. One reason is the skill and speed with which the game is played there. Also, I love the way the fans sing in support of their beloved "sides." For instance, Liverpool has for years had "You'll Never Walk Alone" as its theme. How moving to hear 50,000 fans rise as one to sing the lyrics of that old standard! It's an encouragement to players and fans alike that together they will see each other through to the end. Walk alone? Never.

This sentiment has meaning for everyone. Because each of us is made for community, isolation and loneliness are among the most painful of human experiences. During painful times, our faith is vital.

The child of God never needs to fear abandonment. Even if people turn on us, friends forsake us, or circumstances separate us from loved ones, we are never alone. God has said, "Never will I leave you; never will I forsake you" (Hebrews 13:5). This is not just a nice tune or clever lyrics offering an empty sentiment. It is the promise of God himself to those who are the objects of His love. He is there—and He isn't going away.

With Christ, you will never walk alone.

Bill Crowder

God Promises
Never to Let Us Go

MY FINGERNAILS OR HIS HANDS?
PSALM 37:23–26

The Lord upholds him with his hand.
Psalm 37:24

Tough times can cause us to get our perspective turned around. I was reminded of this when I talked to a fellow griever—another parent who, like Sue and me, lost a teenage daughter to death suddenly and without warning.

She told me she had been missing her daughter terribly, and she told God she felt as if she were hanging on by her fingernails. Then she felt as if God reminded her that His hand of protection was there to hold her up—that she could let go, and He would catch her.

That's a better perspective, isn't it? This picture reminds us that when troubles come and we feel least able to hold on to our faith, it's not up to us. It's up to God to support us with His mighty hand.

Psalm 37:23–24 says: "The Lord makes firm the steps of the one who delights in him; though he may stumble, he will not fall, for the Lord upholds him with his hand." And Psalm 63:8 tells us: "I cling to you; your right hand upholds me."

In tough times, we can become so preoccupied with our role in "clinging to God" that we forget about His promised protection. It's not our fingernails that sustain us—it's His loving, upholding hand.

Dave Branon

God Promises
That Jesus Is the Resurrection and the Life

LETTING GO
JOHN 11:21–36

Precious in the sight of the LORD is the death of his faithful servants.
Psalm 116:15

"Your father is actively dying," said the hospice nurse. "Actively dying" refers to the final phase of the dying process and was a new term to me, one that felt strangely like traveling down a lonely one-way street. On my dad's last day, not knowing if he could still hear us, my sister and I sat by his bed. We kissed the top of his beautiful bald head. We whispered God's promises to him. We sang "Great Is Thy Faithfulness" and quoted the 23rd Psalm. We told him we loved him and thanked him for being our dad. We knew his heart longed to be with Jesus, and we told him he could go. Speaking those words was the first painful step in letting go. A few minutes later, our dad was joyously welcomed into his eternal home.

The final release of a loved one is painful. Even Jesus's tears flowed when His good friend Lazarus died (John 11:35). But because of God's promises, we have hope beyond physical death. Psalm 116:15 says that God's "faithful servants"—those who belong to Him—are "precious" to Him. Though they die, they'll be alive again.

Jesus promises, "I am the resurrection and the life. The one who believes in me will live, even though they die; and whoever lives by believing in me will never die" (John 11:25–26). What comfort it brings to know we'll be in God's presence forever.

Cindy Hess Kasper

God Promises
He Will Care for Us Forever

ROOM AND BOARD
JOHN 14:1–11

I go to prepare a place for you.
John 14:2 NKJV

On a recent trip to England, my wife and I visited Anne Hathaway's Cottage in Stratford-upon-Avon. The house is more than four hundred years old, and it was the childhood and family home of William Shakespeare's wife.

The tour guide drew our attention to a table made with wide boards. One side was used for eating meals and the other for chopping food. In English life, different expressions grew from this usage as the word *board* became associated with food, housing, honesty, and authority. An inn would offer "room and board"—that is, sleeping and eating accommodations. In taverns where customers played cards, they were told to keep their hands "above board" to make sure they weren't cheating. And in the home, the father was given a special chair at the head of the table where he was called "chairman of the board."

As I reflected on this, I thought about how Jesus is our "room and board." He is our source of spiritual nourishment (John 6:35, 54); He empowers us to live a life of integrity (14:21); He is our loving Master (Philippians 2:11); and He is even now preparing our eternal home. He promised: "I go to prepare a place for you" (John 14:2 NKJV; see also 14:1–4, 23). His grace has provided our everlasting room and board.

Dennis Fisher

God Promises

Guidance through the Holy Spirit

EYE IN THE SKY
PSALM 139:1–10

The LORD will guide you always.
Isaiah 58:11

Creating a system by which an "eye in the sky" can help guide cars and planes and boats all the time is complicated. For instance, the Global Positioning System (GPS) that most people are familiar with works because there are always twenty-four to thirty-two satellites orbiting the Earth at an altitude of 12,600 miles. These satellites must maintain a constant speed and altitude if the guidance they provide is to be accurate.

Today's complicated GPS is just a tiny analogy of what God can do. God promised the nation of Israel: "The LORD will guide you always" (Isaiah 58:11). The psalmist was aware that there was no place he could go without God knowing where he was (Psalm 139:7–8). Long before GPS, God sat "above the circle of the earth" (Isaiah 40:22) and saw everything.

The knowledge that there is someone who tracks you wherever you are can bring fear to those who are trying to get away. But for the Christian, this brings great joy and assurance. No matter where he was, the psalmist was confident that God's hand would lead him (Psalm 139:10).

God has promised to guide and lead you today. He's the best Guide you could have, and He wants to lead you along the right paths.

C. P. Hia

God Promises

A Trove of Promises

THE TREASURE CHEST
HEBREWS 11:32–40

*Imitate those who through faith and
patience inherit what has been promised.*
Hebrews 6:12

When I was a young girl, my mother often let me rummage through her button box as I recovered from an illness. It always cheered me to come across old, familiar buttons and remember the garments they once adorned. I especially liked it when she picked out an old, overlooked button and used it again.

Similarly, I often leaf through my Bible during distressing times and recall familiar promises that have strengthened me. But I'm always encouraged to find help from promises I've never noticed before.

I remember one dark morning during my husband's terminal illness when I was looking for a word from God to sustain me in our painful circumstances. In Hebrews 11, I noted that God had rescued His suffering people in some very dramatic ways. Yet I couldn't always identify with their particular situations. Then I read about some "whose weakness was turned to strength" (v. 34). God used that phrase to assure me that I too could be made strong in my weakness. At that very moment I began sensing His strength, and my faith was renewed.

Are you being tested today? Remember, there are many promises in the Bible, God's treasure chest. Generations have proven them true, and so can you.

Joanie Yoder

God Promises
Peace in a Difficult World

TROUBLED TIMES
JOHN 16:21–33

In this world you will have trouble.
But take heart! I have overcome the world.

John 16:33

If you've never heard of Murphy's Law, you've probably experienced it: "If anything can go wrong, it will."

Murphy's maxim reminds me of the principle Jesus shared with His disciples when He told them, "In this world you will have trouble" (John 16:33). In other words, we can count on it—sooner or later we will hit troubled times. It's not the way God originally intended life to be, but when the human race first succumbed to Satan's seduction in the garden, everything on this planet fell into the grip of sin. And the result has been disorder and dysfunction ever since.

The reality of trouble in life is obvious. It's the reality of peace that often eludes us. Interestingly, when Jesus warned His followers about trouble, in the same breath He also promised peace. He even told them to "take heart! I have overcome the world" (v. 33). The word *overcome* indicates a past event that has a continuing effect. Not only did Jesus conquer the fallen world through His death and resurrection but He also continues to provide victory, no matter how much trouble we may face.

So, although we can expect some trouble in this fallen world, the good news is that we can count on Jesus for peace in troubled times.

Joe Stowell

God Promises

To Always Be with Us

DAD, WHERE ARE YOU?
DEUTERONOMY 31:1–8

The LORD himself goes before you and will be with you; he will never leave you nor forsake you. Do not be afraid; do not be discouraged.

Deuteronomy 31:8

"Dad! Where are you?"

I was pulling into our driveway when my daughter, panicking, called me on my cell phone. I needed to be home by 6:00 to get her to play practice; I was on time. My daughter's voice, however, betrayed her lack of trust. Reflexively, I responded: "I'm here. Why don't you trust me?"

But as I spoke those words, I wondered, How often could my heavenly Father ask that of me? In stressful moments, I too am impatient. I too struggle to trust, to believe that God will keep His promises. So I cry out: "Father! Where are you?"

Amid stress and uncertainty, I sometimes doubt God's presence—or even His goodness and purposes for me. The Israelites did too. In Deuteronomy 31, they were preparing to enter the promised land, knowing their leader, Moses, would stay behind. Moses sought to reassure God's people by reminding them, "The LORD himself goes before you and will be with you; he will never leave you nor forsake you. Do not be afraid; do not be discouraged" (v. 8).

That promise—that God is always with us—remains a cornerstone of our faith today (see Matthew 1:23; Hebrews 13:5). Indeed, Revelation 21:3 culminates with these words: "God's dwelling place is now among the people, and he will dwell with them."

Where is God? He is right here, right now, right with us—always ready to hear our prayers.

Adam Holz

God Promises

To Work for Good for His Trusting Ones

STORM CLOUDS
ROMANS 8:18–30

Our light and momentary troubles are achieving
for us an eternal glory that far outweighs them all.
2 Corinthians 4:17

I was feeling down about some circumstances the other day and wondering how I might lift my spirits. I pulled from my shelf the book *Life Is Like Licking Honey Off a Thorn* by Susan Lenzkes, and I read this: "We take the laughter and the tears however they come, and let our God of reality make sense of it all."

Lenzkes says some people are optimists who "camp in pleasures and good memories," denying the brokenness. Others are pessimists who "focus on life's losses, losing joy and victory in the process." But people of faith are realists who "receive it all—all the good and bad of life—and repeatedly choose to know that God really loves us and is constantly at work for our good and His glory."

As I read, I looked outside and noticed dark clouds and a steady rain. A little later, a friendly wind came up and blew the clouds away. Suddenly the skies were bright blue. The storms of life blow in and out like that.

By faith we cling to God's promise of Romans 8:28. And we recall that "our light and momentary troubles are achieving for us an eternal glory that far outweighs them all" (2 Corinthians 4:17). God loves us, and He's getting us ready for the day when skies will be forever blue.

Anne Cetas

God Promises
That Jesus Left Us Great Blessings

A DEPARTING BLESSING
LUKE 24:44-53

*While he was blessing them, he left them
and was taken up into heaven.*
Luke 24:51

A cancer-stricken believer was dying. I was in his room as his family gathered around him. One by one he spoke to his children, to their spouses, and to his young grandchildren. He gave each a loving, tender blessing. Even his warnings were spoken with gentleness. He reminded them to keep the Lord in the center of their lives. We wept together, knowing that soon he would no longer be with us. A few days later he was gone.

Our Savior was doing much the same thing just before He ascended to heaven. Rather than weep as they saw Him leave, His disciples were filled with great joy, even though they understood only dimly how they would experience His blessings. But Jesus would soon send the Holy Spirit to indwell them (Acts 1–2). He would carry on a ministry of intercession for them "at the right hand of God" (Romans 8:34). And the promise of His return would comfort them (1 Thessalonians 4:13–18).

As we think about our Savior ascending to heaven, let's rejoice in the blessings He left us. And as we have occasion, let's encourage our loved ones to keep Jesus at the center of their lives. Someday we will depart from this earth, and our example and words may be the most precious blessing we can leave behind.

David Egner

God Promises
To Be Our Refuge

ABLE AND AVAILABLE
PSALM 46

God is our refuge and strength, an ever-present help in trouble.
Psalm 46:1

My husband was at work when I received news about my mom's cancer diagnosis. I left him a message and reached out to friends and family. None were available. Covering my face with trembling hands, I sobbed. "Help me, Lord." A resulting assurance that God was with me comforted me through those moments when I felt utterly alone.

I thanked the Lord when my husband came home and support from friends and family trickled in. Still, the calming awareness of God's presence I sensed in those first few hours of lonely grieving affirmed that God is readily and faithfully available wherever and whenever I need help.

In Psalm 46, the psalmist proclaims that God is our sanctuary, our strength, and our steadfast supporter (v. 1). When it feels as if we're surrounded by chaos or everything we thought was stable crashes down around us, we don't have to fear (vv. 2–3). God doesn't falter (vv. 4–7). His power is evident and effective (vv. 8–9). Our eternal Sustainer gives us confidence in His unchanging character (v. 10). The Lord, our secure stronghold, remains with us forever (v. 11).

God created His followers to prayerfully support and encourage one another. But He also affirms He is always able and available. When we call on God, we can trust Him to keep His promises to provide for us. He will comfort us through His people as well as through His personal presence.

Xochitl Dixon

God Promises
A Harvest

TIRED OF DOING GOOD?
GALATIANS 6:1-10

---

*Let us not become weary in doing good, for at the
proper time we will reap a harvest if we do not give up.*
Galatians 6:9

George does volunteer work for an inner-city ministry. He picks up boys and girls for club meetings, delivers sacks of groceries to needy families, and tries to coach some of the teens who come to the gym to play basketball. But he's thinking of quitting. He doesn't feel that his efforts are accomplishing anything. In fact, he receives little or no gratitude from the people he's trying to help.

Often we don't see the results of doing good until much later. Leslie B. Flynn tells about Dyson Hague, a chaplain in an English hospital who visited a ward of dying soldiers. One man asked him if he would write his Sunday school teacher and tell her he would die a Christian because of her teaching.

Chaplain Hague wrote the letter. A few weeks later he received this reply: "Just a month ago I resigned my class of young men I had been teaching for years, for I felt that my teaching was getting nowhere. Then came your letter, telling how my teaching had helped win this boy to Christ. I've asked for my class back. May God have mercy on me!"

If you're getting tired of doing good, think carefully before you quit. God promises that you will reap a harvest if you keep at it.

Herb Vander Lugt

God Promises
To Keep Us Secure and Safe

HE WON'T LET US GO
JOHN 10:22–30

I give them eternal life, and they shall never perish;
no one will snatch them out of my hand.

John 10:28

Julio was biking across the George Washington Bridge—a busy, double-decked thoroughfare connecting New York City and New Jersey—when he encountered a life-or-death situation. A man was standing on a ledge over the Hudson River preparing to jump. Knowing that the police wouldn't arrive in time, Julio acted quickly. He got off his bike and spread out his arms toward the man, saying something like: "Don't do it. We love you." Then, like a shepherd with a crook, he grabbed the distraught man, and with the help of another passerby, brought him to safety. According to reports, Julio wouldn't let go of the man, even after he was safe.

Two millennia earlier, in a life-or-death situation, Jesus, the Good Shepherd, said He would lay down His life to save and never let go of those who believed in Him. He summarized how He would bless His sheep: they would know Him personally, have the gift of eternal life, would never perish, and would be secure in His care. This security didn't depend on the ability of the frail and feeble sheep but on the sufficiency of the Shepherd who'll never let one be snatched "out of [His] hand" (John 10:28–29).

When we were distraught and feeling hopeless, Jesus rescued us. Now we can feel safe and secure in our relationship with Him. He loves us, pursues us, finds us, saves us, and promises never to let us go.

Marvin Williams

God Promises

His Mercy

GOD'S PROMISES
GENESIS 9:1–17

*I have set my rainbow in the clouds, and it will be
the sign of the covenant between me and the earth.*

Genesis 9:13

Do you like to look at rainbows? When you see a rainbow, have you ever
thought that God is looking at it too?

The next time that multicolored spectrum of beauty bends over
the landscape, take time to view it in the light of God's promise to
Noah: "Whenever the rainbow appears in the clouds, I will see it and
remember the everlasting covenant between God and all living creatures"
(Genesis 9:16).

The rainbow was a reminder of God's gracious pledge that He would
never again destroy the earth with water. A worse calamity, though, is coming. Peter warned, "The present heavens and earth are reserved for fire,
being kept for the day of judgment" (2 Peter 3:7).

The rainbow, seen against the clouds of judgment, spoke of grace. But
the rainbow fades when compared to God's grace shown at Calvary. At
the cross, God's wrath against sin was placed on Jesus Christ, the believer's
substitute. When the Light of the world met the storm clouds of judgment
at Calvary, a beautiful bow of promise and forgiveness came into view.
And one day believers will gather around God's rainbow-circled throne
(Revelation 4:1–3).

So next time you see a rainbow, celebrate! And remember God's abundant mercy and grace.

Henry Bosch

God Promises
To Care for Us Every Day

UNOPENED TOMORROWS
MATTHEW 6:25–34

We live by faith, not by sight.
2 Corinthians 5:7

We often wish we could see what lies around the corner in life. Then we could prepare for it, control it, or avoid it.

A wise person has said, "Though we can't see around corners, God can!" How much better and more reassuring that is!

One day my ten-year-old granddaughter Emily and I were boiling eggs for breakfast. As we stared into the boiling water and wondered how long it would take to get the eggs just right, Emily said, "Pity we can't open them up to see how they're doing." I agreed! But that would have spoiled them, so we had to rely on guesswork, with no guarantee of results.

We began talking about other things we would like to see but can't—like tomorrow. Too bad we can't crack tomorrow open, we said, to see if it's the way we would like it. But meddling with tomorrow before its time, like opening a partly cooked egg, would spoil both today and tomorrow.

Because Jesus has promised to care for us every day—and that includes tomorrow—we can live by faith one day at a time (Matthew 6:33–34).

Emily and I decided to leave tomorrow safely in God's hands. Have you?

Joanie Yoder

God Promises
To Forgive

THE ERASER OF CONFESSION
1 JOHN 1:5–10

---

*If we confess our sins, he is faithful and just
and will forgive us our sins.*

1 John 1:9

From the time Joseph Dixon (1827–1869) began producing the pencil during the US Civil War, the only substantial change in its design has been the addition of an eraser. Consider for a moment this unique little writing stick. At one end is a hard black point and at the other a small rubber tip. This simple instrument can be used to scribble, sketch, compute complicated formulas, or compose lofty poetry. But it can also quickly correct an error, change a figure, or start all over.

Each day the Christian inscribes words and deeds on the record of his personal history. But as he reflects upon what he's said and done, he becomes aware that some of what's been written is not of the quality that will please the Savior. He remembers attitudes and actions that should never be part of a believer's life. Yet these sins are forgiven and fellowship with God restored through honest confession and repentance.

In John's first epistle, he told us how to walk uprightly and enjoy fellowship with Christ and with one another. But John was a realist, knowing that some of the pages of our composition would be marked by daily flaws and failures. That's why 1 John 1:9 is such a blessed promise. It tells us we can use the eraser of confession and start over.

Dennis DeHaan

God Promises

A Crown of Righteousness

WHAT COMES NEXT?
2 TIMOTHY 4:1–8

There is in store for me the crown of righteousness,
which the Lord . . . will award to me on that day.

2 Timothy 4:8

On the night of April 3, 1968, Dr. Martin Luther King Jr. gave his final speech, "I've Been to the Mountaintop." In it, he hints that he believed he might not live long. He said, "We've got some difficult days ahead. But it doesn't matter with me now. Because I've been to the mountaintop. And I've looked over. And I've seen the promised land. I may not get there with you. . . . [But] I'm happy tonight. I'm not worried about anything. I'm not fearing any man. Mine eyes have seen the glory of the coming of the Lord." The next day, he was assassinated.

The apostle Paul, shortly before his death, wrote to his protégé Timothy: "I am already being poured out like a drink offering, and the time for my departure is near. . . . Now there is in store for me the crown of righteousness, which the Lord, the righteous Judge, will award to me on that day" (2 Timothy 4:6, 8). Paul knew his time on earth was drawing to a close, as did Dr. King. Both men realized lives of incredible significance, yet they never lost sight of the true life ahead. Both men welcomed what came next.

Like them, may we "fix our eyes not on what is seen, but on what is unseen, since what is seen is temporary, but what is unseen is eternal" (2 Corinthians 4:18).

Remi Oyedele

God Promises
To Care for Our Needs

GETTING WHAT YOU WANT
LUKE 12:15, 22–34

Life does not consist in an abundance of possessions.
Luke 12:15

There's a popular idea floating around about how to get whatever you want. It's called "the law of attraction." Just think and feel what you want to attract, and "the law will use people, circumstances, and events to magnetize what you want to you, and magnetize you to it." This positive-thinking philosophy teaches that the "energy" of your dominant thoughts "attracts" your circumstances.

You won't find that idea anywhere in the Bible! As believers, we have good reason to be positive in our thinking, but it's because our heavenly Father understands our needs and meets them. Since He cares for us, we don't have to be anxious (Luke 12:29–30). "Life does not consist in an abundance of possessions" (v. 15), so we make it our aim instead to be "rich toward God" (v. 21). We do that by seeking His kingdom and purpose (v. 31) and by laying up treasures in heaven, not for ourselves in this life.

Jesus said, "Be on your guard against all kinds of greed" (v. 15) because one day, like the foolish rich person in the parable in Luke 12, we will leave it all behind. That's when we'll have more than we ever dreamed of. In the meantime, God promises to care for our needs—no matter what the circumstances. And that's no secret.

Anne Cetas

God Promises

Peace, Perfect Peace

DEALING WITH DELAY
ISAIAH 26:1-9

You will keep in perfect peace those whose minds are steadfast.
Isaiah 26:3

Clouds of ash spewed by a volcano in Iceland closed airports across the UK and Europe for five days. Nearly 100,000 flights were canceled and millions of passengers around the world found themselves in an enormous holding pattern on the ground. People missed important events, businesses lost money, and no one knew when it would end.

When our plans fall apart and there is no remedy, how do we deal with frustration and delay? Isaiah 26:3–4 is an anchor for our souls in every storm of life: "You will keep in perfect peace those whose minds are steadfast, because they trust in you. Trust in the LORD forever, for the LORD, the LORD himself, is the Rock eternal." Whether we're facing annoying inconvenience or heartbreaking loss, this rock-solid promise is worth memorizing and repeating every night when we close our eyes to sleep.

Today, when plans are shattered, do our minds dwell on the circumstances or on the Lord? During frustrating delay, can we still trust the loving heart of God? In the hymn "Like a River Glorious," Frances Havergal so beautifully expressed what we long for, "Finding as He promised, perfect peace and rest."

David McCasland

God Promises
Comfort and Support

AN ANCHOR WHEN WE'RE AFRAID
ISAIAH 51:12–16

I, even I, am he who comforts you.
Isaiah 51:12

Are you a worrier? I am. I wrestle with anxiety almost daily. I worry about big things. I worry about small things. Sometimes, it seems like I worry about everything. During my teenage years, I called the police when my parents were four hours late getting home.

Scripture repeatedly tells us not to be afraid. Because of God's goodness and power, and because He sent Jesus to die for us and His Holy Spirit to guide us, our fears don't have to rule our lives. We may well face hard things, but God has promised to be with us through it all.

One passage that has helped me profoundly in fearful moments is Isaiah 51:12–16. Here, God reminded His people, who had endured tremendous suffering, that He was still with them and that His comforting presence is the ultimate reality. No matter how bad things may seem: "I, even I, am he who comforts you," He told them through the prophet Isaiah (v. 12).

I love that promise. Those eight words have been an emotion-steadying anchor for my soul. I've clung to this promise repeatedly when life has felt overwhelming, when my own "constant terror" (v. 13) has felt oppressive. Through this passage, God reminds me to lift my eyes from my fears and in faith and dependence look to the One who "stretches out the heavens" (v. 13)—the One who promises to comfort us.

Adam Holz

God Promises
To Lovingly Care for Us

STRENGTH IN STILLNESS
EXODUS 14:10–14

In quietness and trust is your strength.
Isaiah 30:15

Early in my Christian life the demands of commitment made me wonder if I could make it past a year without returning to my old sinful ways. But this Scripture verse helped me: "The LORD will fight for you; you need only to be still" (Exodus 14:14). These are the words Moses spoke to the Israelites when they had just escaped from slavery in Egypt and were being pursued by Pharaoh. They were discouraged and afraid.

Since I was a young believer, with temptations engulfing my world, this call "to be still" encouraged me. Now, more than forty years later, remaining still and calm while trusting Him in the midst of stress-laden situations has been a constant desire for my Christian living.

"Be still, and know that I am God," the psalmist says (Psalm 46:10). When we remain still, we get to know God, "our refuge and strength, an ever-present help in trouble" (v. 1). We see our weakness apart from God and recognize our need to surrender to Him. "When I am weak, then I am strong," says the apostle Paul (2 Corinthians 12:10).

Daily we grind through stress and other frustrating situations. But we can trust that He will be faithful to His promise to care for us. May we learn to be still.

Lawrence Darmani

God Promises
That He Will Help Fight Our Battles

NOTHING LEFT BUT GOD
2 CHRONICLES 20:3–17

*Do not be afraid or discouraged because of this
vast army. For the battle is not yours, but God's.*
2 Chronicles 20:15

A wise Bible teacher once said, "Sooner or later God will bring self-sufficient people to the place where they have no resource but Him—no strength, no answers, nothing but Him. Without God's help, they're sunk."

He then told of a despairing man who confessed to his pastor, "My life is really in bad shape." "How bad?" the pastor inquired. Burying his head in his hands, he moaned, "I'll tell you how bad—all I've got left is God." The pastor's face lit up. "I'm happy to assure you that a person with nothing left but God has more than enough for great victory!"

In today's Bible reading, the people of Judah were also in trouble. They admitted their lack of power and wisdom to conquer their foes. All they had left was God! But King Jehoshaphat and the people saw this as reason for hope, not despair. "Our eyes are on you," they declared to God (2 Chronicles 20:12). And their hope was not disappointed as He fulfilled His promise: "The battle is not yours, but God's" (v. 15).

Are you in a position where all self-sufficiency is gone? As you turn your eyes on the Lord and put your hope in Him, you have God's reassuring promise that you need nothing more.

Joanie Yoder

God Promises

To Love His Own Forever

DISPOSABLE CULTURE
PSALM 136:1–9, 23–26

Give thanks to the LORD, for he is good. His love endures forever.
Psalm 136:1

More than ever, we live in a disposable culture. Think for a minute about some of the things that are made to be thrown away—razors, water bottles, lighters, paper plates, plastic eating utensils. Products are used, tossed, and then replaced.

This disposable culture is also reflected in more significant ways. Many times true commitment in relationships is seen as optional. Marriages struggle to survive. Long-term employees are discharged just before retirement for cheaper options. A highly revered athlete leaves to join another team. It seems as if nothing lasts.

Our unchanging God, however, has promised that His loving mercy endures forever. In Psalm 136, the singer celebrates this wonderful promise by making statements about God's wonder, work, and character. He then punctuates each statement about God with the phrase, "His loves endures forever." Whether it is the wonder of His creation (vv. 4–9), the rescue of His people (vv. 10–22), or His tender care for His own (vv. 23–26), we can trust Him because His mercy will never fail. In a temporary world, the permanence of God's mercy gives us hope. We can sing with the psalmist, "Give thanks to the LORD, for he is good. His love endures forever" (v. 1).

Bill Crowder

God Promises
That Jesus Is Returning; Look for Him

COMING SOON
REVELATION 22:7–21

Yes, I am coming soon.
Revelation 22:20

A "COMING SOON!" announcement often precedes future events in entertainment and sports, or the launch of the latest technology. The goal is to create anticipation and excitement for what is going to happen, even though it may be months away.

While reading the book of Revelation, I was impressed with the "coming soon" sense of immediacy permeating the entire book. Rather than saying, "Someday, in the far distant future, Jesus Christ is going to return to earth," the text is filled with phrases like "what must soon take place" (1:1) and "the time is near" (v. 3). Three times in the final chapter, the Lord says, "I am coming soon" (Revelation 22:7, 12, 20). Other versions translate this phrase as, "I'm coming speedily" and "I'm on My way!"

How can this be—since two thousand years have elapsed since these words were written? "Soon" doesn't seem appropriate for our experience of time.

Rather than focusing on a date for His return, the Lord is urging us to set our hearts on His promise that will be fulfilled. We are called to live for Him in this present age as we "wait for the blessed hope—the appearing of the glory of our great God and Savior, Jesus Christ" (Titus 2:13).

David McCasland

God Promises
True and Certain Hope

THE SOURCE
PSALM 23

You have been my hope, Sovereign LORD,
my confidence since my youth.
Psalm 71:5

The ancient road from Jerusalem to Jericho is a narrow, treacherous path along a deep gorge in the Judean wilderness. Its name is Wadi Kelt, but it's known as the valley of the shadow, for this is the location that inspired David's 23rd Psalm. The place itself offers little reason to compose such a hopeful poem. The landscape is bleak, barren, and perilously steep. It's a good place for thieves, but not for anyone else.

When David wrote, "Even though I walk through the valley of the shadow of death, I fear no evil" (v. 4 NASB), he was in a place where evil was an ever-present reality. Yet he refused to give in to fear. He wasn't expressing hope that God would abolish evil so he could pass through safely; he was saying that the presence of God gave him the confidence to pass through difficult places without fear of being deserted by Him. In another psalm, David said that the Lord was his hope (71:5).

Many claim to have hope, but only those whose hope is Christ can claim it with certainty. Hope comes not from strength, intelligence, or favorable circumstances, but from the one true source—the Lord. As Maker of heaven and earth, He alone has the right to promise hope and the power to keep the promise.

Julie Ackerman Link

God Promises
To Give Us Peace

SEND TRANQUILITY
JOHN 14:25–31

The LORD gives strength to his people;
the LORD blesses his people with peace.

Psalm 29:11

When Jesus was with His disciples in the upper room shortly before His crucifixion, He knew they would face turmoil and unrest in the days ahead. First, they would experience the distressing events of His betrayal, arrest, execution, and burial. Then, after His resurrection and ascension, long periods of hard work, opposition, ridicule, and persecution would come. So in the quiet of those final moments together, He gave them these words of comfort: "Peace I leave with you, my peace I give you. I do not give to you as the world gives" (John 14:27).

Peace of mind and heart is still one of mankind's most precious and needed commodities. In his book *A Time to Heal*, President Gerald R. Ford repeated a story he had heard some years earlier. During the civil war in Greece in 1948, a villager was planning to emigrate to the United States. Before he left, he asked his weary, beleaguered, poverty-stricken neighbors, "What should I send when I get to America? Should I send money? Food? Clothing?" "No," one of his neighbors replied, "you should send us a ton of tranquility."

Perhaps the burdens and pressures of life are piling up on you. Like those Greek patriots and Christ's disciples, you need peace. If so, and if you know Jesus as Savior, trust Him to make good on His promise (John 14:27). Stop struggling and just rest by faith in His loving arms. Cast your burden on Him. He is the Prince of Peace, and He has promised to send tranquility.

David Egner

God Promises

A Wonderful Counselor

KING OF OUR LIVES
JOHN 19:16–22

*For what I received I passed on to you as of first importance:
that Christ died for our sins according to the Scriptures.*

1 Corinthians 15:3

Nearly two thousand years ago in Jerusalem, Pontius Pilate commanded that a placard be placed on the cross that read: "Jesus of Nazareth, the King of the Jews." Perhaps Pilate sought to induce fear among the people and discourage them from crowning their own king.

"King of the Jews." Was it an original thought at the time? Perhaps it had been introduced when the wise men asked, "Where is the one who has been born king of the Jews?" (Matthew 2:2). They had sought the fulfillment of this promise: "For to us a child is born . . . ; the government will be on his shoulders. And he will be called Wonderful Counselor, Mighty God, Everlasting Father, Prince of Peace" (Isaiah 9:6). They believed Jesus was this Child.

Later, when Christ was crucified, some jeered, "Come down from the cross, if you are the Son of God" (Matthew 27:40). They wanted to see if Jesus really was King. But Jesus did not come down. The true meaning of the cross is that "Christ died for our sins" (1 Corinthians 15:3). He who paid the penalty of our sins has made God's forgiveness possible.

Those who accept God's forgiveness and ask Jesus Christ to be their Savior and Lord can have only one appropriate response—to serve Him. He is King of our lives.

Albert Lee

APRIL 14

God Promises

His Holy Presence in Our Lives

FROM A DISTANCE
ACTS 17:22–31

Surely the LORD is in this place, and I was not aware of it.

Genesis 28:16

A popular song from years ago titled "From a Distance" envisions a world of harmony and peace. It says, "God is watching us from a distance." Indeed, God is watching us, but not from a distance. He is present in the room with you, right in front of you, gazing at you with unbounded love in His eyes.

I think of the example of Brother Lawrence, who spent long years working in a kitchen washing pots and pans and repairing the sandals of other monks. He wrote: "As often as I could, I placed myself as a worshiper before Him, fixing my mind upon His holy presence."

That is our task as well. But we forget and sometimes need reminders of His presence. I have driven an old handmade nail into the shelf over my desk to remind me that the crucified and resurrected Jesus is always present. Our task is to remember to "keep [our] eyes always on the LORD" (Psalm 16:8)—to know that He is with us to "the very end of the age" (Matthew 28:20) and that God "is not far from any one of us" (Acts 17:27).

Remembering may be as simple as calling to mind that the Lord has promised to be with you all through the day and saying to Him, "Good morning," or "Thank you," or "Help!" or "I love you."

David Roper

God Promises
Eternity with Him through Christ

GREAT SACRIFICE
HEBREWS 10:5–18

The Lord Jesus Christ . . . gave himself for our sins to rescue us.
Galatians 1:3–4

W. T. Stead, an innovative English journalist at the turn of the twentieth century, was known for writing about controversial social issues. Two of the articles he published addressed the danger of ships operating with an insufficient ratio of lifeboats to passengers. Ironically, Stead was aboard the *Titanic* when it struck an iceberg in the North Atlantic on April 15, 1912. According to one report, after helping women and children into lifeboats, Stead sacrificed his own life by giving up his life vest and a place in the lifeboats so others could be rescued.

There is something very stirring about self-sacrifice. No greater example of that can be found than in Christ himself. The writer of Hebrews says, "This Man, after He had offered one sacrifice for sins forever, sat down at the right hand of God. . . . For by one offering He has perfected forever those who are being sanctified" (Hebrews 10:12, 14 NKJV). In his letter to the Galatians, Paul opened with words describing this great sacrifice: "The Lord Jesus Christ . . . gave himself for our sins to rescue us from the present evil age" (Galatians 1:3–4).

Jesus's offering of himself on our behalf is the measure of His love for us. That willing sacrifice continues to rescue men and women and offer assurance of eternity with Him.

Bill Crowder

God Promises

Rest for Our Burdened Hearts

A WORD TO THE WEARY
ISAIAH 50:4-10

The Sovereign LORD has given me a well-instructed tongue,
to know the word that sustains the weary.

Isaiah 50:4

The people of Israel were struggling. They had been taken captive by the Assyrians and forced to live in a country far from home. What could the prophet Isaiah give these weary people to help them?

He gave them a prophecy of hope. It was a message from God relating to the promised Messiah. In Isaiah 50:4, the Savior himself described the comfort and consolation He would one day bring: "The Sovereign LORD has given me a well-instructed tongue, to know the word that sustains the weary."

These were words of dual comfort—both to the people in exile and to future generations whose lives would be touched by Jesus's compassion. In the Gospels we see how Christ fulfilled the prophecy with "the word that sustains the weary." To the crowds who followed Him, Christ proclaimed: "Come to me, all you who are weary and burdened, and I will give you rest" (Matthew 11:28). Words of compassion indeed!

Jesus left us an example of how to minister to people who have grown weary. Do you know someone who needs a timely word of encouragement or the listening ear of a concerned friend? A word of comfort to the weary can go a long way.

Dennis Fisher

God Promises
To Care Deeply for His Children

STAR SHEPHERD
EZEKIEL 34:11–16

Why do you say, . . . "My way is hidden from the LORD"?
Isaiah 40:27

In the spring, shepherds in Idaho move their flocks from the lowlands into the mountains. Thousands of sheep move up the passes into the high country to summer pasture.

My wife and I came across a flock on Shaw Mountain. It was bedded down in a meadow by a quiet stream—a picturesque scene that evoked thoughts of Psalm 23.

But where was the shepherd? The sheep appeared to be alone—until a few broke away from the flock and began to wander toward a distant gully. Then we heard a shrill whistle from above. Looking up, we saw the shepherd sitting high on a hill above the sheep, keeping watch over his flock. A mountain dog and two Border collies stood at his side. The dogs, responding to the shepherd's signal, bounded down the hill and herded the drifting sheep back to the flock where they belonged.

In the same way, the Good Shepherd is watching over you. Even though you cannot see Him, He can see you! He knows you by name and knows all about you. You are the sheep of His pasture (Ezekiel 34:31). God promises that He "looks after" His sheep, He will "tend them in a good pasture," and "bind up the injured" (vv. 12, 14, 16).

You can trust in God's watchful care.

David Roper

God Promises
A Fresh Identity

OUR NEW NAME
REVELATION 2:12–17

---

*I will also give that person a white stone
with a new name written on it.*

Revelation 2:17

She called herself a worrier, but when her child was hurt in an accident, she learned how to escape that restricting label. As her child was recovering, she met each week with friends to talk and pray, asking God for help and healing. Through the months as she turned her fears and concerns into prayer, she realized that she was changing from being a worrier to a prayer warrior. She sensed that the Lord was giving her a new name. Her identity in Christ was deepening through the struggle of unwanted heartache.

In Jesus's letter to the church at Pergamum, the Lord promises to give to the faithful a white stone with a new name on it (Revelation 2:17). Biblical commentators have debated over the meaning, but most agree that this white stone points to our freedom in Christ. In biblical times, juries in a court of law used a white stone for a not-guilty verdict and a black stone for guilty. A white stone also gained the bearer entrance into such events as banquets; likewise, those who receive God's white stone are welcomed to the heavenly feast. Jesus's death brings us freedom and new life—and a new name.

What new name do you think God might give to you?

Amy Boucher Pye

God Promises
That He Will Welcome Us Home

BLESSED ASSURANCE
2 CORINTHIANS 5:1–10

*We are confident, I say, and would prefer to be
away from the body and at home with the Lord.*

2 Corinthians 5:8

As I was talking with a gentleman whose wife had died, he shared with me that a friend said to him, "I'm sorry you lost your wife." His reply? "Oh, I haven't lost her; I know exactly where she is!"

To some this may seem like a rather bold or even flippant assertion. With so many after-death theories, one might wonder how we can be really sure where our loved ones go after death, let alone where we ourselves will end up.

Yet confidence is appropriate for followers of Jesus Christ. We have the assurance from God's Word that when we die we will immediately be with our Lord (2 Corinthians 5:8). Thankfully, this is more than just wishful thinking. It is grounded in the historic reality of Jesus, who came and died to cancel our penalty for sin so we could receive eternal life (Romans 6:23). He then proved that there was life after death by exiting His grave and ascending into heaven where, as He promised, He is preparing a place for us (John 14:2).

So, rejoice! Since the benefits of this reality are out of this world, we can boldly say with Paul that "we are confident, I say, and would prefer to be away from the body and at home with the Lord" (2 Corinthians 5:8).

Joe Stowell

God Promises

Security in Christ's Presence

UNIMAGINABLE PROMISES
2 PETER 1:2–8

He has given us his very great and precious promises.

2 Peter 1:4

In our moments of greatest failure, it can be easy to believe it's too late for us, that we've lost our chance at a life of purpose and worth. That's how Elias, a former inmate at a maximum-security prison in New York, described feeling as a prisoner. "I had broken . . . promises, the promise of my own future, the promise of what I could be."

It was Bard College's "Prison Initiative" college degree program that began to transform Elias's life. While in the program, he participated on a debate team, which in 2015 debated a team from Harvard—and won. For Elias, being "part of the team . . . [was] a way of proving that these promises weren't completely lost."

A similar transformation happens in our hearts when we begin to understand that the good news of God's love in Jesus is good news for us too. *It's not too late*, we begin to realize with wonder. *God still has a future for me.*

And it's a future that can be neither be earned nor forfeited, for it is dependent only on God's extravagant grace and power (2 Peter 1:2–3). It's a future where we're set free from the despair in the world and in our hearts. That future is filled with His "glory and goodness" (v. 3)—a future secure in Christ's unimaginable promises (v. 4). We are transformed into the "freedom and glory of the children of God" (Romans 8:21).

Monica La Rose

God Promises
To Notice What You Do in His Name

THE FORGOTTEN WORKER
HEBREWS 6:9–20

God is not unjust; he will not forget your work and the love you have shown him as you have helped his people.

Hebrews 6:10

People around the world are familiar with Mount Rushmore, the South Dakota site where the heads of former American presidents are carved in gigantic scale on a cliff wall. Yet, while millions know of Mount Rushmore, relatively few know the name Doane Robinson—the South Dakota state historian who conceived the idea of the magnificent sculpture and managed the project. The monument is admired and appreciated, but he is the forgotten man behind the masterpiece. His name is largely unrecognized or was never even known by some.

Sometimes, in the service of the Master, we may feel that we have been forgotten or are behind the scenes and not recognized. Ministry can be a life of effort that often goes unappreciated by the very people we are seeking to serve in Jesus's name. The good news, however, is that while people may not know, God does. Hebrews 6:10 says, "God is not unjust; he will not forget your work and the love you have shown him as you have helped his people and continue to help them."

What a promise! Our heavenly Father will never forget our service to Him. That is infinitely more important than being applauded by the crowds.

Bill Crowder

God Promises
That Jesus Will Return

ARE YOU LOOKING UP?
TITUS 2

We wait for the blessed hope—the appearing of . . . Jesus Christ.
Titus 2:13

Are you so eager for Christ's return that you hope it will take place today? Many of us wouldn't be honest if we answered an unqualified yes to this question. We enjoy life as it is. We love what we're doing. We enjoy our families and watching kids or grandkids moving toward maturity. And there are still people and places we would like to visit during our retirement years—whether now or in the future.

Does this mean that we're not waiting "for the blessed hope—the appearing of the glory of our great God and Savior, Jesus Christ" (Titus 2:13)? No, it doesn't. I believe that His return is indeed "the blessed hope." Earthly pleasures are only temporary and cannot compare with the joys of heaven. Besides, I am troubled by the sin, sorrow, and suffering all around me.

All Christians are thankful for Jesus's promise, "I will come back and take you to be with me" (John 14:3). But our own circumstances affect how eagerly we anticipate His return. Whether life for us today is a joy or a struggle, we are to "say 'No' to ungodliness and worldly passions" and to "live self-controlled, upright and godly lives" (Titus 2:12).

God wants us to enjoy life. But He also wants us to live each day as if it may be the one in which He will return. Are you looking up?

Herb Vander Lugt

God Promises
To Be Our Rock

UNBREAKABLE FAITH
ISAIAH 26:3–13

*Trust in the LORD forever, for the LORD,
the LORD himself, is the Rock eternal.*
Isaiah 26:4

After doctors diagnosed their firstborn son with autism, Diane Dokko Kim and her husband grieved facing a lifetime of caring for a cognitively disabled child. In her book *Unbroken Faith*, she admits to struggling with adjusting their dreams and expectations for their beloved son's future. Yet through this painful process, they learned that God can handle their anger, doubts, and fears. When their son reached adulthood, Diane used her experiences to encourage parents of children with special needs. She tells others about God's unbreakable promises, limitless power, and loving faithfulness. She assures people that He gives us permission to grieve when we experience the death of a dream, an expectation, a way, or a season of life.

In Isaiah 26, the prophet declares that God's people can trust in the Lord forever, "for the LORD . . . is the Rock eternal" (v. 4). He's able to sustain us with supernatural peace in every situation (v. 12). Focusing on His unchanging character and crying out to Him during troublesome times revitalizes our hope (v. 15).

When we face any loss, disappointment, or difficult circumstance, God invites us to be honest with Him. He can handle our ever-changing emotions and our questions. He remains with us and refreshes our spirits with enduring hope. Even when we feel like our lives are falling apart, God can make our faith unbreakable.

Xochitl Dixon

God Promises

To Always Look Out for Us

NONE FORGOTTEN
LUKE 12:1–7

Are not five sparrows sold for two pennies?
Yet not one of them is forgotten by God.

Luke 12:6

Jesus chose a sparrow, a lowly feathered creature, to illustrate the great truth that God cares for us in a tender and wonderful way. Jesus said the Father in heaven thought about and individually remembered every bird. He then reminded His audience that if God has a tender regard for such insignificant creatures, certainly He has an infinitely greater love for us.

The cure for all loneliness is found in the encouraging thought that He never forgets us and never considers us unimportant. The psalmist was thrilled when he contemplated this comforting truth and exclaimed, "I am poor and needy; may the Lord think of me" (Psalm 40:17).

An orchestra leader was having rehearsal. One of the piccolo players thought that in all the din of the great chorus and orchestra his instrument would not be missed. So he didn't play. Suddenly the conductor threw his hands in the air, and all was still. He asked, "Where is the piccolo?" The music was spoiled because one man failed to carry his part.

Your contribution to life is important, small as it may seem. Remember, you and your efforts are always significant to God! You are never out of the circle of His attention and concern, for "he cares for you" (1 Peter 5:7).

Henry Bosch

God Promises
True Security

A SECRET PLACE
PSALM 91

*He will command his angels concerning you
to guard you in all your ways.*

Psalm 91:11

Feeling secure is a high priority in this unsafe, volatile world. A private investigation agency in Florida promises to "work diligently to restore the sense of security and safety that you and your family deserve."

The psalmist found a "secret place" where he felt safe (Psalm 91:1 NKJV). And we can rest secure in that same place. He described it with these phrases:

"In the shadow of the Almighty" (v. 1). Shadows provide protection from the direct heat of the sun. If the heat is severe, the shade reduces what we actually feel. When we're under God's shadow, we do not face the full heat of our difficulties.

"My refuge and my fortress" (v. 2). God is the strongest protector we could ever have, and we can run to Him for help. Nothing can penetrate Him to get to us unless it's part of His loving plan for our ultimate good.

"Under his wings" (v. 4). God is soft and tender like a caring mother bird. When troubles rage, He draws us close. We don't need to fear that He will cast us out—we are His.

"A dwelling" (v. 9). Our Father will be our home, our abiding place—now and forever.

True security can be found only in our Lord, who promises to save us and be near us (vv. 15–16).

Anne Cetas

God Promises
To Bless Us

ANCIENT PROMISES
NUMBERS 6:22–27

The LORD bless you and keep you.
Numbers 6:24

In 1979, Dr. Gabriel Barkay and his team discovered two silver scrolls in a burial ground outside the Old City of Jerusalem. In 2004, after twenty-five years of careful research, scholars confirmed that the scrolls were the oldest biblical text in existence, having been buried in 600 BC. What I find particularly moving is what the scrolls contain—the priestly blessing that God wanted spoken over His people: "The LORD bless you and keep you; the LORD make his face shine on you" (Numbers 6:24–25).

In giving this benediction, God showed Aaron and his sons (through Moses) how to bless the people on His behalf. The leaders were to memorize the words in the form God gave so they would speak to them just as God desired. Note how these words emphasize that God is the one who blesses, for three times they say, "the Lord." And six times He says, "you," reflecting just how much God wants His people to receive His love and favor.

Ponder for a moment that the oldest existing fragments of the Bible tell of God's desire to bless. What a reminder of God's boundless love and how He wants to be in a relationship with us. If you feel far from God today, hold tightly to the promise in these ancient words, which were preserved for us. May the Lord bless you; may the Lord keep you.

Amy Boucher Pye

God Promises
Strength for the Trusting

WAIT FOR THE LORD
PSALM 27

Wait for the LORD; be strong and take heart and wait for the LORD.
Psalm 27:14

In Cantonese, a Chinese dialect, the word for *wait* sounds like the word for *class*. Making a pun on this word, some senior folks in one region identify themselves as "third-class citizens," which also means "people of three waits." They wait for their children to return home from work late at night. They wait for the morning sun to dispel their sleepless nights. And with a sigh of resignation, they wait for death.

In the Bible, the word *wait* is more an attitude than an activity. To "wait for the Lord" is to trust Him. Psalm 27 is David's exuberant declaration of faith in God. He sees the Lord as his salvation (v. 1). In times of danger, he knows for certain that God will hide him (v. 5). He remembers that God has asked him to seek His face, so he asks God not to hide from him. For, like a child, he longs to see God's approving face (vv. 8–10). In his darkest moments, David declares: "I remain confident of this: I will see the goodness of the LORD in the land of the living" (v. 13).

Though no one knows how life will unfold, we can decide to trust God and to focus our mind on Him. For to those who wait on the Lord, the promise is given: Our heart will be strengthened (v. 14).

Albert Lee

God Promises
Abundant Life

MUCH IN BETWEEN
EPHESIANS 3:14–21

That you may be filled to the measure of all the fullness of God.
Ephesians 3:19

In the western panhandle of Texas is a small town named Texline. It had an ostentatious beginning in the late 1800s as a thriving center along a new railroad line. Within a few years, though, most of the shops had closed and the town's population shriveled to about four hundred. In 2000, the population was still just over five hundred.

One online description of Texline says that it has "a city limits sign at one end, another at the other end, and not much in between."

What a waste if the same description could be given of our spiritual journey! The journey of the Christian life on earth begins at the moment of faith in Jesus and ends when the believer goes to be with the Lord. This raises an important question: What happens in between?

A rich and full life is available to all who believe in and serve Jesus. The apostle Paul prayed that believers would "be filled to the measure of all the fullness of God" (Ephesians 3:19). He wanted them to know life "to the full" (John 10:10). But how many of us experience even a small part of the abundant life Christ promised to those who are faithful to Him?

God desires to give us a marvelous beginning with salvation and a great ending in Glory—with much in between.

David Egner

God Promises
Benefits Worth Reviewing

BEING CARED FOR
PSALM 46

The LORD Almighty is with us.
Psalm 46:11

Debbie, the owner of a housecleaning service, was always searching for more clients to build up her business. On one call she talked with a woman whose response was, "I won't be able to afford that now; I'm undergoing cancer treatment." Right then Debbie decided that "no woman undergoing cancer treatment would ever be turned away. They would even be offered a free housecleaning service." So she started a nonprofit organization where companies donated their cleaning services to women battling cancer. One such woman felt a rush of confidence when she came home to a clean house. She said, "For the first time, I actually believed I could beat cancer."

A feeling of being cared for and supported can help sustain us when we're facing a challenge. An awareness of God's presence and support can especially bring hope to encourage our spirit. Psalm 46, a favorite of many people going through trials, reminds us: "God is our refuge and strength, an ever-present help in trouble" and "Be still, and know that I am God; . . . I will be exalted in the earth. The LORD Almighty is with us" (vv. 1, 10–11).

Reminding ourselves of God's promises and His presence with us can be a means to help renew our hearts and give us the courage and confidence to go through hard times.

Anne Cetas

God Promises
That We Can Trust His Faithfulness

PROMISES YOU CAN BANK ON
2 CHRONICLES 6:1–11

*No matter how many promises God
has made, they are "Yes" in Christ.*

2 Corinthians 1:20

After a global financial crisis, the US government enacted stricter laws to protect people from questionable banking practices. Banks had to change some of their policies to comply. To notify me of such changes, my bank sent me a letter. But when I got to the end, I had more questions than answers. The use of phrases like "we may" and "at our discretion" certainly didn't sound like anything I could depend on!

In contrast, the Old Testament quotes God as saying "I will" numerous times. God promises David: "I will raise up your offspring to succeed you, your own flesh and blood, and I will establish his kingdom. He is the one who will build a house for my Name, and I will establish the throne of his kingdom forever" (2 Samuel 7:12–13). There's no uncertainty in those words! Recognizing God's faithfulness to His promises, King Solomon says in his prayer of dedication for the temple: "You have kept your promise to your servant David my father; with your mouth you have promised and with your hand you have fulfilled it" (2 Chronicles 6:15). Centuries later, the apostle Paul said that all of God's promises are "yes" in Christ (2 Corinthians 1:20).

In a world of uncertainty, our trust is in a faithful God who will always keep His promises.

Julie Ackerman Link

God Promises
That Our Patience Pays Off

Waiting in Anticipation
Psalm 130:1-6

I wait for the Lord more than watchmen wait for the morning,
more than watchmen wait for the morning.

Psalm 130:6

Every May Day (May 1) in Oxford, England, an early morning crowd gathers to welcome spring. At 6:00, the Magdalen College Choir sings from the top of Magdalen Tower. Thousands wait in anticipation for the dark night to be broken by song and the ringing of bells.

Like the revelers, I often wait. I wait for answers to prayers or guidance from the Lord. Although I don't know the exact time my wait will end, I'm learning to wait expectantly. In Psalm 130 the psalmist writes of being in deep distress facing a situation that feels like the blackest of nights. In the midst of his troubles, he chooses to trust God and stay alert like a guard on duty charged with announcing daybreak. "I wait for the Lord more than watchmen wait for the morning, more than watchmen wait for the morning" (v. 6).

The anticipation of God's faithfulness breaking through the darkness gives the psalmist hope to endure even in the midst of his suffering. Based on the promises of God found throughout Scripture, that hope allows him to keep waiting even though he has not yet seen the first rays of light.

Be encouraged if you are in the middle of a dark night. The dawn is coming—either in this life or in heaven! In the meantime, don't give up hope but keep watching for the deliverance of the Lord. He will be faithful.

Lisa Samra

God Promises
To Be Unchangeable

PREDICTING THE FUTURE
ISAIAH 54:4–10

Though the mountains be shaken and the hills be removed,
yet my unfailing love for you will not be shaken.
Isaiah 54:10

During the 1893 Chicago World's Fair, a group of social analysts gazed one hundred years into the future and tried to forecast what the world would be like in 1993. Some of their predictions were:

- Many people will live to be 150.
- The government will have grown more simple, as true greatness always tends toward simplicity.
- Prisons will decline, and divorce will be considered unnecessary.

They were wrong on all counts! So, what does the future really hold? Two things are certain: Circumstances will change; God will not.

We know these truths from observation. We see them throughout the Bible. Yet, we must prove them for ourselves when our life turns upside down and everything seems out of control.

We can give way to fear and panic, or we can choose to trust God's promise: "'Though the mountains be shaken and the hills be removed, yet my unfailing love for you will not be shaken nor my covenant of peace be removed,' says the LORD, who has compassion on you." (Isaiah 54:10).

Although circumstances will change, God will never change. We can be confident that He will always be faithful. Therefore, we can be at peace.

David McCasland

God Promises

A Joyous Eternity Eventually

IF I STOP THE CLOCK
1 KINGS 10:23–11:4

The glory of the LORD filled his temple.
1 Kings 8:11

Every year when May rolls around in Michigan, I want to stop the clock. I rejoice when death is defeated by fragile sprouts that refuse to be confined by hardened clay and brittle branches. Over a few weeks, the naked landscape transforms into fully clothed trees adorned by bright, fragrant flowers. I can't get enough of the sights, sounds, and scents of springtime. I want time to stop moving.

Also in May, I come to 1 Kings in my Bible reading schedule. When I get to chapter 10, I have the same feeling: I want the story to stop. The nation of Israel has bloomed. Solomon has become king and has built a magnificent dwelling place for God, who moved in with a blaze of glory (8:11). Finally united under a righteous king, the people are at peace. I love happy endings!

But the story doesn't end there. It continues: "King Solomon, however, loved many foreign women" (11:1), and "his wives turned his heart after other gods" (v. 4).

Just as the seasons of the year continue, so do the cycles of life—birth and death, success and failure, sin and confession. Although we have no power to stop the clock while we're enjoying good times, we can rest in God's promise that eventually all bad times will end (Revelation 21:4).

Julie Ackerman Link

God Promises
Comfort and Help

A MEASURE OF HEALING
2 CORINTHIANS 1:3–7

My comfort in my suffering is this: Your promise preserves my life.
Psalm 119:50

When I asked a friend how she was doing four years after the sudden death of her husband, she said, "I feel I am healing. Tears tend to burn my eyes rather than pour down my face. To me, that is a measure of healing."

How fitting are those words to describe the changes that happen as the years pass for grievers who have endured an unexpected loss.

Scripture promises comfort in our suffering (2 Corinthians 1:3–7), but that help does not come all at once. In fact, from what I have heard, our desired healing may not arrive completely in this life. This is what others have told me—others who are further down the road of grief than our family is after losing our teenager Melissa in a car accident. In the midst of our pain, we entrust our lives to God's sovereign direction, but we also realize that gnawing sadness will always reside in our hearts.

Indeed, God has promised that He will wipe away all tears in heaven (Revelation 7:17), but until then the healing will be incomplete. Grief lessens but does not dissipate. The psalmist said that while God's Word gives life, there is still the combination of "comfort in my suffering" (Psalm 119:50). Even in life's toughest circumstances, we can, with God's help, enjoy a measure of healing.

Dave Branon

God Promises
Joy Forever

BETWEEN THE ETERNITIES
HEBREWS 11:8–16

*These people were still living by faith when they died.
They did not receive the things promised; they only
saw them and welcomed them from a distance.*
Hebrews 11:13

In the television western *Broken Trail*, cowboy Prentice Ritter must provide words of comfort at the funeral of a friend. Uncomfortable in the situation, he quietly says, "We are all travelers in this world. From the sweet grass to the packing house, birth till death, we travel between the eternities."

In a sense, he was right. We are travelers—pilgrims—in a world that offers no lasting peace or rest. And while there is only one eternity, we travel between eternity past and eternity future, waiting for promises of a home and a hope that will last forever—promises yet to be fulfilled.

In those times of struggle and despair when our pilgrimage of life is difficult, it is helpful to remember that though we are pilgrims who travel between the eternities, we have a Savior who is the Lord and Master of eternity. He has offered us the promise of life with Him forever and has secured that promise with His own sacrifice. This was the promise spoken of by the writer of Hebrews 11:13.

We are locked into the moments and hours and days of life, but we look ahead by faith in Christ. One day, we will experience the promises of eternity when faith will become sight as we see Him. That hope is what lifts us beyond life between the eternities to a joy that is eternal.

Bill Crowder

God Promises
That He Is Our Joy

NOT WHAT I PLANNED
PSALM 37:1–8

Be still before the LORD and wait patiently for him.

Psalm 37:7

This isn't the way I expected my life to be. I wanted to marry at nineteen, have a half dozen children, and settle into life as a wife and mother. Instead, I went to work, married in my forties, and never had children. For a number of years I was hopeful that Psalm 37:4 might be for me a God-guaranteed promise: "He will give you the desires of your heart."

But God doesn't always "do this" (v. 5) my way, and unmet desires stir up occasional sadness. Like mine, your life may have turned out differently than you planned. A few thoughts from Psalm 37 may be helpful (even though the psalm is primarily about comparing ourselves to the wicked).

We learn from verse 4 that unfulfilled desires don't have to take the joy out of life. As we get to know God's heart, He becomes our joy.

"Commit your way to the LORD" (v. 5). The word commit means "to roll." Bible teacher Herbert Lockyer Sr., says, "'Roll thy way upon the Lord,' as one who lays upon the shoulders of one stronger than himself a burden which he is not able to bear."

"Trust in him" (v. 5). When we confidently entrust everything to God, we can "wait patiently for [the LORD]" (v. 7), for He is bringing about His best for our lives.

Anne Cetas

God Promises
His Forever Love for Us

"LOVABLE!"
JEREMIAH 31:1–6

I have loved you with an everlasting love;
I have drawn you with unfailing kindness.

Jeremiah 31:3

"Lovable!"

That exclamation came from my daughter as she got ready one morning. I didn't know what she meant. Then she tapped her shirt, a hand-me-down from a cousin. Across the front was that word: "Lovable." I gave her a big hug, and she smiled with pure joy. "You are lovable!" I echoed. Her smile grew even bigger, if that was possible, as she skipped away, repeating the word over and over again.

I'm hardly a perfect father. But that moment was perfect. In that spontaneous, beautiful interaction, I glimpsed in my girl's radiant face what receiving unconditional love looked like: It was a portrait of delight. She knew the word on her shirt corresponded completely with how her daddy felt about her.

How many of us know in our hearts that we are loved by a Father whose affection for us is limitless? Sometimes we struggle with this truth. The Israelites did. They wondered if their trials meant God no longer loved them. But in Jeremiah 31:3, the prophet reminds them of what God said in the past: "I have loved you with an everlasting love." We too long for such unconditional love. Yet the wounds, disappointments, and mistakes we experience can make us feel anything but lovable. But God opens His arms—the arms of a perfect Father—and invites us to experience and rest in His love.

Adam Holz

God Promises
To Reach Out to Us

GOD HOLDS US
ISAIAH 41:1–10

I will uphold you with my righteous right hand.
Isaiah 41:10

South African Fredie Blom turned 116 in May 2020, widely recognized at the time as the oldest living man. Born in 1904, the year the Wright Brothers built their Flyer II, he lived through both World Wars, apartheid, and the Great Depression. When asked for the secret for his longevity, Blom shrugged. Like many of us, he didn't always choose the foods and practices that promote wellness. However, Blom did offer one reason for his remarkable health: "There's only one thing, it's [God]. He's got all the power. . . . He holds me." Mr. Blom died in August 2020.

Blom echoes words similar to what God spoke to Israel, as the nation wilted under the oppression of fierce enemies. "I will strengthen you and help you," God promised. "I will uphold you with my righteous right hand" (Isaiah 41:10). No matter how desperate the Israelites' situation was or how impossible the odds that they would ever find relief might have been, God assured His people that they were held in His tender care. "Do not fear, for I am with you," He insisted. "Do not be dismayed, for I am your God" (v. 10).

No matter how many years we're given, life's hardships will come knocking at our door. A troubled marriage. A child abandoning the family. Terrifying news from the doctor. Even persecution. No matter what, our God reaches out to us and holds us firmly. He gathers us and holds us in His strong, tender hand.

Winn Collier

God Promises

To Walk Through the Valley with Us

THE FEAR OF FALLING
PSALM 46

The eternal God is your refuge,
and underneath are the everlasting arms.
Deuteronomy 33:27

Have you ever dreamed that you were falling out of bed or from some great height, and you awoke in fright? I remember that as a boy I would often be awakened by such a terrifying feeling.

I heard about a man who had this sensation as soon as he slipped into sleep. He was so rudely awakened by his sense of falling that he was afraid to go back to sleep. He feared he would die, and he imagined he was falling into a bottomless pit.

Then one evening as he was strolling through a cemetery, he saw this phrase engraved on a tombstone:

Underneath Are
The Everlasting Arms

These words reminded him that when believers die, they are safely carried by the Lord to their home in heaven. He recalled the assurance of the psalmist, "Even though I walk through the darkest valley, I will fear no evil, for you are with me" (Psalm 23:4).

The once-fearful man realized that in life and in death— and even in sleep—the "everlasting arms" of our loving Lord are there to catch and hold us. That night he was able to sing what he was taught in childhood, "Teach me to live that I may dread the grave as little as my bed!" At last he could fall asleep without fear.

M. R. DeHaan

God Promises

To Join Us to His Grace

CLAIMING THE PROMISE
GENESIS 12:1–4; 21:1–7

---

*Sarah became pregnant and bore a son to Abraham
in his old age, at the very time God had promised him.*

Genesis 21:2

When people say with a sigh, "Promises, promises," it's often when they've been disappointed by someone who failed to keep a commitment. The more it happens, the greater the sadness and the deeper the sigh.

Have you ever felt that God doesn't keep His promises? It's an attitude that can subtly develop over time.

After God promised Abraham, "I will make you into a great nation" (Genesis 12:2), twenty-five years elapsed before the birth of his son Isaac (21:5). During that period, Abraham questioned God about his lack of a child (15:2), and he even resorted to fathering a son through his wife's handmaiden (16:15).

Yet, through the ups and downs, God kept reminding Abraham of His promise to give him a child, while urging him to walk faithfully with Him and believe (17:1–2).

When we claim one of God's promises in the Bible, whether it is for peace of mind, courage, or provision of our needs, we place ourselves in His hands and on His schedule. As we wait, it may at times seem as if the Lord has forgotten us. But trust embraces the reality that when we stand on a promise of God, He remains faithful. The assurance is in our hearts, and the timing is in His hands.

David McCasland

God Promises
Loving Protection

WELCOME WINGS
PSALM 36:5–9

How priceless is your unfailing love, O God!
People take refuge in the shadow of your wings.

Psalm 36:7

One spring a pair of blue jays built a nest in the persimmon tree in our backyard. I enjoyed watching the mother bird as she sat patiently on her eggs. In a matter of days, I noticed a new development as I peered from beneath the eaves of the carport. The father would fly in, the mother would perch on the side of that little home, and four little mouths could be seen gaping above the edge of the nest. To get a better look, I would edge closer to the tree. Then I would stand very still and watch the mother. When I got too close, however, she would spread her wings over her little brood. Her head would cautiously protrude as she looked first to one side and then to the other. She was always on guard, protecting her little ones by sheltering them with her wings.

This beautiful picture of protection reminds me of David's words in Psalm 36:7. When he said that we can find safety "in the shadow of [God's] wings," he may have been referring to the words of his ancestor Boaz (Ruth 2:12). Boaz had said to Ruth, "May the LORD repay you for what you have done. May you be richly rewarded by the LORD, the God of Israel, under whose wings you have come to take refuge."

Surely that's a promise we still need. Life is filled with dangers, both physical and spiritual. Yet we can rest securely because we know that God is aware of them all. We are covered by His omnipotent protection. What better refuge could we have than to live under the shadow of His wings!

Paul Van Gorder

God Promises
That He Is Trustworthy

A NEW PURPOSE
ACTS 9:1–9

"I know the plans I have for you," declares the LORD, *"plans to prosper you and not to harm you, plans to give you a hope and a future."*
Jeremiah 29:11

A sixty-year-old hotel in Kansas was renovated into apartments. A rusty ocean liner on the East Coast is slated to be restored into a hotel. Hangar 61, an admired piece of architecture at the old Stapleton Airport in Colorado, is now a church. Each structure had a specific use that is no longer viable. Yet someone was able to see promise and a new purpose in each one.

If structures can find new life and purpose, why not people? Think about these men in the Bible whose lives took an unexpected direction. There was Jacob, who wrestled with the angel of the Lord (Genesis 32); Moses, who talked to a burning bush (Exodus 3); Paul, who was temporarily blinded (Acts 9). Their stories were different, but all had a change of purpose when their encounter with God sent them down a new path.

We too may experience circumstances that change the course of our lives. But God reminds us of this, in effect: I loved you before you loved me. I want to give you hope and a future. Give all your worries to me because I care about you (1 John 4:19; Jeremiah 29:11; 1 Peter 5:7; John 10:10).

As you cling to God's promises, ask Him to reveal new direction and purpose for your life.

Cindy Hess Kasper

God Promises

To Guide Us on Uncertain Paths

THE WINDING ROAD
PSALM 121

---

*He will not let your foot slip—he who
watches over you will not slumber.*

Psalm 121:3

In his book *A Sweet and Bitter Providence*, John Piper offers these thoughts about God's providence and guidance: "Life is not a straight line leading from one blessing to the next and then finally to heaven. Life is a winding and troubled road. . . . God is not just showing up after the trouble and cleaning it up. He is plotting the course and managing the troubles with far-reaching purposes for our good and for the glory of Jesus Christ."

The Jews journeying to Jerusalem for the annual feasts (Deuteronomy 16:16) had the assurance of knowing that the Lord was plotting their course and managing the winding and troubled roads for them. They expressed this assurance in Psalm 121, a pilgrim song. The question, "Where does my help come from?" did not express doubt but affirmation in the Lord who rules supreme (vv. 1–2). Unlike a guard who sometimes slumbered, or the god Baal who needed to be rustled out of his stupor (1 Kings 18:27), the Lord is fully alert and secured the journey of His people with providential care (vv. 3–4). The Lord, who rescued Israel, would continue to help, preserve, and walk with His people.

Life is a winding road with unknown perils and troubles, but we can be certain of God's providence, security, and care.

Marvin Williams

God Promises

No One Will Snatch Us from His Hand

IN HIS GRIP
ROMANS 8:31–39

I press on to take hold of that for which Christ Jesus took hold of me.
Philippians 3:12

When we cross a busy street with small children in tow, we put out our hand and say, "Hold on tight," and our little ones grasp our hand as tightly as they can. But we would never depend on their grasp. It is our grip on their hand that holds them and keeps them secure. So Paul insists, "Christ Jesus took hold of me" (Philippians 3:12). Or more exactly, "Christ has a grip on me!"

One thing is certain: It is not our grip on God that keeps us safe, but the power of Jesus's grasp. No one can take us out of His grasp—not the devil, not even ourselves. Once we're in His hands, He will not let go.

We have this assurance: "I give them eternal life, and they shall never perish; no one will snatch them out of my hand. My Father, who has given them to me, is greater than all; no one can snatch them out of my Father's hand" (John 10:28–29).

Doubly safe: Our Father on one side and our Lord and Savior on the other, clasping us in a viselike grip. These are the hands that shaped the mountains and oceans and flung the stars into space. Nothing in this life or the next "will be able to separate us from the love of God that is in Christ Jesus our Lord" (Romans 8:39).

David Roper

God Promises

The Freedom of Forgiveness

PEACE AND RECONCILIATION
MATTHEW 18:21–35

*Shouldn't you have had mercy on your
fellow servant just as I had on you?*

Matthew 18:33

When the US Civil War ended in 1865, more than half a million soldiers lay dead, the economy was shattered, and people remained deeply divided politically. The observance of Mother's Day in the United States began with two women's efforts for peace and reconciliation during this time of anguish. In 1870, Julia Ward Howe called for an International Mother's Day on which women would unite in opposing war in all its forms. A few years later, Anna Reeves Jarvis began her annual Mother's Friendship Day in an effort to reunite families and neighbors alienated by the war. There is always great suffering when friends and families are fractured and unwilling to forgive.

The gospel of Jesus Christ brings the promise of peace and reconciliation with God and with each other. When Peter asked Jesus how often he should forgive a brother who sinned against him (Matthew 18:21), the Lord surprised everyone with His answer of "seventy-seven times" (v. 22). Then He told an unforgettable story about a servant who had received forgiveness and failed to pass it on (vv. 23–35). As God freely forgives us, so He requires that we extend what we have received to others.

With God's love and power, forgiveness is always possible.

David McCasland

God Promises
An Ongoing Connection

ACCESS TO GOD
1 JOHN 5:6–15

Let us then approach God's throne of grace with confidence, so that we may receive mercy and find grace to help us in our time of need.
Hebrews 4:16

Technology is a blessing in so many ways. Need a bit of information about a health problem? All you have to do is access the internet to get a list of options to guide your search. Need to contact a friend? Just send a text, email, or Facebook post. But technology can also be frustrating at times. The other day I needed to access some information in my bank account and was asked a list of security questions. Unable to recall the exact answers, I was blocked from my own account. Or think of the times when an important conversation is cut off because of a dead cell phone battery, with no way to reconnect until you find a way to recharge it.

All of this makes me delighted with the reality that when I need to access God in prayer, there are no security questions or chargers required. I love the assurance that John gives when he says, "This is the confidence we have in approaching God: that if we ask anything according to his will, he hears us" (1 John 5:14).

God is always accessible, for He never slumbers nor sleeps (Psalm 121:4). No password needed! He is waiting and ready to listen.

Joe Stowell

God Promises
Life After Death

WHEN THE WOODS WAKE UP
JOHN 11:14–27

*I am the resurrection and the life. He who believes
in Me, though he may die, he shall live.*
John 11:25 NKJV

Through cold, snowy winters, the hope of spring sustains those of us who live in Michigan. May is the month when that hope is rewarded. The transformation is remarkable. Limbs that look lifeless on May 1 turn into branches that wave green leafy greetings by month's end. Although the change each day is imperceptible, by the end of the month the woods in my yard have changed from gray to green.

God has built into creation a cycle of rest and renewal. What looks like death to us is rest to God. And just as rest is preparation for renewal, death is preparation for resurrection.

I love watching the woods awaken every spring, for it reminds me that death is a temporary condition and that its purpose is to prepare for new life, a new beginning, for something even better. "Unless a kernel of wheat falls to the ground and dies, it remains only a single seed. But if it dies, it produces many seeds" (John 12:24).

While pollen is a springtime nuisance when it coats my furniture and makes people sneeze, it reminds me that God is in the business of keeping things alive. And after the pain of death, He promises a glorious resurrection for those who believe in His Son.

Julie Ackerman Link

God Promises
Spiritual Food

OPEN WIDE
PSALM 81

I am the LORD your God . . . .
Open wide your mouth wide and I will fill it.
Psalm 81:10

As a boy, I was always thrilled to discover a newly constructed robin's nest. It was fascinating to watch for the eggs and then to wait for those featherless little creatures with bulging eyes and gaping mouths to break out of their shells. Standing at a distance, I could see their heads bobbing unsteadily and their mouths wide open, expecting Mother Robin to give them their dinner.

As I recall those childhood scenes, I think of God's promise: "I am the LORD your God . . . ; Open wide your mouth and I will fill it" (Psalm 81:10). In spite of this gracious offer to ancient Israel, the people ignored God, and He "gave them over to their stubborn heart to follow their own devices" (v. 12). If they had accepted God's offer, "You would be fed with the finest of wheat; with honey from the rock I would satisfy you" (v. 16).

So too God longs to give us spiritual food. And He will satisfy our spiritual hunger as we study His Word, worship with others, listen to faithful Bible teachers, read literature with good biblical content, and daily depend on Him.

If we refuse God's provisions, we will suffer spiritual malnutrition and fail to grow. But if we open our mouth wide, we can be sure that God will fill it.

Richard DeHaan

God Promises

That Our Sins Can Be Forgiven

WITHIN A STONE'S THROW
JOHN 7:53–8:11

*"Let any one of you who is without sin
be the first to throw a stone at her."*

John 8:7

As a group of religious leaders herded an adulterous woman toward Jesus, they couldn't know they were carrying her within a stone's throw of grace. Their hope was to discredit Him. If He told them to let the woman go, they could claim He was breaking Mosaic law. But if He condemned her to death, the crowds following Him would have dismissed His words of mercy and grace.

But Jesus turned the tables on the accusers. Scripture says that rather than answering them directly, He started writing on the ground. When the leaders continued to question Him, He invited any of them who had never sinned to throw the first stone, and then He started writing on the ground again. The next time He looked up, all the accusers were gone.

Now the only person who could have thrown a stone—the only sinless One—looked at the woman and gave her mercy. "'Then neither do I condemn you,' Jesus declared. 'Go now and leave your life of sin'" (John 8:11).

Whether today finds you needing forgiveness for judging others or desiring assurance that no sin is beyond His grace, be encouraged by this: No one is throwing stones today; go and be changed by God's mercy.

Randy Kilgore

God Promises
That His Love Never Ends

LONGING FOR GOD
1 JOHN 4:13-16

My soul yearns, even faints, for the courts of the LORD;
my heart and my flesh cry out for the living God.

Psalm 84:2

One day my daughter was visiting with our one-year-old grandson. I was getting ready to leave the house on an errand, but as soon as I walked out of the room my grandson began to cry. It happened twice, and each time I went back and spent a moment with him. As I headed out the door the third time, his little lip began to quiver again. At that point my daughter said, "Dad, why don't you just take him with you?"

Any grandparent could tell you what happened next. My grandson went along for the ride, just because I love him.

How good it is to know that the longings of our hearts for God are also met with love. The Bible assures us that we can "know and rely on the love God has for us" (1 John 4:16). God doesn't love us because of anything we have or haven't done. His love isn't based on our worthiness at all, but on His goodness and faithfulness. When the world around us is unloving and unkind, we can rely on God's unchanging love as our source of hope and peace.

Our heavenly Father's heart has gone out to us through the gift of His Son and His Spirit. How comforting is the assurance that God loves us with love that never ends!

James Banks

God Promises
To Do a Fresh Thing

SOMETHING NEW
ISAIAH 43:14-21

See, I am doing a new thing! . . .
I am making . . . streams in the wasteland.
Isaiah 43:19

Farming is difficult in areas that lack fresh water. To help solve this problem, the Seawater Greenhouse company has created something new: "cooling houses" in Somaliland, Africa, and other countries with similar climates. Cooling houses use solar pumps to drizzle saltwater over walls made of corrugated cardboard. As the water moves down each panel, it leaves its salt behind. Much of the remaining fresh water evaporates inside the structure, which becomes a humid place where fruit and vegetable crops can flourish.

Through the prophet Isaiah, God promised to do a "new thing" as He provided "streams in the wasteland" for ancient Israel (Isaiah 43:19). This new thing contrasted with the old thing He had done to rescue His people from the Egyptian army. Remember the Red Sea account? God wanted His people to recall the past but not let it overshadow His current involvement in their lives (v. 18). He said, "See, I am doing a new thing! Now it springs up; do you not perceive it? I am making a way in the wilderness" (v. 19).

While looking to the past can bolster our faith in God's provision, living in the past can blind us to all the fresh work of God's Spirit today. We can ask God to show us how He's currently moving—helping, remaking, and sustaining His people. May this awareness prompt us to partner with Him to meet the needs of others, both near and far.

Jennifer Benson Schuldt

God Promises

Strength When You Need It

TEST YOUR TIREDNESS
ISAIAH 40:18–31

Those who hope in the LORD will renew their strength.
Isaiah 40:31

Someone confided in me that she was feeling guilty. She said, "Even though I'm a Christian, I still get so tired!" As I reviewed the Scriptures, I found that God's people sometimes suffered fatigue and even exhaustion. Unfortunately, in the name of victorious Christian living, some people view all weariness as a failure to trust and obey God.

But according to Isaiah, our Creator anticipates weariness in His finite creatures. He promises to renew our strength if we hope on Him (40:30–31). He also understands that our need for strength, like our need for food, isn't a once-for-all provision.

Our choice is not whether we will experience weariness but what we will be weary about. In my own life, I suffered exhaustion during a long period of time because of worry, fear, and bitterness. Thanks to the Lord, these negative feelings no longer dominate me. But I still get very tired because of my involvement in worthy causes and my desire to live faithfully as a servant of Christ.

Give yourself a "tiredness test." If you are tired for the wrong reasons, humbly seek God's loving correction. If you are tired for the right reasons, seek God's renewing strength. You don't need to feel guilty about feeling weary.

Joanie Yoder

God Promises
A Complete Awareness

HE KNOWS US
PSALM 139:1–14

---

*You have searched me, LORD, and you know me. You know
when I sit and when I rise; you perceive my thoughts from afar.*
Psalm 139:1–2

Did God know about me as I drove at night on a one-hundred-mile jour-ney to my village in Ghana? Given the condition I was in, the answer was not simple. My temperature ran high and my head ached. I prayed, "Lord, I know you are with me, but I'm in pain!"

Tired and weak, I parked by the road near a small village. Ten minutes later, I heard a voice. "Hello! Do you need any help?" It was a man with his companions from the community. Their presence felt good. When they told me the name of their village, Naa mi n'yala (meaning, "The King knows about me!"), I was amazed. I had passed this community dozens of times without stopping. This time, the Lord used its name to remind me that, indeed, He, the King, was with me while I was alone on that road in my ailing condition. Encouraged, I pressed on toward the nearest clinic.

God knows us thoroughly as we go about our everyday chores, at dif-ferent locations and situations, no matter our condition (Psalm 139:1–4, 7–12). He does not abandon us or forget us; nor is He so busy that He neglects us. Even when we are in trouble or in difficult circumstanc-es—"darkness" and "night" (vv. 11–12)—we are not hidden from His pres-ence. This truth gives us such hope and assurance that we can praise the Lord who has carefully created us and leads us through life (v. 14).

Lawrence Darmani

MAY 24

God Promises

To Walk Beside Us in Hard Times

HIS COMFORTING PRESENCE
ACTS 7:54–60

"Look," he said, "I see heaven open and the
Son of Man standing at the right hand of God."
Acts 7:56

When Jesus told His disciples that He would build His church and the gates of Hades would not overcome it (Matthew 16:18), He was saying that although the outcome was sure, they would encounter difficult times along the way. Later He warned Peter that Satan would try to sift him as wheat. Then He said, "But I have prayed for you" (Luke 22:32). This was Christ's assurance that in the face of adversity they could depend on His loving presence and care.

Persecution fell early upon the infant church. The faithful Stephen was the first person martyred for the Christian faith. As the stones fell upon him, he experienced the comforting presence of Christ (Acts 7:56). Commenting about that incident, H. A. Ironside wrote, "Here is a very significant thing. We are told in the epistle to the Hebrews that when Jesus had by Himself purged our sin, He sat down on the right hand of the Majesty on high; and here, as Stephen looked up, he saw the Lord standing. What does this mean? It is just as though the blessed Lord, in His great compassion for Stephen, has risen from His seat and is looking over the battlements of heaven to strengthen and cheer the martyr."

God gives no guarantees that His people will escape hardship. Even now you may be enduring opposition or trouble. If so, take comfort—you are not alone. The Lord is "standing," as it were, at the Father's right hand, watching over you. Call upon Him. He has promised to care for you, and He has assured you of His comforting presence.

David Egner

God Promises

More Power for Those Who Need It

STRENGTH FOR THE WEARY
ISAIAH 40:27–31

They will run and not grow weary, they will walk and not be faint.

Isaiah 40:31

On a beautiful, sunny day, I was walking in a park and feeling very weary in spirit. It wasn't just one thing weighing me down—it seemed to be everything. When I stopped to sit on a bench, I noticed a small plaque placed there in loving memory of a "devoted husband, father, brother, and friend." Also on the plaque were these words, "But they who wait for the LORD shall renew their strength; they shall mount up with wings like eagles; they shall run and not be weary, they shall walk and not faint" (Isaiah 40:31 ESV).

Those familiar words came to me as a personal touch from the Lord. Weariness—whether physical, emotional, or spiritual—comes to us all. Isaiah reminds us that although we become tired, the Lord, the everlasting God, the Creator of the ends of the earth "will not grow tired or weary" (v. 28). How easily I had forgotten that in every situation "[the Lord] gives strength to the weary and increases the power of the weak" (v. 29).

What's it like on your journey today? If fatigue has caused you to forget God's presence and power, why not pause and recall His promise. "Those who hope in the LORD will renew their strength" (v. 31). Here. Now. Right where we are.

David McCasland

God Promises
Forgiveness and Love

GOD FORGIVES DISOBEDIENCE
HOSEA 14

I will heal their waywardness and love them freely.
Hosea 14:4

I'll never forget the painful lesson I learned in early childhood about disobedience. My father, who had been mowing our lawn, interrupted his work to go shopping. He left the push mower standing near some flowers and ordered me not to touch it while he was gone. But I disobeyed him and gave it a push. To my shock, the mower veered and knocked over several flowers.

When Dad returned, I blubbered, "I didn't mean to do it!" Wisely, he replied, "Why did you do it then?" I knew the truth—I did mean to push the mower. My sin wasn't that I mowed the flowers down, it was that I disobeyed my father.

This childhood lesson is a reminder to be sorry for disobedience and not just the consequences. Rather than blubber to God, "I didn't mean to do it," do what Hosea told wayward Israel to do: "Take words [of repentance] with you, and return to the LORD" (Hosea 14:2). Tell the Lord honestly that you knew His will but chose to disobey, and cry out for His mercy. Praise God, He forgives!

Are you grieved that you chose to disobey and are not merely sorry about the consequences? Then "take words with you and return to the Lord" today. He promises to forgive you of your sin, for He loves you freely (v. 4).

Joanie Yoder

God Promises
A Life of Joy and Hope

BELIEVING OR TRUSTING?
PSALM 16

Keep me safe, my God, for in you I take refuge.
Psalm 16:1

Some people touring a mint where coins are made were shown the caldrons filled with molten metal. The tour guide told the guests that if a person were to dip his hand into water and then have someone pour the hot liquid over his hand, he would neither be injured nor feel any pain.

Picking out one couple, he suggested that perhaps they would like to prove the truthfulness of what he had just said. The husband quickly replied, "No, thanks. I'll take your word for it." But his wife said, "Sure, I'll give it a try!" Matching action to her words, she thrust her hand into a bucket of water and then held it out as the molten metal was poured over it. The hot liquid rolled off harmlessly just as the guide had said it would. (This is called the Leidenfrost Effect, and while it works, we do not recommend that you try it!) In the story, the host turned to the husband and remarked, "Sir, you claimed to believe what I said. But your wife truly trusted."

When it comes to the promises of the Bible, many Christians react like that husband. They claim to believe them, but they don't really trust God. Consequently, they fail to experience the life of joy and hope that He alone can give. In Psalm 16, David spoke of having a goodly heritage, a glad heart, stability, hope, and the assurance of "eternal pleasures" (v. 11). He knew the meaning of faith.

Let's not miss out on God's marvelous blessings by claiming to believe but never acting on the promises. Instead, let's learn to be like the woman at the mint. She truly trusted.

Richard DeHaan

God Promises
To Carry Our Burdens

RINGING REMINDERS
PSALM 37:21–31

Though he may stumble, he will not fall,
for the LORD upholds him with his hand.
Psalm 37:24

The clock tower at Westminster, which contains the bell known as Big Ben, is an iconic landmark in London, England. It is traditionally thought that the melody of the tower chimes was taken from the tune of "I Know That My Redeemer Liveth" from Handel's *Messiah*. Words were eventually added and put on display in the clock room:

Lord, through this hour be Thou our guide;
So by Thy power no foot shall slide.

These words allude to Psalm 37: "The LORD directs the steps of the godly. He delights in every detail of their lives. Though they stumble, they will never fall, for the LORD holds them by the hand" (vv. 23–24 NLT). Notice how intimately involved God is in His children's experience: "He delights in every detail of their lives" (v. 23 NLT). Verse 31 adds, "The law of their God is in their hearts; their feet do not slip."

How extraordinary! The Creator of the universe not only upholds us and helps us but He also cares deeply about every moment we live. No wonder the apostle Peter was able to confidently invite us to "cast all your anxiety on him because he cares for you" (1 Peter 5:7). As the assurance of His care rings in our hearts, we find courage to face whatever comes our way.

Bill Crowder

God Promises
And We Respond

THE GROWTH EQUATION
JAMES 1:22–27

*Do not merely listen to the word,
and so deceive yourselves. Do what it says.*
James 1:22

Growing in grace and in the knowledge of our Lord and Savior Jesus Christ calls for more than simply putting new information into the computer of our brain—important as that is. A Christian who has memorized Scripture can still remain spiritually ignorant. On the other hand, an unlearned believer whose mind can scarcely retain the exact words of a text but who is applying what he knows can be a spiritual giant by comparison. That's why, when we listen to a sermon, read a devotional message, or gain new insight from a book, we must determine to put into practice what we have learned. Only then can God's truth become a personal possession.

I've read that when Edward VI, the king of England in the sixteenth century, attended a worship service, he stood while the Word of God was read. He took notes during this time and later studied them with great care. Through the week he earnestly tried to apply them to his life. That's the kind of serious-minded response to truth the apostle James calls for in today's Scripture reading. A single revealed fact cherished in the heart and acted upon is more vital to our growth than a head filled with lofty ideas about God.

Do you feel as if you've reached a spiritual plateau? Check and see if there is any biblical promise you've not claimed. New light is not given unless you are walking in the light you already have. The growth equation for the Christian is always hearing + doing = growing.

Dennis DeHaan

God Promises
To Rule Righteously and Protect Us

IT LOOKS BAD
PSALM 12

I will protect them from those who malign them.
Psalm 12:5

King David looked out at the world and was troubled. He didn't need the internet to paint a bleak picture of society or *The New York Times* to remind him of crime and suffering. Even without a cable news show to give him all the bad news, he saw the evil.

He looked around and saw that "no one is faithful anymore." He noticed that "those who are loyal have vanished." In his world, "everyone lies to their neighbor; they flatter with their lips but harbor deception in their hearts" (Psalm 12:1–2).

This description may sound like the theme of a TV show, but it was life circa 1,000 BC. While we may view society's evils as much worse than anything before, David reminds us that evil is not a twenty-first-century innovation.

But David's words also give us hope. Notice his reaction to the bad news he bore. In verse 1, he turned to God and cried, "Help!" Then he implored God with specific needs. The response he got was positive. God promised that because He rules righteously, He would provide protection and safety (vv. 5–7).

When you are discouraged by all the bad news, cry out for God's help. Then bask in the confidence of His assurance. Three thousand years after David, God is still, and always will be, in control.

Dave Branon

God Promises

The Spirit's Help in Our Weakness

CLEAR COMMUNICATION
ROMANS 8:18–27

*The Spirit helps us in our weakness. We do not know
what we ought to pray for, but the Spirit himself
intercedes for us through wordless groans.*

Romans 8:26

While I was traveling in Asia, my iPad (containing my reading material and many work documents) suddenly died, a condition described as "the black screen of death." Seeking help, I found a computer shop and encountered another problem—I don't speak Chinese and the shop's technician didn't speak English. The solution? He pulled up a software program in which he typed in Chinese, but I could read it in English. The process reversed as I responded in English, and he read in Chinese. The software allowed us to communicate clearly, even in different languages.

At times, I feel like I'm unable to communicate and express my heart when I pray to my heavenly Father—and I'm not alone. Many of us struggle sometimes with prayer. But the apostle Paul wrote, "The Spirit helps us in our weakness. We do not know what we ought to pray for, but the Spirit himself intercedes for us through wordless groans. And he who searches our hearts knows the mind of the Spirit, because the Spirit intercedes for God's people in accordance with the will of God" (Romans 8:26–27).

How amazing is the gift of the Holy Spirit! Better than any computer program, He clearly communicates my thoughts and desires in harmony with the Father's purposes. The work of the Spirit makes prayer work!

Bill Crowder

God Promises
His Unfailing Love

LOCKED IN LOVE
ROMANS 8:31–39

Give thanks to the LORD, for he is good; his love endures forever.
Psalm 106:1

In June 2015, the city of Paris removed forty-five tons of padlocks from the railings of the Pont des Arts pedestrian bridge. As a romantic gesture, couples would etch their initials onto a lock, attach it to the railing, click it shut, and throw the key into the River Seine.

After this ritual was repeated thousands of times, the bridge could no longer bear the weight of so much "love." Eventually the city, fearing for the integrity of the bridge, removed the "love locks."

The locks were meant to symbolize everlasting love, but human love does not always last. The closest of friends may offend each other and never resolve their differences. Family members may argue and refuse to forgive. A husband and wife may drift so far apart that they can't remember why they once decided to marry. Human love can be fickle.

But there is one constant and enduring love—the love of God. "Give thanks to the LORD, for he is good; his love endures forever," proclaims Psalm 106:1. The promises of the unfailing and everlasting nature of God's love are found throughout Scripture. And the greatest proof of this love is the death of His Son so that those who put their faith in Him can live eternally. And nothing will ever separate us from His love (Romans 8:38–39).

Fellow believers, we are locked into God's love forever.

Cindy Hess Kasper

God Promises
To Be with His People

ALWAYS THERE
PSALM 55:6–23

*Evening, morning and noon I cry out
in distress, and he hears my voice.*

Psalm 55:17

The radio engineers who work at Our Daily Bread Ministries were getting ready to broadcast a program via satellite. They had prepared everything, including the satellite link. But just as they were to begin uploading, the signal to the satellite was lost. Confused, the engineers labored to reconnect the link, but nothing worked. Then they got the word—the satellite was gone. Literally. The satellite had suddenly and surprisingly fallen from the sky. It was no longer there.

I suspect that sometimes when we pray, we think something similar has happened to God—that for some reason He isn't there. But the Bible offers us comfort with the assurance that God hasn't "fallen from the sky." He is always available to us. He hears and He cares.

In a time of desperation, David wrote, "Evening, morning and noon I cry out in distress, and he hears my voice" (Psalm 55:17). No matter when we call on God, He hears the cries of His children. That should encourage our hearts. What was David's response to having a God who hears prayer? "Cast your burden on the LORD and he will sustain you" (v. 22). Although God may not answer as we would like or when we would like, we know that at "evening, morning and noon" He is always there.

Bill Crowder

God Promises

That Jesus Will Return

HEADLINE EVENT!
JOHN 13:33–14:3

"Look, he is coming with the clouds," and "every eye will see him."
Revelation 1:7

When the Lord Jesus told His disciples that He would be leaving them (John 13:33), they reacted with disbelief and dismay. But He quickly gave His fearful followers the promise, "I will come again." And what a coming that will be! One who died generations ago will actually return to this earth. Yes, when our Lord comes back, it will be such a phenomenal occurrence that it will command worldwide attention.

Did you know that the printing type most newspapers use for astounding events is called "second coming" type? These are large, heavy, black letters reserved for only the most stupendous, amazing, front page news—such as the return of Jesus Christ. This type of banner headline was used to announce the surrenders of Germany and Japan, marking the end of World War II. It also told the news of the assassination of John F. Kennedy and the shooting of President Ronald Reagan. This bold heading style signaled Apollo 11's manned landing on the moon and other dramatic events of universal importance.

One day the world will witness the great event for which the "second coming" type was named—the return of Jesus Christ. Yes, the Savior will literally come back to this planet He left so long ago. He will fulfill the promise He gave to His disciples before He ascended to heaven. And when He does, it will command the attention of all earth's inhabitants. The whole world will know that the Lord Jesus is alive. Truly it will be a "headline event"!

David Egner

God Promises
A Transformed City

A GOOD ENDING
REVELATION 22:1–5

*The throne of God and of the Lamb will be in the city,
and his servants will serve him. They will see his face.*
Revelation 22:3–4

As the lights dimmed and we prepared to watch *Apollo 13*, my friend said under his breath, "Shame they all died." I watched the movie about the 1970 spaceflight with apprehension, waiting for tragedy to strike, and only near the closing credits did I realize I'd been duped. I hadn't known or remembered the end of the true story—that although the astronauts faced many hardships, they made it home alive.

In Christ, we can know the end of the story—that we too will make it home alive. By that I mean we will live forever with our heavenly Father, as we see in the book of Revelation. The Lord will create a "new heaven and a new earth" as He makes all things new (21:1, 5). In the new city, the Lord God will welcome His people to live with Him, without fear and without the night. We have hope in knowing the end of the story.

What difference does this make? It can transform times of extreme difficulty, such as when people face the loss of a loved one or even their own death. Though we recoil at the thought of dying, we can embrace the joy of the promise of eternity. We long for the city where no longer will there be any curse—where we'll live forever by God's light (22:5).

Amy Boucher Pye

= *God Promises* =
His Care No Matter Our Age

HOW TO GROW OLD
ISAIAH 45:4–13

*Even to your old age and gray hairs I am he,
I am he who will sustain you.*

Isaiah 46:4

"How are you today, Mama?" I asked casually. My eighty-four-year-old friend, pointing to aches and pains in her joints, whispered, "Old age is tough!" Then she added earnestly, "But God has been good to me."

"Growing old has been the greatest surprise of my life," said Billy Graham in his book *Nearing Home.* "I am an old man now, and believe me, it's not easy." However, Graham noted, "While the Bible doesn't gloss over the problems we face as we grow older, neither does it paint old age as a time to be despised or a burden to be endured with gritted teeth." He then mentions some of the questions he has been forced to deal with as he has aged, such as, "How can we not only learn to cope with the fears and struggles and growing limitations we face but also actually grow stronger inwardly in the midst of these difficulties?"

In Isaiah 46 we have God's assurance: "Even to your old age and gray hairs . . . I am he who will sustain you. I have made you and I will carry you; I will sustain you and I will rescue you" (v. 4).

We don't know how many years we will live on this earth or what we might face as we age. But one thing is certain: God will care for us throughout our life.

Lawrence Darmani

God Promises
That Jesus Is a Light in the Dark

A BAD DREAM
JOHN 6:15–31

*Have no fear of sudden disaster or of the
ruin that overtakes the wicked.*

Proverbs 3:25

All of us have had bad dreams. Perhaps we were falling from a high building, fleeing from a hideous creature, or standing before an audience and forgetting our speech.

My wife once had a nightmare. She dreamed she was in a small room when two men appeared out of the mist. Fear overwhelmed her. Just as the men were about to grab her, she said, "Let me tell you about Jesus." Immediately she was awakened by the sound of her own voice. The name Jesus had freed her from fear.

We read in John 6 that Jesus's disciples were afraid when in the dimness of nightfall they saw a strange figure walking on the stormy Sea of Galilee. But the mysterious figure was not part of a bad dream—He was real. Matthew reports that they "cried out in fear" (14:26). Then the disciples heard a familiar voice: "It is I; don't be afraid" (John 6:20). It was Jesus. Their fears were calmed, as well as the sea.

The Savior speaks the same assurance to us today amid the many fears along our Christian journey. Solomon said, "The name of the LORD is a fortified tower; the righteous run to it and are safe" (Proverbs 18:10).

Fears will come, but we are assured that Jesus is always a light in the darkness.

Dennis DeHaan

God Promises

To Rescue Seekers

HE'S THERE ALL THE TIME
ISAIAH 45:18–25

I have not said . . . , "Seek me in vain."
Isaiah 45:19

I'll never forget my frustrating experience when I went to Chicago's Union Station early one morning to pick up an elderly relative who was arriving by train. When I got there, she wasn't where I thought she would be. With increasing anxiety I scoured the place—to no avail. Thinking she had missed her train, I was about to leave when I glanced down a hallway toward the baggage area. There she was, luggage at her feet, patiently waiting for me to arrive. She had been there all the time. And, to my chagrin, she was right where she was supposed to be.

It's that way with God. He's there, patiently waiting for us. He assures us, "I have not said . . . , 'Seek me in vain'" (Isaiah 45:19). Why, then, do we often have trouble finding Him? Probably because we are looking in all the wrong places.

You'll find Him right where He is supposed to be—in His Word, in prayer, and in the voice of the Holy Spirit who lives within you. The God who says "seek and you will find" (Matthew 7:7) also promises that "he rewards those who earnestly seek him" (Hebrews 11:6). So you can rejoice that God is right where He is supposed to be, and He's waiting for you right now.

Joe Stowell

God Promises

A Rich Feast in Jesus's Presence

SWEET AGAIN
ISAIAH 25:1–9

On this mountain the LORD Almighty
will prepare a feast of rich food for all peoples.
Isaiah 25:6

Russian wedding customs are filled with beauty and significance. One such custom takes place during the reception as the toastmaster proposes a toast in honor of the couple. Everyone takes a sip from his or her raised glass and then shouts, "Gor'ko! Gor'ko!" meaning "Bitter! Bitter!" When the guests shout that word, the newlyweds must rise and kiss each other in order to make the drink sweet again.

Isaiah prophesies that the bitter drink of desolation, ruin, and the curse upon the earth (chapter 24) will give way to the sweet hope of a new heaven and new earth (chapter 25). God will prepare a feast of rich foods and the finest and sweetest of drinks. It will be a banquet of continual blessing, fruitfulness, and provision for all people (25:6). There's more. Under the sovereign reign of the righteous King, death is swallowed up, bitter tears are wiped away, and the shroud of disgrace is removed (vv. 7–8). And His people will rejoice because the One they trusted in and waited for will bring salvation, tuning the bitter cup of life sweet again (v. 9).

One day, we'll be together with Jesus at the wedding supper of the Lamb. When He welcomes His bride (the church) home, the promise of Isaiah 25 will be fulfilled. The life once bitter will be made sweet again.

Marvin Williams

God Promises
To Strengthen Us

HELP FROM HIS SPIRIT
MICAH 6:3–8

What does the LORD require of you? To act justly,
and to love mercy and to walk humbly with your God.

Micah 6:8

Many of us make promises to ourselves to mark the beginning of a new year. We make pledges such as I'm going to save more, exercise more, or spend less time on social media. We begin the year with good intentions, but before long old habits tempt us to take up our old ways. We slip up occasionally, then more frequently, and then all the time. Suddenly, it's the middle of the year, and those resolutions are long forgotten.

Instead of choosing our own self-improvement goals, a better approach might be to ask ourselves: "What does the Lord desire of me?" Through the prophet Micah, God has revealed that He wants us to do what is right, to be merciful, and to walk humbly with Him (Micah 6:8). All of these things relate to soul-improvement rather than self-improvement.

Thankfully, we don't have to rely on our own strength. The Holy Spirit has the power to help us as believers in our spiritual growth. God's Word says that, He is able to "strengthen you with power through his Spirit in your inner being" (Ephesians 3:16).

So let's resolve to be more Christlike. The Spirit will help us as we seek to walk humbly with God.

Jennifer Benson Schuldt

God Promises
To Be with Us, No Matter What

CAPE TRIBULATION
JAMES 1:1–8

*Consider it pure joy, my brothers and sisters, whenever
you face trials of many kinds, because you know that the
testing of your faith produces perseverance.*
James 1:2–3

On June 10, 1770, British navigator James Cook's ship hit a reef off the
northeast coast of Australia. He sailed the ship out into deeper water only
to hit the reef again, and this time the collision almost sank the ship. This
experience moved Cook to write in the ship's log: "The north point [was
named] Cape Tribulation because here began all our troubles."

Many of us have experienced a trial that has seemed to trigger a string
of other trials. The loss of a job, the death of a loved one, an unwanted
divorce, or a decline in health could all be part of the list.

Even though a crisis may seem to be our "Cape Tribulation," God is
still sovereign and He most certainly is in control. It is His purpose to use
tribulation to build resilience into us. James writes: "Consider it pure joy,
my brothers and sisters, whenever you face trials of many kinds, because you
know that the testing of your faith produces perseverance" (James 1:2–3).

In the midst of your life-changing trial, remember that God is still at
work. He wants to use your "Cape Tribulation" experience to build your
character. He has promised His grace to see you through (2 Corinthians 12:9).

Dennis Fisher

God Promises
And It Happens!

WHAT ARE THE ODDS?
HEBREWS 11:23–29

---

*By faith Moses, when he had grown up, refused
to be known as the son of Pharaoh's daughter.*
Hebrews 11:24

The problem of compulsive gambling may seem foreign to most of us. Yet experts believe that millions of Americans are psychologically addicted to gambling. It gives them the excitement of hope and risk, but it usually ends in defeat. It is indeed a temporary pleasure. For those who engage in it, losing is the name of the game; winning means not losing everything.

Some Christians have a similar problem—spiritual gambling. It's a way of living that involves taking chances by seeing how far we can stretch God's patience. Although we know there is no such thing as "luck," too often we gamble away our time or dabble in sinful pleasures. We live as if it were possible to ignore the will of God and still come out ahead. We seem to be addicted to the excitement of risk.

There's not one chance in five that God won't keep His word. There's not even one chance in a thousand. We can be absolutely sure that what He's promised will come true. That's why it makes so much sense to be like Moses and believe God. He was willing to trust in the reliable word of the Lord rather than take his chances with the temporary excitement of sin (Hebrews 11:24–26). He believed that God was one hundred percent trustworthy. Do you?

Mart DeHaan

God Promises
That Sins Will Be Washed Away

NOT GOOD ENOUGH
1 TIMOTHY 1:12–17

Though your sins are like scarlet, they shall be as white as snow.
Isaiah 1:18

A friend told me recently of a young mother who was trying to explain her father's death to her four-year-old. The girl wondered where Grandpa was. "I'm sure he's in heaven," the mother answered, "because he was very good." The girl replied sadly, "I guess I won't be in heaven." "Why not?" her mother asked in surprise. "'Cause I'm not very good."

The story saddened me, as I'm saddened when I hear of others who believe they must be very good to get into heaven, especially since we all know deep down in our hearts that we're not very good at all.

Perhaps like this little girl you're thinking about your sins and asking, "What must I do to get to heaven?" The answer has already been given: Jesus, by His death, has paid in full the price of your sins, no matter how sordid, tawdry, or shameful they may be. Your salvation is free.

God promises, "Though your sins are like scarlet, they shall be as white as snow; though they are red as crimson, they shall be like wool" (Isaiah 1:18). John Donne wrote:

Or wash thee in Christ's blood, which hath this might,

That being red, it dyes red souls to white.

No one is good enough to get into heaven. Eternal life is a gift. Receive Jesus by faith.

David Roper

JUNE 13

God Promises
Redirection

WHEN GOD CORRECTS US
PROVERBS 3:15–18

Do not despise the LORD's discipline, and do not resent his rebuke.
Proverbs 3:11

Solomon warned us not to lean on our own understanding (Proverbs 3:5). That implies we are prone to make mistakes in judgment. And how we hate having our mistakes corrected!

Some people detest correction so much that their main goal in life seems to be attempting to avoid mistakes or hide the ones they make. But let's be practical. Correction, if well received, can save us a lot of grief.

A personal experience told by Eugene Peterson illustrates the value of correction. With his lawn mower tipped on its side, Eugene struggled to remove the blade so he could sharpen it. When his biggest wrench wouldn't budge the nut, he slipped a four-foot length of pipe over the wrench handle for more leverage. When that failed, he started banging on the pipe with a huge rock. Finally, his neighbor pointed out that the threads on the bolt went the other way. When Eugene reversed his exertions, the nut turned easily. He said, "I was saved from frustration and failure."

Are you forcing your life in the wrong direction? Welcome the correction of your heavenly Father, who delights in you. Trust His wisdom instead of your own, and He will redirect your life. That's a promise (Proverbs 3:6).

Joanie Yoder

God Promises

To Reveal His Faithfulness

PROMISES, PROMISES
2 PETER 1:1–9

He has given us his very great and precious promises, so that through them you may participate in the divine nature.

2 Peter 1:4

My youngest daughter and I have a game we call "Pinchers." When she goes up the stairs, I'll chase her and try to give her a little pinch. The rules are that I can only pinch her (gently, of course!) when she's on the stairs. Once she's at the top, she's safe. Sometimes, though, she's not in the mood to play. And if I follow her up the stairs, she'll sternly say, "No pinchers!" I'll respond, "No pinchers. I promise."

Now, that promise may seem a little thing. But when I do what I say, my daughter begins to understand something of my character. She experiences my consistency. She knows my word is good, that she can trust me. It's a little thing, keeping such a promise. But promises—or keeping them, I should say—are the glue of relationships. They lay a foundation of love and trust.

I think that's what Peter meant when he wrote that God's promises enable us to "participate in the divine nature" (2 Peter 1:4). When we take God at His word, trusting what He says about himself and about us, we encounter His heart toward us. It gives Him an opportunity to reveal His faithfulness as we rest in what He says is true. I'm thankful that Scripture brims with His promises—rock-solid reminders that "his compassions never fail. They are new every morning" (Lamentations 3:22–23).

Adam Holz

God Promises

Help for Us in Our Weakness

PROMISE KEEPERS
HEBREWS 6:13–20

After waiting patiently, Abraham received what was promised.
Hebrews 6:15

Gripped by the gravity of the promises he was making to LaShonne, Jonathan found himself stumbling as he repeated his wedding vows. He thought, *How can I make these promises and not believe they're possible to keep?* He made it through the ceremony, but the weight of his commitments remained. After the reception, Jonathan led his wife to the chapel where he prayed—for more than two hours—that God would help him keep his promise to love and care for LaShonne.

Jonathan's wedding-day fears were based on the recognition of his human frailties. But God, who promised to bless the nations through Abraham's offspring (Galatians 3:16), has no such limitations.

To challenge his Jewish Christian audience to perseverance and patience to continue in their faith in Jesus, the writer of Hebrews recalled God's promises to Abraham, the patriarch's patient waiting, and the fulfillment of what had been promised (Hebrews 6:13–15). Abraham and Sarah's status as senior citizens was no barrier to the fulfillment of God's promise to give Abraham "many descendants" (v. 14).

Are you challenged to trust God despite being weak, frail, and human? Are you struggling to keep your commitments, to fulfill your pledges and vows? In 2 Corinthians 12:9, God promises to help us: "My grace is sufficient for you, for my power is made perfect in weakness."

For more than thirty-six years God has helped Jonathan and LaShonne to remain committed to their vows. As they have done, why not trust Him to help you?

Arthur Jackson

God Promises
That Our Trust in Him Is Worthwhile

FRUSTRATING PROMISES
PSALM 37:1–24

Delight in the LORD, and he will give you the desires of your heart.

Psalm 37:4

Do any Bible promises frustrate you? Some people say that Psalm 37:4 is a guarantee that you'll get whatever you want—a spouse, a job, money. This has made me wonder at times, Why don't I always get what I want?

When a promise frustrates us because it seems that God is not fulfilling it, maybe it's because we don't understand what the verse really means. Here are three suggestions to help, using Psalm 37 as an example.

Consider the context. Psalm 37 is telling us not to worry or be envious of the wicked. Our focus is not to be on what they have, nor on what they seem to be getting away with (vv. 12–13). Instead, we are commanded to trust and delight in the Lord (vv. 3–-4).

Consider other verses. We're taught in 1 John 5:14 that our requests need to be according to God's will for us. Other Scriptures on the same topic can give us a balance.

Consult a Bible commentary. In *The Treasury of David*, C. H. Spurgeon says this about verse 4: "[Those] who delight in God desire or ask for nothing but what will please God." Doing a little deeper study can help us understand frustrating Bible verses like this one.

As we learn to delight in the Lord, His desires will become our own. And He will grant them.

Anne Cetas

God Promises
A Perfect World to Come

DEPRESSING NEWS?
2 PETER 3:1–13

The day of the Lord will come like a thief.
The heavens will disappear with a roar.
2 Peter 3:10

Some scientists tell us that in the far distant future Earth will be unable to sustain life because the sun will be too hot. This is depressing news for those who put all their hope in this world. It means that all of humankind's accomplishments will one day be wiped out.

For those who believe the Bible, though, this information is not surprising. We know that the earth in its present form will one day be destroyed "by fire" (2 Peter 3:10). But that's not depressing news. On the contrary, we gladly anticipate the day when our sin-marred planet will be replaced by a world "where righteousness dwells" (v. 13). This expectation becomes for us a powerful incentive for "holy and godly lives" (v. 11).

We also realize that our earthly lives have great significance, because through our prayers, our behavior, and our Christian witness we become partners with God as He works in the world. And one day, when He replaces our present cosmos with the perfect world, we will be given a place in our eternal home (John 14:2).

Because of our faith in Christ, we can be filled with joy and hope. The Lord wants to use our life in this world and He promises us a perfect world to come.

Herb Vander Lugt

God Promises
Spiritual Victory

DEFEAT OR VICTORY?
1 JOHN 5:1–13

*Everyone born of God overcomes the world. This is
the victory that has overcome the world, even our faith.*

1 John 5:4

Each year on June 18 the great Battle of Waterloo is recalled in what is now Belgium. On that day in 1815, Napoleon's French army was defeated by a multinational force commanded by the Duke of Wellington. Since then, the phrase "to meet your Waterloo" has come to mean "to be defeated by someone who is too strong for you or by a problem that is too difficult for you."

When it comes to our spiritual lives, some people feel that ultimate failure is inevitable and it's only a matter of time until each of us will "meet our Waterloo." But John refuted that pessimistic view when he wrote to followers of Jesus: "Everyone born of God overcomes the world. This is the victory that has overcome the world, even our faith" (1 John 5:4).

John weaves this theme of spiritual victory throughout his first letter as he urges us not to love the things this world offers, which will soon fade away (2:15–17). Instead, we are to love and please God. "And this is what he promised us—eternal life" (2:25).

While we may have ups and downs in life, and even some battles that feel like defeats, the ultimate victory is ours in Christ as we trust in His power.

David McCasland

God Promises

To Temper Our Temptation

FINDING THE WAY OUT
1 CORINTHIANS 10:1–13

---

*No temptation has overtaken you except what is common
to mankind. And God is faithful; he will not let you
be tempted beyond what you can bear. But when you are tempted,
he will also provide a way out so that you can endure it.*

1 Corinthians 10:13

There's a street with an intriguing name in the city of Santa Barbara, California. It's called "Salsipuedes," which means "leave if you can." When the street was first named, the area bordered on a marsh that sometimes flooded, and the Spanish-speaking city planners dubbed the location with a not-so-subtle warning to stay away.

God's Word cautions us to stay away from the "wrong road" of sin and temptation: "Avoid it, do not travel on it; turn from it and go on your way" (Proverbs 4:15). But Scripture doesn't just say "leave if you can." It offers assurance and tells us where to turn: "God is faithful; he will not let you be tempted beyond what you can bear. But when you are tempted, he will also provide a way out so that you can endure it" (1 Corinthians 10:13).

The promise that God will not allow us to be tempted above our ability to withstand is an encouraging reminder. When we turn to God in the moments when temptation comes, we know He is more than willing to help us stay away.

The Bible affirms that Jesus is able "to empathize with our weaknesses." But He was "tempted in every way, just as we are—yet he did not sin" (Hebrews 4:15). Jesus knows the way out of every temptation. He will show us as we run to Him!

James Banks

God Promises
That We Will Bear Fruit

DESERT PETE
EXODUS 17:1–7

The message they heard was of no value to them,
because they did not share the faith of those who obeyed.
Hebrews 4:2

In the 1960s, the Kingston Trio released a song called "Desert Pete." The ballad tells of a thirsty cowboy who is crossing the desert and finds a hand pump. Next to it, Desert Pete has left a note urging the reader not to drink from the jar hidden there but to use its contents to prime the pump.

The cowboy resists the temptation to drink and uses the water as the note instructs. In reward for his obedience, he receives an abundance of cold, satisfying water. Had he not acted in faith, he would have had only a jar of unsatisfying, warm water to drink.

This reminds me of Israel's journey through the wilderness. When their thirst became overwhelming (Exodus 17:1–7), Moses sought the Lord. He was told to strike the rock of Horeb with his staff. Moses believed and obeyed, and water gushed from the stone.

Sadly, Israel would not consistently follow Moses's example of faith. Ultimately, "the message they heard was of no value to them, because they did not share the faith of those who obeyed" (Hebrews 4:2).

Sometimes life can seem like an arid desert. But God can quench our spiritual thirst in the most unlikely circumstances. When by faith we believe the promises of God's Word, we can experience rivers of living water and grace for our daily needs.

Dennis Fisher

God Promises
To Remember Our Sins No More

WHEN OTHERS WON'T FORGIVE
PHILIPPIANS 3:12–16

Forgetting what is behind . . . I press on toward the goal.
Philippians 3:13–14

I was having lunch with two men who had opened their lives to Christ while they were in prison. The younger man had been discouraged by the fact that the family from whom he had stolen would not forgive him.

"My crime was violent," the older man said. "It continues to haunt and affect the family to this day. They have not forgiven me, . . . the pain is just too great. At first, I found myself paralyzed by this longing for their forgiveness." He continued his story: "Then one day I realized I was adding selfishness to my brokenness. It's a lot to expect that the family forgive me. I was focused on what I felt I needed to heal from my past. It took some time to realize that their forgiveness of me was a matter between them and God."

"How can you stand it?" the younger man asked.

The older man explained that God did for him what he didn't deserve and what others simply can't do: He died for our sins, and He keeps His promise to move our sins "as far as the east is from the west" (Psalm 103:12). And He "remembers your sins no more" (Isaiah 43:25).

In the face of such great love, we honor Him by accepting His forgiveness as sufficient. We must forget what lies behind and keep pressing forward (Philippians 3:13–14).

Randy Kilgore

God Promises
A Formula for Successful Living

A NO-FAIL RECIPE
2 PETER 1:1–11

If you do these things, you will never stumble.
2 Peter 1:10

Like most people who cook, I have a favorite recipe. Mine is for a scrumptious banana cake. Handed down from my mother, it's a no-fail recipe—that is, if you follow the directions exactly. I've shared it with friends, and most of them have had good results. One or two, however, said the recipe was no good. Later I discovered they had omitted some ingredients and substituted others.

The apostle Peter gave us the recipe for effective Christian living. The two main ingredients God provides are His divine power (2 Peter 1:3) and His precious promises (v. 4). As we thoroughly blend His power and promises into our believing and living, we'll be more like Christ.

Then Peter listed the ingredients we must add to our faith: goodness, knowledge, self-control, perseverance, godliness, mutual affection, and love (vv. 5–7). If we include each of these, we'll not be unfruitful, nor will we stumble in our walk with the Lord (v. 8). All who omit these vital ingredients are shortsighted, even blind, and have forgotten that they were "cleansed from their past sins" (v. 9).

Don't change God's ingredients and then blame His recipe when things go wrong. Instead, follow His instructions diligently. His recipe brings spiritual success.

Joanie Yoder

God Promises

Holy Spirit Direction

GUIDANCE NEEDED
JOHN 16:13–17

---

*When he, the Spirit of truth, comes,
he will guide you into all the truth.*

John 16:13

St. Nicholas Church in Galway, Ireland, has both a long history and an active present. It's the oldest church in Ireland, and it provides guidance in a very practical way. The church towers over the town, and its steeple is used by ships' captains as a guide for navigating their way safely into Galway Bay. For centuries, this church has reliably pointed the way home for sailors.

We can all certainly identify with the need for guidance. In fact, Jesus addressed this very need during His Upper Room Discourse. He said that after His departure the Holy Spirit would play a crucial role in the lives of believers. As part of that role, Jesus promised, "When he, the Spirit of truth, comes, he will guide you into all the truth" (John 16:13).

What a marvelous provision! In a world of confusion and fear, guidance is often needed. We can easily be misdirected by the culture around us or by the brokenness within us (1 John 2:15–17). God's Spirit, however, is here to help, to direct, and to guide. How thankful we can be that the Spirit of truth has come to give us the guidance we often so desperately need. Set your course by His life, and you will reach safe harbor.

Bill Crowder

God Promises
Never to Leave Us

EVER-PRESENT PRESENCE
MATTHEW 28:16–20

Surely I am with you always, to the very end of the age.
Matthew 28:20

During the 2018 World Cup of soccer, Colombian forward Radamel Falcao scored in the seventieth minute against Poland, securing a victory. The dramatic goal was Falcao's thirtieth in international play, earning him the distinction of scoring the most goals by a Colombian player in international competition.

Falcao has often used his success on the soccer pitch to share his faith, frequently lifting his jersey after a score to reveal a shirt with the words, *Con Jesus nunca estará solo*: "With Jesus you'll never be alone."

Falcao's statement points us to the reassuring promise from Jesus, "I am with you always, to the very end of the age" (Matthew 28:20). Knowing He was about to return to heaven, Jesus comforted His disciples by assuring them that He would always be with them, through the presence of His Spirit (v. 20; John 14:16–18). Christ's Spirit would comfort, guide, protect, and empower them as they took the message of Jesus to cities both near and far. And when they experienced periods of intense loneliness in unfamiliar places, Christ's words would likely echo in their ears, a reminder of His presence with them.

No matter where we go, whether close to home or far away, as we follow Jesus into the unknown we too can cling to this promise. Even when we experience feelings of loneliness, as we reach out in prayer to Jesus, we can receive comfort. We know He's with us.

Lisa Samra

God Promises
To Take Us through Our Hardship

THE OTHER SIDE
MARK 4:35–41

---

*When evening came, he said to his disciples, "Let us go over
to the other side." . . . A furious squall came up, and the
waves broke over the boat, so that it was nearly swamped.*

Mark 4:35, 37

Even when we follow Christ's guidance, we may face hardships.

For example, Jesus's disciples were doing God's will when they took
Him across the lake, for He had commanded them to do so. Yet they were
buffeted by a dreadful tempest, and they seemed to be in danger of drowning. A storm—and Christ on board! It seems a contradiction. Shouldn't
His presence ensure a peaceful journey?

Not at all! Life at times becomes more difficult after a person has
accepted Christ as Savior and Lord. But a storm—and Christ asleep! That
even deepens the perplexity! Our Lord's silence, the frustrating delays, the
mysteries of His dealings—these are too profound for us to understand.
Yet we can be certain that His purpose in testing our faith is to strengthen
it. God will surely fulfill His plan for us through our struggles, and His
deliverance will lead us to praise Him.

Unnecessary fears troubled the disciples because they did not trust
Jesus's words. If they had just thought for a moment, they would have
remembered that He had said, "Let us go over to the other side" (Mark
4:35). He didn't say, "Let us go to the middle of the lake and be drowned."

Our trust should be like that today. No matter what the trial, we may
rest assured that God's help has already been promised. He'll go with us to
"the other side."

Henry Bosch

God Promises
Wisdom and Strength

HAPPY ADVERSITY
JAMES 1:1–12

Consider it pure joy, my brothers and sisters,
when you face trials of many kinds.

James 1:2

On the back of a wedding anniversary card were some wiggly lines drawn by our three-year-old grandson. Alongside was a note from our daughter explaining that Trevor told her what he had written: "I'm writing a letter for your love and happy adversity."

Trevor's "mistake" has become our watchword, because "happy adversity" embodies the biblical principle of facing difficulties with joy: "Consider it pure joy, my brothers and sisters, whenever you face trials of many kinds, because you know that the testing of your faith produces perseverance" (James 1:2–3).

From our perspective, adversity is anything but happy. We sometimes think that the Christian life is supposed to be trouble-free, and we see little value in hardship. But God sees it differently.

J. B. Phillips's translation of James 1:2–3 reads: "When all kinds of trials and temptations crowd into your lives my brothers, don't resent them as intruders, but welcome them as friends! Realise that they come to test your faith and to produce in you the quality of endurance."

Affliction does not come as a thief to steal our happiness but as a friend bringing the gift of staying power. Through it all, God promises us His wisdom and strength.

So don't be offended if I wish you "Happy Adversity" today.

David McCasland

God Promises
His Faithfulness

A REASON FOR HOPE
LAMENTATIONS 3:19–33

Because of the LORD's great love we are not consumed,
for his compassions never fail. They are new every morning.
Lamentations 3:22–23

It's one of the saddest stories of the Bible, yet it inspired one of the most hopeful hymns of the twentieth century.

The prophet Jeremiah witnessed unimaginable horrors when the Babylonians invaded Jerusalem in 586 BC. Solomon's temple was reduced to ruins, and with it went not only the center of worship but also the heart of the community. The people were left with no food, no rest, no peace, no leader. But in the midst of suffering and grief, one of their prophets found a reason for hope. "Because of the LORD's great love we are not consumed," wrote Jeremiah, "for his compassions never fail. They are new every morning; great is your faithfulness" (Lamentations 3:22–23).

Jeremiah's hope came from his personal experience of the Lord's faithfulness and from his knowledge of God's promises in the past. Without these, he would have been unable to comfort his people.

This hope of Lamentations 3 is echoed in a hymn by Thomas Chisholm (1866–1960). Although suffering sickness and setbacks throughout his life, he wrote "Great Is Thy Faithfulness." It assures us that even in times of great fear, tragic loss, and intense suffering we can find comfort and confidence as we trust in God's great faithfulness.

Julie Ackerman Link

God Promises

Present and Future Rewards

I'LL PAY YOU LATER
LUKE 14:7–14

You will be repaid at the resurrection of the righteous.
Luke 14:14

Suppose a boss were to say to an employee, "We really appreciate what you're doing around here, but we've decided to change the way we pay you. Starting today, we're going to pay you later—after you retire." Would the employee jump for joy? Of course not. That's not the way things work in this world. We like our payment now—or at least every payday.

Did you know that God promises to "pay" us later—much later? And He asks us to be happy about it!

Jesus suggested that our ultimate reward for the good things we do in His name comes after we die. In Luke 14, Jesus said that if we care for the poor, the lame, and the blind, our reward for such kindness will come at the resurrection of the righteous (v. 14). He also said that if we are persecuted, we should "rejoice in that day and leap for joy, because great is your reward in heaven" (Luke 6:22–23). Surely, the Lord gives us comfort, love, and guidance today, but what wonderful things He has planned for us in the future!

This may not be the way we would have planned it; we don't enjoy waiting for things. But imagine how glorious it will be when we receive our rewards in Jesus's presence. What a grand time we'll have as we enjoy what God has reserved for later.

Dave Branon

God Promises

To Care for Us in Hard Times

RIDING THE RAPIDS
ISAIAH 43:1–7

When you pass through the rivers, they will not sweep over you.
Isaiah 43:2

The rafting guide escorted our group to the river's edge and directed us all to put on life jackets and grab paddles. As we climbed into the boat, he assigned us seats to balance the boat's weight, providing stability when we encountered rapids. After highlighting the thrills that the watery voyage ahead would hold for us, he detailed a series of directions we could expect to hear—and would need to follow—to effectively steer the boat through the white water. He assured us that even though there might be tense moments on the way, our journey would be both exciting and safe.

Sometimes life feels like a white-water rafting trip, one that contains more rapids than we might like. God's promise to Israel, through the prophet Isaiah, can guide our feelings when we fear the worst is happening: "When you pass through the rivers, they will not sweep over you" (Isaiah 43:2). The Israelites faced an overwhelming fear of rejection by God as they went into exile as a consequence of their sin. Instead, He affirms them and promises to be with them because He loves them (vv. 2, 4).

God won't abandon us in the rough waters. We can trust Him to guide us through the rapids—our deepest fears and most painful troubles—because He also loves us and promises to be with us.

Kirsten Holmberg

God Promises
Ongoing Renewal

SPRINGS OF LIVING WATER
JOHN 4:5–15

Whoever believes in me, as the Scripture has said,
rivers of living water will flow from within them.

John 7:38

In 1896, Sherwood Eddy enthusiastically began his ministry as a missionary to India. But after just a year he was ready to quit—his energy depleted, his spirit broken.

One morning after a sleepless night he begged God for help. Then he remembered the promise of Jesus to the woman at Jacob's well, "The water I give them will become in them a spring of water welling up to eternal life" (John 4:14).

Eddy wrote, "I resolved to stop drawing on myself so constantly and begin instead drawing on God." From then on, he daily set aside time for prayerfully drinking from the well that never runs dry—the inexhaustible, soul-renewing wellspring of God's grace. "Since that day," Eddy said, "I have known not one hour of darkness and despair. The eternal God has been my refuge, and underneath me I have felt the everlasting arms."

No matter how much energy or talent we have, sooner or later we discover that the well of our personal resources is running dry. But when Christ, the source of living water, indwells our lives, we aren't locked into the drudgery of drawing on our human abilities. Jesus becomes our unfailing source of spiritual renewal. We find that when we have nothing left, He is the well that never runs dry.

Vernon Grounds

God Promises
Hope for Heroes

PLODDER FOR GOD
HEBREWS 11:32–40

---

*They went about . . . destitute, persecuted
and mistreated—the world was not worthy of them.*
Hebrews 11:37–38

Columnist Leonard Pitts Jr. writes about the need for heroes: "My middle son, Marlon, complained to me just the other day that his generation is coming of age 'in a world without heroes.' . . . His words tugged at me. . . . Our children have learned to wait for the other shoe to drop, for 'heroes' to be unmasked and values betrayed."

In spite of all the scandals in the world of sports, politics, and business, countless people in all walks of life still remain faithful to God under incredible odds. I know of a Christian whose wife lay sick in the hospital for ten years. He stayed true to her and visited her every day until she died.

I can't forget the US Congressman from Michigan who when he died was praised by colleagues for his compassion and high moral principles. Then there are the many parents of physically or mentally impaired children, who rely on Christ for the grace and strength to get through each day.

Through faith in God's promises, the unnamed people in Hebrews 11:32–40 stayed true to their convictions. Some even paid with their lives. They are described as people "the world was not worthy of" (v. 38).

Let's keep our eyes on people who show that kind of faith today. They are this world's true heroes.

Joanie Yoder

God Promises

His Continual Presence

God's Astonishing Promise
Hebrews 13:5-6

Never will I leave you; never will I forsake you.
Hebrews 13:5

The writer to the Hebrews quotes God as saying to His people, "Never will I leave you; never will I forsake you" (Hebrews 13:5). How does that strike you? Is it just some pleasant piety that evokes a wide yawn?

This isn't like saying we have coffee with the president or a Supreme Court justice. Knowing people like that would say something significant about us. But to claim that God is with us every moment of every day, as close as our skin, in every turn of life, tear-stained or drenched in smiles— some would say that borders on insanity.

Yet throughout history men and women have staked their lives on that truth. Abraham, Moses, Rahab, Joshua, David, Esther, just to name a few. The promise was true for them, but how can we know it's true for us?

It is true for us because of Jesus. By His coming, He says, in effect, "I want to be with you; I gave myself to you; I gave myself for you. Do you really think I would ever forsake you?"

How do you respond to this astonishing promise? You can say it's too good to be true. You can say it sounds unbelievable. But don't ignore it. In your hurts, your fears, your struggles, your temptations, there is no more wonderful promise than this: "I will never leave you nor forsake you."

Haddon Robinson

God Promises

That We Can Know Him

UNPREDICTABLE
PSALM 46

Be still, and know that I am God; I will be exalted among the nations, I will be exalted in the earth.

Psalm 46:10

In the 2003 US Women's Open, the relatively unknown Hilary Lunke secured the greatest prize in women's golf—and a place in history. Not only did she win the US Open in an 18-hole playoff but it was also her only professional victory. Her surprising and inspiring win underscores the fact that one of the most exciting things about sports is its unpredictability.

The unpredictability of life is not always so thrilling, however. We devise and strategize. We make plans, projections, and proposals about what we would like to see happen in life, but often they are little more than our best guess. We have no idea what a year, a month, a week, or even a day might bring. So we pray and plan, and then we trust the God who knows fully and completely what we can never predict. That is why I love the promise of Psalm 46:10: "Be still, and know that I am God; I will be exalted among the nations, I will be exalted in the earth."

Life is unpredictable. There are countless things I can never know with certainty. What I can know, however, is that there is a God who knows all and loves me deeply. And by knowing Him, I can "be still"—I can be at peace.

Bill Crowder

God Promises
Joy and Contentment

BEYOND OUR DREAMS
LUKE 12:15–31

*Watch out! Be on your guard against all kinds of greed;
life does not consist in an abundance of possessions.*

Luke 12:15

According to research by university professors Richard Ryan and Tim Kasser, there's a dark side to the "American dream" of prosperity, and the problem isn't confined to the United States. Based on data collected from subjects in twelve countries, Kasser says that in every culture he's studied, there are psychologically unhelpful and often destructive results from pursuing wealth. The problem is not having money but "living a life where that's your focus."

In today's Scripture, Jesus warned His followers: "Watch out! Be on your guard against all kinds of greed; life does not consist in an abundance of possessions " (Luke 12:15). But our lingering conviction that more money will bring us more happiness and satisfaction makes it difficult to believe either the psychologists or the Son of God.

To counter our natural tendency toward covetousness, Christ urged us to be rich toward God and to trust Him for all our needs. He commands us to "seek his kingdom," and promises that " these things" (life's necessities) will be added to us (v. 31).

Making Christ our focus does not guarantee prosperity but joy and contentment beyond our dreams.

David McCasland

God Promises
A Forever Life

DRINK UP
JOHN 4:7–14

Whoever drinks the water I give them will never thirst.

John 4:14

Ida's Pastry Shoppe in Jenison, Michigan, advertised this special offer: "Buy one of our coffee mugs for $4.79 and fill up your cup for a dime each time you visit."

But the owners never expected that twenty-five years later, four longtime customers would still be getting their cup of java every day—for ten cents.

You won't find many deals like that anymore. But Jesus offered something far greater to the woman at the well (John 4:10). He said, "Everyone who drinks this water will be thirsty again, but . . . the water I give them will become in them a spring of water welling up to eternal life" (vv. 13–14).

The woman at the well was ready to listen. None of her many personal relationships had ever filled up her emptiness. Then Jesus offered her "water" that would soothe her parched life and give her something more—the promise of eternal life.

That same promise is ours as well. Jesus said, "I have come that they may have life, and have it to the full" (John 10:10).

God's grace and love come from a bottomless reservoir. Drink from the water He offers, and you will never thirst again.

Cindy Hess Kasper

God Promises
Abundant Life

AS IS
2 CORINTHIANS 5:14–21

If anyone is in Christ, the new creation has come:
The old has gone, the new is here!
2 Corinthians 5:17

The beat-up old car sits on the used-car lot, rusty and forsaken. Years of abuse and hard driving have taken their toll on the formerly shiny automobile.

A man walks onto the lot and is attracted to this rust bucket. He plunks down cash, and the salesperson hands over the keys while saying, "I'm selling you this car 'as is.' We're not fixing anything." The new owner just smiles; he knows his cars, and he's about to restore this castoff to its former beauty.

Across town, a troubled woman sits in forlorn sadness, contemplating where she went wrong. Years of abuse and hard living have taken their toll on what was once a vibrant young girl. She's been mistreated by others so many times that she feels she has little value anymore. And after making her own mistakes and living with her own bad choices, she's sure she will be left on life's junk heap forever.

But then someone tells her about Jesus. Someone mentions that Jesus specializes in castoffs, that He is waiting to transform anyone who trusts Him—even her. Someone tells her that Jesus will take her "as is." She believes. She trusts. And Jesus begins to restore another lost person to the abundant life He has promised.

Dave Branon

JULY 7

God Promises
That Generosity Is Rewarded

GIVING TO THE POOR
PROVERBS 11:24-31

*Those who give to the poor will lack nothing, but those
who close their eyes to them receive many curses.*
Proverbs 28:27

In the latter part of the seventeenth century, German preacher August H.
Francke founded an orphanage to care for homeless children. According to
Francke's book *The Footsteps of Providence*, one day Francke, though desperately needing funds for the orphanage, sent a destitute Christian widow
a ducat—a gold coin.

Later, Francke received a letter of thanks from the woman. She
explained that the gift had come at a time when "she extremely wanted
such help." She also said that because of his generosity she had asked the
Lord to shower the orphanage with gifts. Soon after, Francke received a gift
of one ducat from one benefactor and twelve double ducats from another
on the same day. A friend from Sweden sent two more. He thought he had
been amply rewarded for helping the widow, but he was soon informed
that the orphanage was to receive five hundred gold pieces from the estate
of Prince Lewis of Wurtemburg. When he heard this, Francke recalled the
prayer of the woman who "entreated the Lord to reward our [children].

As Christians, we must give with pure motives, "without expecting to
get anything back" (Luke 6:35). But we can be certain that if we do give
out of love for Christ, we will have God's blessing. "Those who give to
the poor will lack nothing" (Proverbs 28:27) is a promise from God that
never fails.

Henry Bosch

God Promises
To Give Confidence during Hard Times

CONFIDENT HOPE
PHILIPPIANS 1:19–26

For to me, to live is Christ and to die is gain.

Philippians 1:21

Dr. William Wallace was serving as a missionary surgeon in Wuzhou, China, in the 1940s when Japan attacked China. Wallace, who was in charge of Stout Memorial Hospital at the time, ordered the hospital to load his equipment on barges and continue to function as a hospital while floating up and down rivers to avoid infantry attacks.

During dangerous times, Philippians 1:21—one of Wallace's favorite verses—reminded him that if he lived, he had work to do for the Savior; but if he died, he had the promise of eternity with Christ. The verse took on special meaning when he died while falsely imprisoned in 1951.

The apostle Paul's writing reflects a deep devotion we can aspire to as followers of Jesus, enabling us to face trials and even danger for His sake. It is devotion enabled by the Holy Spirit and the prayers of those closest to us (v. 19). It's also a promise. Even when we surrender ourselves to continued service under difficult circumstances, it is with this reminder: when our life and work end here, we still have the joy of eternity with Jesus ahead of us.

In our hardest moments, with hearts committed to walking with Christ now, and with our eyes firmly fixed on the promise of eternity with Him, may our days and our acts bless others with the love of God.

Randy Kilgore

God Promises
The Companionship of our Savior

CHRIST IS NEAR
HEBREWS 13:1–6

---

*Keep your lives free from the love of money
and be content with what you have.*

Hebrews 13:5

A diver from Genoa, Italy, loved to explore the crystal-clear waters in the sea near his home. As he was enjoying the undersea world one day, he thought about how wonderful it would be to place a statue of Christ down there. Then all who lived by the sea or died in its waters would have Christ near. Later, when he presented his idea to others, it caught on. People from all over Italy sent bronze and copper articles to be melted down. Soon an eight-foot statue of Christ was completed. On the day the nine-hundred-pound artifact was lowered to its place fifty-six feet below the surface of the sparkling waters, the diver said, "Now Christ is near the sailors and people who live on the seashore."

Although that man meant well, perhaps he failed to comprehend the wonderful truth of Scripture that Jesus is not limited by time or space. A statue or a picture, therefore, can't bring Him any closer. He is with us wherever we are, whether on land, in the air, or on the sea. Some believers have difficulty acknowledging Christ's nearness because He can't be seen. What they fail to appreciate is that the indwelling Holy Spirit is the one who manifests the Savior to them. When Jesus promised His disciples, "surely I am with you always" (Matthew 28:20); He was guaranteeing His ever-abiding presence, even though He would no longer be with them in a physical body.

As twenty-first-century followers of the Savior, we have the same assurance. Wherever we go, and whatever the situation, Christ is always near.

David Egner

God Promises
Ultimate Security

YOUR SAFE PLACE
PROVERBS 18:10–11

The name of the LORD is a fortified tower;
the righteous run to it and are safe.

Proverbs 18:10

My daughter and I were arranging to attend an extended family gathering. Because she was nervous about the trip, I offered to drive. "Okay. But I feel safer in my car. Can you drive it?" she asked. I assumed she preferred her more spacious vehicle to my compact one, so I responded, "Is my car too cramped?" "No, it's just that my car is my safe place. Somehow I feel protected there."

Her comment challenged me to consider my own personal "safe place." Immediately I thought of Proverbs 18:10, "The name of the LORD is a fortified tower; the righteous run to it and are safe." In Old Testament times, the walls and watchtower of a city provided warning of danger from without and shielding for its citizens within. The writer's point is that God's name, which stands for His character, person, and everything that He is, provides true protection for His people.

Certain physical places promise longed-for safety in moments that seem dangerous. A sturdy roof overhead in the midst of a storm. A hospital offering medical care. The embrace of a loved one.

What is your "safe place"? Wherever we seek safety, it is God's presence with us in that place that provides the strength and protection we really need.

Elisa Morgan

God Promises
Comfort

HOPE ANYWAY
PSALM 34:15–18

My comfort in my suffering is this: Your promise preserves my life.
Psalm 119:50

Among the hundreds of articles I've written for *Our Daily Bread* since 1988, a few stick in my mind. One such article is from the mid-1990s when I told of a time our three girls were away at camp or on mission trips, so six-year-old Steve and I had some guy time.

As we were enjoying an excursion to the airport, Steve turned to me and said, "It's not as much fun without Melissa," his eight-year-old sister and sidekick. Neither of us knew then how poignant those words would turn out to be. Life indeed has not been "as much fun" for the years since Mell died in a car accident as a teenager. The passage of time may dull the ache, but nothing takes the pain away completely. Time cannot heal that wound. But here's something that can help: listening to, meditating on, and savoring the solace promised by the God of all comfort.

Listen: "Because of the LORD's great love we are not consumed, for his compassions never fail" (Lamentations 3:22).

Meditate: "In the day of trouble he will keep me safe in his dwelling" (Psalm 27:5).

Savor: "My comfort in my suffering is this: Your promise preserves my life" (Psalm 119:50).

Life can never be the same again when someone we love is gone. But God's promises bring hope and comfort.

Dave Branon

God Promises

Freedom from Imperfection After Death

LIFELONG BUT TEMPORARY
1 CORINTHIANS 15:35–49

*The body that is sown in perishable, it is raised imperishable;
it is sown in dishonor, it is raised in glory.*

1 Corinthians 15:42–43

When Paul Schneider was two years old, a medical specialist said he would never walk or have understandable speech because of brain damage that occurred at birth.

Paul proved the experts wrong. He not only learned to walk but he also earned a college degree and spoke to audiences more than three hundred times.

Closest to Paul's heart, though, was his love for Christ, the One who saved him from his sins and gave him the courage to persevere against enormous odds. And it was his hope in Christ that inspired the phrase he used to describe his cerebral palsy: "Lifelong but temporary."

Paul Schneider's outlook was rooted in 1 Corinthians 15. Because Jesus conquered sin and death and rose from the grave, He promises a new "spiritual body" to all who trust Him. This body will be free from all the imperfections of our current existence. It will be a transformed body, having abilities beyond anything we now know (Philippians 3:21).

In 1995 Paul Schneider entered the presence of Christ, free from his cerebral palsy. All Christians have the promise of receiving a new body at the resurrection. We may have a lifelong limitation that is physical, mental, emotional, or all three, but it is still only temporary.

Dennis DeHaan

God Promises
Peace

UNCERTAIN TIMES
PHILIPPIANS 4:6–9

The peace of God, which transcends all understanding,
will guard your hearts and your minds in Christ Jesus.
Philippians 4:7

During a major economic downturn several years ago, many people lost their jobs. Sadly, my brother-in-law was one of them. Writing to me about their situation, my sister shared that although there were uncertainties, they had peace because they knew that God would care for them.

Believers in Jesus can have peace in the midst of uncertainties because we have the assurance that our heavenly Father loves His children and cares for our needs (Matthew 6:25–34). We can bring all our concerns to Him with an attitude of thankfulness, trusting Him to meet our needs and give us peace (Philippians 4:6–7).

"The peace of God, which transcends all understanding," writes the apostle Paul, "will guard your hearts and your minds in Christ Jesus" (v. 7). To say the peace of God surpasses all understanding reveals that we can't explain it, but we can experience it as He guards our hearts and minds.

Our peace comes from the confidence that the Lord loves us and He is in control. He alone provides the comfort that settles our nerves, fills our minds with hope, and allows us to relax even in the midst of changes and challenges.

Poh Fang Chia

God Promises
A Beacon of Hope

LIMITLESS LOVE
PSALM 36

Your love, LORD, reaches to the heavens, your faithfulness to the skies.
Psalm 36:5

Recently, a friend sent me the history of a hymn that I often heard in church when I was a boy:

> Could we with ink the ocean fill,
> And were the skies of parchment made;
> Were every stalk on earth a quill,
> And every man a scribe by trade;
> To write the love of God above
> Would drain the ocean dry;
> Nor could the scroll contain the whole
> Tho' stretched from sky to sky.

These words were originally part of an ancient Jewish poem, and centuries later were found on the wall of a patient's room in an insane asylum.

Frederick M. Lehman was so moved by the poem that he desired to expand on it. In 1917, while seated on a lemon box during his lunch break from his job as a laborer, he added the words of the first two stanzas and the chorus, completing the song "The Love of God."

The psalmist describes the comforting assurance of God's love in Psalm 36: "Your steadfast love, O LORD, extends to the heavens" (v. 5 ESV). Regardless of the circumstances of life—whether in a moment of sanity in a mind otherwise muddled with confusion or during a dark time of trial—God's love is a beacon of hope, our ever-present, inexhaustible source of strength and confidence.

Joe Stowell

God Promises
To Show Us the Way

LOOKING BACK
GENESIS 48:8–16

God . . . has been my shepherd all my life to this day.
Genesis 48:15

George Matheson, best known for the hymn "O Love That Wilt Not Let Me Go," wrote another song titled "Ignored Blessings," in which he looks back to "the road gone by." By looking back he could see that his heavenly Father had led him all the way.

God has an itinerary for each of us—a "course" we must run (see Acts 20:24 and 2 Timothy 4:7). Our route is charted in the councils of heaven and rooted in the sovereign purposes of God.

Yet our choices are not irrelevant. We make decisions every day, large and small, some of which have life-altering consequences. The question—aside from the confounding mystery of God's sovereignty and human choice—is this: How can we discern the course to be run?

The answer is clearer to me now that I'm older and have more of the past to look back on. By looking back, I see that God has led me all the way. I can truthfully say, "God . . . has been my shepherd all my life to this day" (Genesis 48:15). Though clouds surround the present, and I do not know what the future may hold, I have the assurance that the Shepherd will show me the way. My task is to follow Him in love and obedience, and entrust each step to Him.

David Roper

God Promises
His Faithful Care

GROWING THROUGH GRIEF
PSALM 119:65–80

It was good for me to be afflicted so that I might learn your decrees.
Psalm 119:71

A woman who lost her husband of forty years to a sudden heart attack said that the resulting grief had caused her to value love more. When she heard couples arguing, she sometimes spoke to them, saying, "You don't have time for this." She noted that the wasted moments in all our lives become more precious when they cannot be repeated.

Grief changes our perspective on life. It is trite but true that how we deal with sorrow will make us either bitter or better. In a remarkable statement, the psalmist actually thanked God for a difficult experience: "Before I was afflicted I went astray, but now I obey your word. . . . It is good for me to be afflicted so that I might learn your decrees" (Psalm 119:67, 71).

We don't know the nature of the psalmist's affliction, but the positive outcome was a longing to obey the Lord and a hunger for His Word. Rarely can we use this truth to comfort those who hurt. Instead, it is the Lord's word to us from His compassionate heart and the touch from His healing hand.

When we grieve, it feels more like dying than growing. But as God wraps His loving arms around us, we have the assurance of His faithful care.

David McCasland

God Promises
To Teach Us

NAVIGATING LIFE'S RAPIDS
PSALM 32:5-11

I will instruct you and teach you in the way you should go;
I will counsel you with my loving eye on you.

Psalm 32:8

"Everybody on the left, give me three strong forward strokes!" our white-water raft guide shouted. Those on the left dug in, pulling our raft away from a churning vortex. For several hours, we learned the importance of listening to our guide's instructions. His steady voice enabled six people with little rafting experience to work together to plot the safest course down a raging river.

Life has its share of whitewater rapids, doesn't it? One moment, it's smooth sailing. Then, in a flash, we're paddling like mad to avoid suddenly swirling whirlpools. Those tense moments make us keenly aware of our need for a skilled guide, a trusted voice to help us navigate turbulent times.

In Psalm 32, God promises to be that voice: "I will instruct you and teach you in the way you should go" (v. 8). Backing up, we see that confessing our sins (v. 5) and prayerfully seeking Him (v. 6) play a role in hearing Him too. Still, I take comfort in the fact that God promises, "I will counsel you with my loving eye on you" (v. 8), a reminder that His guidance flows from His love. Near the end of the chapter, the psalmist concludes, "The LORD's unfailing love surrounds the one who trusts in him" (v. 10). And as we trust Him, we can rest in His promise to guide us through life's most difficult passages.

Adam Holz

God Promises
To Be with Us Always

UNLIGHTED PATHS
JOSHUA 1:1–9

The LORD your God will be with you wherever you go.
Joshua 1:9

As we ventured home from a family vacation, the road took us through some desolate parts of central Oregon. For nearly two hours after dusk we drove through deep canyons and across desert plateaus. Fewer than twenty sets of headlights punctuated the darkness. Eventually the moon rose on the horizon, visible to us when the road crested hills but eclipsed when we traveled through the lowlands. My daughter remarked on its light, calling it a reminder of God's presence. I asked whether she needed to see it to know He was there. She replied, "No, but it sure helps."

After Moses's death, Joshua inherited leadership of the Israelites and was charged to take God's chosen people into the promised land. Despite his divine commission, Joshua must have felt challenged by the daunting nature of his task. God graciously offered Joshua assurance to be with him on the journey ahead (Joshua 1:9).

The road of life often travels through uncharted territory. We voyage through seasons when the path ahead isn't clearly visible. God's plan may not always be apparent to us, but He has promised to be with us "always, to the very end of the age" (Matthew 28:20). What greater assurance could we hope for—no matter what uncertainty or challenge we might face? Even when the path is unlit, the Light is with us.

Kirsten Holmberg

God Promises
To Hear Our Prayers

EQUAL ACCESS
PSALM 145:14-27

Let us then approach God's throne of grace with confidence, so that we may receive mercy and find grace to help us in our time of need.
Hebrews 4:16

Pastor Stuart Silvester told me of a conversation he had with an acquaintance who frequently flew his small private plane in and out of Toronto International Airport. He asked the pilot if he ever encountered problems taking off and landing a small craft at an airport that was dominated by so many large jets. His friend responded, "My plane may be small, but I have the same rights, the same privileges, and the same access to that airport as anyone else—even the jumbo jets!"

Pastor Silvester then made this spiritual application: "It's the same with prayer, with the believer's approach to the throne of grace. No matter who we are or how small we are in comparison with others or how low our station in life, we take a back seat to no one. No one is given priority treatment."

In a world that offers preferential treatment to the wealthy, the famous, and the influential, it's encouraging to know that every child of God has equal access to the Father in heaven. The psalmist said, "The LORD is near to all who call on him, to all who call on him in truth" (Psalm 145:18).

With that assurance, we can "come boldly to the throne of grace" in prayer, knowing that our loving God will never turn us away.

Richard DeHaan

God Promises
To Reveal His Awesomeness

THE MAKER OF THE MOON
JEREMIAH 31:3–37

*[The Lord said,] "I will be their God,
and they will be my people."*
Jeremiah 31:33

Soon after astronauts set the Eagle down in the Sea of Tranquility on July 20, 1969, Neil Armstrong planted his foot on the moon's surface and said, "That's one small step for man, one giant leap for mankind." He was the first human to walk on the moon. Other space travelers followed, including the commander of the last Apollo mission, Gene Cernan. "There I was, and there you are, the Earth—dynamic, overwhelming, and I felt . . . it was just too beautiful to happen by accident," Cernan said. "There has to be somebody bigger than you and bigger than me." Even from their unique view in deep space, these men understood their smallness in comparison to the vastness of the universe.

The prophet Jeremiah also considered the immensity of God as Creator and Sustainer of the earth and beyond. The Maker of all promised to reveal himself intimately as He offered His people love, forgiveness, and hope (Jeremiah 31:33–34). Jeremiah affirms God's enormity as "he who appoints the sun to shine by day, who decrees the moon and stars to shine by night" (v. 35). Our Creator and Lord Almighty will reign above all as He works to redeem all of His people (vv. 36–37).

We'll never finish exploring the immeasurable vastness of the heavens and depths of the earth's foundations. But we can stand in awe at the complexity of the universe and trust the maker of the moon—and everything else.

Xochitl Dixon

$\mathcal{G}od\ Promises$

To Offer Peace and Assurance

A SAFE PLACE
PSALM 17:1–9

I call on you, my God, for you will answer me;
turn your ear to me and hear my prayer.

Psalm 17:6

My brothers and I grew up on a wooded hillside in West Virginia that provided a fertile landscape for our imaginations. Whether swinging from vines like Tarzan or building tree houses like the Swiss Family Robinson, we played out the scenarios we found in the stories we read and movies we watched. One of our favorites was building forts and then pretending we were safe from attack. Years later, my kids built forts out of blankets, sheets, and pillows—constructing their own "safe place" against imaginary enemies. It seems almost instinctive to want a hiding place where you can feel safe and secure.

When David, the singer-poet of Israel, sought a safe place, he looked no further than God. Psalm 17:8 asserts, "[God,] keep me as the apple of your eye; hide me in the shadow of your wings." When you consider the Old Testament record of David's life and the almost constant threats he faced, these words reveal an amazing level of confidence in God (v. 6). In spite of those threats, he was convinced his true safety was found in Him.

We can know that same confidence. The God who promises to never leave or forsake us (Hebrews 13:5) is the One we trust with our lives every day. Although we live in a dangerous world, our God gives us peace and assurance—both now and forever. He is our safe place.

Bill Crowder

God Promises
======================================
That Even in Sadness He Gives Hope
======================================

JOY IN THE MIDST OF GRIEF
EZRA 3:10–13

---

*No one could distinguish the sound of the shouts of joy from
the sound of weeping, because the people made so much noise.*

Ezra 3:13

After only a few art lessons, ten-year-old Joel decided to try his hand at painting a flower. By looking at a color photograph of a Rose of Sharon, Joel was able to paint a beautiful mixture of blue, purple, red, green, and white. This made the flower, which had been photographed on the day Joel's aunt died, seem to come to life. To the family, his painting symbolized a bittersweet mixture of feelings. While it provided a lasting reminder of the loss they had suffered, it also carried a celebration of Joel's newly discovered artistic gift. The painting gave joy in the midst of grief.

When the people of Judah returned to Jerusalem from captivity in Babylon, they too had a bittersweet experience. As they began rebuilding Solomon's temple, many in the crowd sang songs of praise. At the same time, some older people, who had seen the beauty of the original temple that had been destroyed by war, wept aloud. We are told that "no one could distinguish the sound of the shouts of joy from the sound of weeping" (Ezra 3:13).

Grieving can be like that. While there is sadness in looking back, it also includes a promise of joy in trusting God for the future. Even in a devastating loss, we have this hope: The Lord provides joy in the midst of grief.

Dennis Fisher

God Promises
His Power

PLUGGED IN
ISAIAH 40:27–31

He gives strength to the weary and increases the power of the weak.
Isaiah 40:29

My wife was working at home on her computer recently when she suddenly noticed her laptop battery power was low, and the computer was about to shut down. The computer was plugged in, though, so it shouldn't have been using the battery. Following the laptop cord to the extension cord, she finally noticed that the extension cord was actually plugged back into itself instead of the wall outlet! She looked at me, amused, and said, "There's a devotional in there somewhere."

As she said it, I was reminded of a passage of Scripture on the power of God: Isaiah 40:27–31. Isaiah identifies the true and unending Source of strength from which we must draw ours—"the everlasting God, the Creator of the ends of the earth" (v. 28). Then he speaks to those whose strength is ebbing, encouraging them to wait on the Lord to find their strength renewed (vv. 29–31).

Jesus spoke of us as branches abiding in Him as the Vine (John 15:4–5). It's a parallel to Isaiah's powerful closing, which promises that if we're plugged into God we will "run and not grow weary, . . . walk and not be faint" (Isaiah 40:31).

When we find ourselves weary and distressed, we need to plug into the true Source of strength and life.

Randy Kilgore

God Promises
That He'll Never Desert Us

A FAITHFUL HELPER
JEREMIAH 20:7-13

The LORD is with me like a mighty warrior.
Jeremiah 20:11

As a young boy, my father had to deliver slop to hungry pigs on the farm where he grew up. He hated this job because the hogs would knock him over when he entered their pen. This task might have been impossible except for a faithful helper who accompanied my dad—a German shepherd named Sugarbear. She would maneuver herself between my father and the pigs and hold them back until my dad finished his chore.

The prophet Jeremiah had the difficult job of proclaiming God's messages to the Israelites. This required him to endure physical abuse, verbal attacks, imprisonment, and isolation. Although Jeremiah struggled with deep discouragement, he had a Helper through all of his trouble. God promised him, "I am with you and will rescue you" (Jeremiah 1:19).

God did not desert Jeremiah, and He will not desert us. We have His continual aid through the power of the Spirit, who lives inside every believer (John 14:16–17). The Helper gives us hope (Romans 15:13), steers us toward spiritual truth (John 16:13), and pours out God's love in our hearts (Romans 5:5). We can trust that God faithfully helps us as we endure hardship. We can say with Jeremiah, "The LORD is with me like a mighty warrior" (Jeremiah 20:11).

Jennifer Benson Schuldt

God Promises

Strength, Help, and His Right Hand

THE FIGHT AGAINST FEAR
HEBREWS 2:9–18

Even though I walk through the darkest valley,
I will fear no evil, for you are with me.

Psalm 23:4

In his landmark book *The Denial of Death*, author and anthropologist Ernest Becker argues that all of our anxieties and fears are rooted in our dread of death. Although Becker was not a Christ-follower, his scholarly study could serve as a commentary on Hebrews 2, which tells us that in our natural state we are subject to the fear of death throughout life (v.15).

We all know something about fear. And certainly the men and women we meet in the Bible were subject to fear, ranging from a mere tremor of anxiety all the way to terrifying panic. But there is never a need to panic, even in the face of death. Our Lord has experienced death and conquered it!

The author of Hebrews tells us that Jesus "was made lower than the angels for a little while, . . . so that by the grace of God he might taste death for everyone" (2:9). Through His death Christ has defeated "him who holds the power of death—that is, the devil," making us "free" from the "fear of death" (vv. 14–15).

Are you victimized by your fears? Recall the wonderful, dread-dispelling promise of Scripture: "Do not fear, for I am with you; do not be dismayed, for I am your God. I will strengthen you and help you; I will uphold you with my righteous right hand" (Isaiah 41:10).

Vernon Grounds

God Promises
To Provide for Our Needs

LEARNING TO TRUST
MATTHEW 6:25–34

Every good and perfect gift is from above, coming down from the Father of the heavenly lights, who does not change like shifting shadows.

James 1:17

When I was a teenager, I sometimes challenged my mother when she tried to encourage me to have faith. "Trust God. He will take care of you," she would tell me. "It's not that simple, Mom!" I would bark back. "God helps those who help themselves!"

But those words, "God helps those who help themselves" are nowhere to be found in Scripture. Instead, God's Word teaches us to depend on Him for our daily needs. Jesus tells us, "Look at the birds of the air; they do not sow or reap or store away in barns, and yet your heavenly Father feeds them. Are you not much more valuable than they? Can any one of you by worrying add a single hour to your life?" (Matthew 6:26–27).

Everything we enjoy—even the strength to earn a living and "help ourselves"—are gifts from a heavenly Father who loves us and values us beyond our ability to fathom.

As Mom neared the end of her life, Alzheimer's disease robbed her of her creative mind and memories, but her trust in God remained. She lived in our home for a season, where I was given a "front-row seat" to observe God's provision for her needs in unexpected ways—ways that helped me see she had been right all along. Instead of worrying, she entrusted herself to the One who promised to take care of her. And He showed himself faithful.

James Banks

God Promises

The Presence of the Holy Spirit

SWEET COMPANY
JOHN 14:15–26

The Spirit of truth . . . lives with you and will be in you.
John 14:17

The elderly woman in the nursing home didn't speak to anyone or request anything. It seemed she merely existed, rocking in her creaky old chair. She didn't have many visitors, so one young nurse would often go into her room on her breaks. Without asking the woman questions to try to get her to talk, she simply pulled up another chair and rocked with her. After several months, the elderly woman said to her, "Thank you for rocking with me." She was grateful for the companionship.

Before He went back to heaven, Jesus promised to send a constant companion to His disciples. He told them He would not leave them alone but would send the Holy Spirit to be in them (John 14:17). That promise is still true for believers in Jesus today. Jesus said that the triune God makes His "home" in us (v. 23).

The Lord is our close and faithful companion throughout our entire life. Recording artist Scott Krippayne expresses this truth in his song titled "Sweet Company." In it he refers to Jesus as his "guiding star," providing sweet company for this life and for eternity.

Let's enjoy Jesus's sweet company today.

Anne Cetas

God Promises
To Guide Us with His Spirit

WALKING GOD'S WAY
ISAIAH 30:15–21

Whether you turn to the right or to the left, your ears will hear a voice behind you, saying, "This is the way; walk in it."
Isaiah 30:21

"We're going this way," I said as I touched my son's shoulder and redirected him through the crowd to follow his mom and sisters in front of us. I'd done this more often as the day wore on at the amusement park our family was visiting. He was getting tired and more easily distracted. *Why can't he just follow them?* I wondered.

Then it hit me: How often do I do exactly the same thing? How often do I veer from obediently walking with God, enchanted by the temptations to pursue what I want instead of seeking His ways?

Think of Isaiah's words from God for Israel: "Whether you turn to the right or to the left, your ears will hear a voice behind you, saying, 'This is the way; walk in it'" (Isaiah 30:21). Earlier in that chapter, God had rebuked His people for their rebelliousness. But if they would trust His strength instead of their own ways (v. 15), He promised to show His graciousness and compassion (v. 18).

One expression of God's graciousness is His promise to guide us by His Spirit. That happens as we talk to Him about our desires and ask in prayer what He has for us. I'm thankful God patiently directs us, day-by-day, step-by-step, as we trust Him and listen for His voice.

Adam Holz

God Promises

That We Will Live Forever with Jesus

THE CROSS AND THE CROWN
JOHN 19:21–30

*Jesus said to her, "I am the resurrection and the life.
The one who believes in me will live, even though they die.*

John 11:25

Westminster Abbey in London has a rich historical background. In the tenth century, Benedictine monks began a tradition of daily worship there that still continues today. The Abbey is also the burial place of many famous people, and every English monarch since AD 1066 has been crowned at the Abbey. In fact, sixteen of those monarchs are also buried there—their rule ending where it began.

No matter how grandiose their burial, world rulers rise and fall; they live and die. But another king, Jesus, though once dead, is no longer buried. In His first coming, Jesus was crowned with thorns and crucified as the "king of the Jews" (John 19:3, 19). Because Jesus rose from the dead in victory, we who are believers in Christ have hope beyond the grave and the assurance that we will live with Him forever. Jesus said, "I am the resurrection and the life. The one who believes in me will live, even though they die; and whoever lives by believing in me will never die" (11:25–26).

We serve a risen King! May we gladly yield to His rule in our lives now as we look forward to the day when the "Lord God Almighty" will reign for all eternity (Revelation 19:6).

Bill Crowder

God Promises
And We Can Claim Them

THE FAITHFUL PROMISES
HEBREWS 10:19–25

Let us hold unswervingly to the hope we profess,
for he who promised is faithful.

Hebrews 10:23

It has been said that God's promises are dated in heaven. And since we know only "in part," as the Bible says (1 Corinthians 13:12), we don't always know when they will be fulfilled. But that shouldn't matter, for we do have the confidence that God will keep them.

Suppose a wealthy man were to give you a note saying "Sometime in the future, a time I've decided upon, you will receive $50,000 that I have set aside for you." Although you might become impatient as you wait for the money, you confidently expect to get it. But if that same man were to say, "If everything works out, I might give you $50,000," you'd expect the money only if he didn't go bankrupt, change his mind, forget his promise, or die.

Of course, the first situation carries the greatest certainty. And that's the way it is in God's economy. He dates, as it were, many of His promises according to His sovereign will and in keeping with His perfect knowledge of what is best for us. This in no way diminishes the value of God's promises, for He backs them all with the infinite riches of His character. He never changes His mind. He never forgets His word. He never dies. God may seem to delay the fulfillment of a promise, but we can be encouraged that every promise is as good as His word.

God is neither slow nor tardy. So don't be discouraged. Keep on claiming the promises. God is the faithful promiser.

Paul Van Gorder

God Promises

That There Is Joy in Praises

FOR YOUNG AND OLD
PSALM 119:9–16

Praise be to you, LORD.
Psalm 119:12

Kerri's grandpa was having health problems and hadn't been himself lately. To cheer him up, Kerri visited him to recite a Bible passage she had memorized for a speech contest.

Grandpa knew that she had won, so he wanted to reward her. Opening his Bible to his favorite passage, he hid some money there. When Kerri arrived, she recited her winning entry, Psalm 119:9–16. Then Grandpa gave Kerri the Bible, and she opened it to find the hidden gift—located at Psalm 119. They had both chosen the same passage!

For Kerri and her grandpa, God's direction led them to a portion of Scripture of vital importance for both young and old. It details how to stay pure in a world of impurity (Psalm 119:9)—something all young people need to do. It explains the importance of hiding God's Word in our hearts (v. 11)—something many older believers depend on as life becomes more difficult. The verses also remind us to praise God, value His standards, meditate on Scripture, and delight in His teachings (vv. 13–16).

Sometimes God surprises us with the way He speaks to us through His Word. He can even use an amazing grandfather-grandchild "coincidence" to put them, and us, face-to-face with some of His most precious promises.

Dave Branon

God Promises

Never to Leave Us

A FRIEND TO THE END
PROVERBS 18:14–24

There is a friend who sticks closer than a brother.

Proverbs 18:24

Traditionally, medical schools have trained their students to help patients live, while offering little instruction in helping them face death. But that is changing with the addition of courses in end-of-life care. Physicians are now taught that when they have used all their medical expertise without achieving a cure, they should seize the opportunity to stand compassionately beside their dying patients and be a friend.

Death frightens many of us and makes us feel awkward in the presence of a terminally ill person. But our greatest opportunities to help someone in Jesus's name may come during a person's final days on earth.

The Bible speaks of a friendship that knows no limits. "A friend loves at all times," said the wise man (Proverbs 17:17). And "there is a friend who sticks closer than a brother" (18:24). Jesus said, "Greater love has no one than this: to lay down one's life for one's friends" (John 15:13).

Jesus is both our Great Physician and our Friend, and He promised that He would never leave us nor forsake us (Hebrews 13:5). He calls us to stand with our friends and family in His name as their earthly journey nears its end. That's what a true friend would do.

David McCasland

God Promises

Rest for the Weary Soul

BEAUTIFULLY BURDENED
MATTHEW 11:28–30

My yoke is easy and my burden is light.
Matthew 11:30

I awoke to pitch darkness. I hadn't slept more than thirty minutes and my heart sensed that sleep wouldn't return soon. A friend's husband lay in the hospital, having received the dreaded news, "The cancer is back—in the brain and spine now." My whole being hurt for my friends. What a heavy load! And yet, somehow my spirit was lifted through my sacred vigil of prayer. You might say I felt beautifully burdened for them. How could this be?

In Matthew 11:28–30, Jesus promises rest for our weary souls. Strangely, His rest comes as we bend under His yoke and embrace His burden. He clarifies in verse 30, "For my yoke is easy and my burden is light." When we allow Jesus to lift our burden from our backs and then tether ourselves to Jesus's yoke, we become harnessed with Him, in step with Him and all He allows. When we bend under His burden, we share in His sufferings, which ultimately allows us to share in His comfort as well (2 Corinthians 1:5).

My concern for my friends was a heavy burden. Yet I felt grateful that God would allow me to carry them in prayer. Gradually I ebbed back to sleep and awoke—still beautifully burdened but now under the easy yoke and light load of walking with Jesus.

Elisa Morgan

God Promises
Living Water

SHOWERS OF BLESSINGS
PSALM 85

Will you not revive us again, that your people may rejoice in you?
Psalm 85:6

When it rains, most people go inside to avoid getting wet. But I remember a summer day in Texas when people ran outside their offices and homes to stand in a downpour. Some shouted, others danced, and everyone was happy. After months of scorching temperatures and crippling drought, the sheer joy of a life-giving rain made getting soaked a pleasure.

Just as a physical drought teaches us that there is no substitute for rain, a time of spiritual dryness burns into us the truth that we cannot live without God's renewing Spirit. Hymnwriter Daniel W. Whittle expressed his longing for spiritual revival in these words: "Showers of blessing, showers of blessing we need; mercy drops round us are falling, but for the showers we plead."

During times of spiritual dryness, when we long for a sense of the presence and power of God, we echo the psalmist's prayer: "Will you not revive us again, that your people may rejoice in you? Show us your unfailing love, LORD, and grant us your salvation" (Psalm 85:6–7).

The spiritual refreshing we crave comes only from above. Christ alone can satisfy our spiritual thirst with the "spring of water welling up to eternal life" He promised to all who come to Him (John 4:14).

David McCasland

God Promises
To Carry Us

TRUST HIM FIRST
ISAIAH 46:3-13

Praise the Lord; praise God our savior!
For each day he carries us in his arms.

Psalm 68:19 NLT

"Don't let go, Dad!"

"I won't. I've got you. I promise."

I was a little boy terrified of the water, but my dad wanted me to learn to swim. He would purposefully take me away from the side of the pool into a depth that was over my head, where he was my only support. Then he would teach me to relax and float.

It wasn't just a swimming lesson; it was a lesson in trust. I knew my father loved me and would never let me be harmed intentionally, but I was also afraid. I would cling tightly to his neck until he reassured me all would be well. Eventually his patience and kindness won out, and I began to swim. But I had to trust him first.

When I feel "over my head" in a difficulty, I sometimes think back on those moments. They help me call to mind the Lord's reassurance to His people: "Even to your old age . . . I am he who will sustain you. I have made you and I will carry you" (Isaiah 46:4).

We may not always be able to feel God's arms beneath us, but the Lord has promised that He will never leave us (Hebrews 13:5). As we rest in His care and promises, He helps us learn to trust in His faithfulness. He lifts us above our worries to discover new peace in Him.

James Banks

God Promises

Sowing and Reaping

FUN IN GOD'S SERVICE
PSALM 126

Our mouths were filled with laughter, our tongues with songs of joy. . . .
"The LORD has done great things for us, and we are filled with joy."
Psalm 126:2–3

When my grandnephew, his wife, and their daughter were serving as missionaries in New Guinea, he always closed his newsletters with these words: "Having fun serving Him."

With the word *fun*, he means "pleasure," not a sense of amusement. How pleasurable it is to be an instrument in God's hand—leading people to the Savior, comforting the sick and sorrowing, bringing transformation to troubled marriages, and doing good in the name of Jesus.

I'm quite sure the writer of Psalm 126 would agree. The six verses radiate with a spirit of joy and gladness from beginning to end. The psalm opens with a reminder of a time when God "restored the fortunes of Zion" (v. 1). God had miraculously delivered His people from a grave situation (exactly what it was we don't know). It was like a dream come true—and His people were filled with joy as they responded with refreshing laughter and hearty singing. It was a revival!

After a prayer for another such revival, the psalmist made a promise to all who serve God: "Those who sow with tears will reap with songs of joy" (v. 5).

An abundant spiritual harvest can lead to laughter and singing. Yes, serving Him is fun!

Herb Vander Lugt

God Promises
A Full Life

LIVING TO THE MAX
JOHN 10:7–11

I have come that they may have life, and have it to the full.
John 10:10

A veteran mountain climber was sharing his experiences with a group of novices preparing for their first major climb. He had conquered many of the world's most difficult peaks, so he was qualified to give them some advice. "Remember this," he said, "your goal is to experience the exhilaration of the climb and the joy of reaching . . . the peak. Each step draws you closer to the top. If your purpose for climbing is just to avoid death, your experience will be minimal."

I see an application to the Christian's experience. Jesus did not call us to live the Christian life just to escape hell. It's not to be a life of minimum joy and fulfillment, but a life that is full and overflowing. Our purpose in following Christ should not be merely to avoid eternal punishment. If that's our primary motivation, we are missing the wonders and joys and victories of climbing higher and higher with Jesus.

The Lord promised us "life . . . to the full" (John 10:10). We cannot experience a full and abundant life if we are living in fear. When we walk by faith, we will see each day of the Christian life as a challenge to be met, and as one more upward step to glory!

Do not live minimally. Live life to the maximum! Climb that mountain with confidence!

David Egner

God Promises

That His Love Never Stops

WHAT CAN'T YOU GIVE UP?
HOSEA 11:8–11

*Neither height nor depth, nor anything else in
all creation, will be able to separate us from the
love of God that is in Christ Jesus our Lord.*

Romans 8:39

"What's one thing you can't give up?" the radio host asked. Listeners called in with some interesting answers. Some mentioned their families, including a husband who shared memories of a deceased wife. Others shared that they can't give up on their dreams, such as making a living in music or becoming a mother. All of us have something we treasure dearly—a person, a passion, a possession—something we can't give up.

In the book of Hosea, God tells us that He won't give up on His chosen people Israel, His treasured possession. As Israel's loving husband, God provided her with everything she needed: land, food, drink, clothing, and security. Yet like an adulterous spouse, Israel rejected God and sought her happiness and security elsewhere. The more God pursued her, the further she drifted away (Hosea 11:2). However, though she had hurt Him deeply, He would not give her up (v. 8). He would discipline Israel so as to redeem her; His desire was to re-establish His relationship with her (v. 11).

Today, all of God's children can have the same assurance: His love for us is a love that will never let us go (Romans 8:37–39). If we've wandered from Him, He yearns for us to return. When God disciplines us, we can be comforted that it's a sign of His pursuit, not of His rejection. We are His treasure; He won't give up on us.

Poh Fang Chia

God Promises

Full Redemption

NO RECORD OF OUR SINS
PSALM 130

If you, LORD, keep a record of sins, Lord, who could stand?
Psalm 130:3

"Out of the depths" the psalmist cries to God (Psalm 130:1). His problem surfaces: terrible guilt for things done and undone in the past. "If you, LORD, keep a record of sins, Lord, who could stand?" (v. 3).

But thankfully, God forgives. He does not keep an account of past sins, no matter how many or how grievous they have been. "Therefore, there is now no condemnation for those who are in Christ Jesus" (Romans 8:1). God's forgiveness then leads us to fear Him (Psalm 130:4). We worship and adore God, for grace and forgiveness cause us to love Him all the more.

But what happens if we slide back into old sins? What if sin lingers? We are to repent and "wait for the LORD" (v. 5). And we are to be patient while God works. We are not hopeless cases. We can "hope" in the One who will deliver us in His time.

We now have these two assurances: God's unfailing love—He will never leave us nor forsake us (Hebrews 13:5). And God's promise of full redemption in due time—He will redeem us from all our iniquities (Psalm 130:8) and present us before His glorious presence without fault and with great joy (Jude v. 24).

We're forgiven! We're free! With the psalmist, let's worship the Lord as we await His coming.

David Roper

God Promises
To Be Close When We Need Comfort

COMING ALONGSIDE
2 CORINTHIANS 1:3–11

*Praise be to the God and Father of our
Lord Jesus Christ, . . . who comforts us in all our troubles,
so that we can comfort those in any trouble.*

2 Corinthians 1:3–4

When my sister Carole was diagnosed with breast cancer, our family worried. That diagnosis, with its surgeries and treatments, caused us to fear for her well-being, which drove our family to prayer on her behalf. Over the ensuing months, Carole's updates were honest about the challenges. But we all celebrated when the report came back that the surgery and treatments had been successful. Carole was on the road to recovery!

Then, less than a year later, my sister Linda faced the same battle. Immediately, Carole came alongside Linda, helping her understand what to expect and how to prepare for what she would face. Carole's experience had equipped her to walk with Linda through her own trial.

This is what Paul calls for in 2 Corinthians 1:3–4, where we read, "Praise be to the God and Father of our Lord Jesus Christ, the Father of compassion and the God of all comfort, who comforts us in all our troubles, so that we can comfort those in any trouble with the comfort we ourselves receive from God."

Thankfully, the Lord doesn't waste anything. Our struggles not only give us an opportunity to experience His comfort but they also open the door for us to share that comfort with others in their struggles.

Bill Crowder

God Promises

His Never-failing Presence

ALWAYS
1 THESSALONIANS 4:13–18

*We will be with the Lord forever. Therefore
encourage one another with these words.*
1 Thessalonians 4:17–18

I love the words *always* and *never.* They hold so much hope! I would like to think that I could always be happy and that life would never fail me. But reality says that I won't always be happy and that the things I hope would never happen just might. So, as good as these words sound, they struggle to live up to their potential—unless you are thinking about the promise of Jesus's presence.

To a group of troubled disciples who feared facing life on their own, Jesus said, "I am with you always" (Matthew 28:20). The writer to the Hebrews reminds us that Jesus said, "'Never will I leave you; never will I forsake you.' So we say with confidence: 'The Lord is my helper; I will not be afraid'" (Hebrews 13:5–6). And the apostle Paul assures believers that after death, "We will be with the Lord forever" (1 Thessalonians 4:17). How encouraging!

No matter how scary our journey may feel today or how hopeless our future may look, the assurance of His never-failing presence can provide us with the courage and comfort to make it through. And best of all, when this short life is over, we will always be with Him. No wonder Paul says to "encourage one another with these words" (v. 18).

Joe Stowell

God Promises
To Forgive and Forget

RINGS AND GRACE
HEBREWS 8:6–13

*For I will forgive their wickedness and
will remember their sins no more.*
Hebrews 8:12

When I look at my hands, I am reminded that I lost my wedding and engagement rings. I was multitasking as I packed for a trip, and I still have no idea where they ended up.

I dreaded telling my husband about my careless mistake—worried how the news would affect him. But he responded with more compassion and care for me than concern over the rings. However, there are times when I still want to do something to earn his grace! He, on the contrary, doesn't hold this episode against me.

So many times, we remember our sins and feel we must do something to earn God's forgiveness. But God has said it is by grace, not by works, that we are saved (Ephesians 2:8–9). Speaking of a new covenant, God promised Israel, "I will forgive their wickedness and will remember their sins no more" (Jeremiah 31:34). We have a God who forgives and no longer calls to mind the wrongs we have done.

We may still feel sad about our past, but we need to trust His promise and believe that His grace and forgiveness are real through faith in Jesus Christ. This news should lead us to thankfulness and the assurance faith brings. When God forgives, He forgets.

Keila Ochoa

God Promises
A Way Around Our Concerns

FOLLY OF WORRY
MATTHEW 6:25-34

*Therefore I tell you, do not worry about your life, what
you will eat or drink; or about your body, what you will wear.*
Matthew 6:25

As Christians, we don't need to worry. Yet it's one of those things we're all guilty of doing. We often become concerned over matters that shouldn't trouble us. I read somewhere that there are two things we should never worry about. First, we must not be anxious about things we can't control. Turning them over to the Lord in prayer, we should leave them in His hands. Second, we should never worry about things we can control. We are to stop our worrying and start doing something about them.

Hudson Taylor, missionary to China and founder of what is today known as OMF International, gave this excellent advice: "Let us give up our work, our plans, ourselves, our lives, our loved ones, our influence, our all, right into [God's] hand; and then, when we have given all over to Him, there will be nothing left for us to be troubled about."

We should avoid worry—not because of the distress it brings to us, but because it displeases the Lord. Charles Wesley is reported to have said that it would be just as inconsistent for him to swear as it would be for him to worry. What he had in mind, no doubt, was the fact that both are sinful. For the child of God, to worry is to doubt the heavenly Father—and that's an insult to Him. He merits our confidence.

Placing our trust firmly in God and His promises will help us avoid the folly of worry.

Richard DeHaan

God Promises
To Keep Us Secure

SAFE IN GOD'S KEEPING
1 PETER 1:1–9

Who through faith are shielded by God's power until the coming of the salvation that is ready to be revealed in the last time.

1 Peter 1:5

One of the most comforting truths in the Bible is the revelation that God has the power to keep and protect all who have received Jesus as Savior. Our eternal safety is further assured through the present ministry of our Lord as our advocate and the one who intercedes (1 John 2:1; Hebrews 7:25).

A magazine carried a testimony of assurance given by Scottish preacher McLeod Campbell. One day a friend who was filled with doubt and spiritual confusion asked, "Pastor, you always seem to have peace of soul. Tell me, how can you feel that you've got such a tight hold on God?" With a smile Campbell exclaimed, "I don't always feel that I have hold of Him, but praise the Lord, I know that He always has hold of me!"

This truth also brings comfort in trial. A poet once wrote:

Able to keep! Yes, able to keep, Though rough the path,
all rugged and steep; Tender the heart that's caring for me,
Mighty the grace, sufficient for thee.
Able to keep—my weakness He knows, Strong the
temptation, crafty the foes; God
is my refuge, He is my shield,
Power almighty that never shall yield.

What a wonderful truth for Christians to cling to in a world that is so uncertain! There's great peace in the promise that God keeps us safe.

Henry Bosch

God Promises

Hope for Difficulty and Doubt

KEY PROMISES
2 CORINTHIANS 1:18–22

No matter how many promises
God has made, they are "Yes" in Christ.

2 Corinthians 1:20

The promises in God's Word are like keys that unlock doors of difficulty, despair, and doubt. A scene from *Pilgrim's Progress* illustrates the point.

The author John Bunyan portrays Christian, the main character in his allegory, as temporarily at a standstill on his journey to heaven. He finds himself locked in a dungeon beneath Doubting Castle. Then one morning Christian says in amazement, "What a fool am I, to lie in a stinking dungeon, when I may as well walk with liberty! I have a key in my bosom called Promise, that will, I am persuaded, open any lock in Doubting Castle." To which Hopeful, his traveling companion, exclaims, "That is good news, good brother; pluck it out of your bosom and try!"

So Christian pulls out the key and tries it in the dungeon door. The bolt opens with ease, and Christian and Hopeful hurry out. They then proceed to the outside door that leads into the castle yard, and the key opens it too. One last barrier stands between them and freedom—an iron gate. At first the lock resists. Christian keeps working the key of promise, and finally the heavy gate swings open.

Do you find yourself locked in Doubting Castle, held prisoner by despair? Choose to trust one of God's promises and act upon it today.

Paul Van Gorder

God Promises
To Strengthen Us

DRAINED OF ALL STRENGTH
ISAIAH 40:25–31

He gives strength to the weary and increases the power of the weak.

Isaiah 40:29

When I was a teenager, my dad and I went on many hunting and fishing trips together. Most became happy memories, but one fishing expedition was nearly a disaster. We drove up into a high mountain range and set up camp in a remote area. Then Dad and I trudged a long way down the mountain to get to a stream to fish.

After a long day fishing in the hot sun, it was time to return to camp. But as we began to head back, Dad's face grew pale. He was dizzy and nauseated, and he had almost no strength.

Trying not to panic, I had him sit down and drink liquids. Then I prayed aloud to God for help. Bolstered by prayer, rest, and nourishment, Dad improved, and we began to go slowly back up the mountain. He held on to my loosened belt as I crawled upward—leading the way back to camp.

Sometimes we find ourselves in what feels like a hopeless valley without the strength to go on. When this happens, it's important to recall God's promise: "He gives strength to the weary and increases the power of the weak" (Isaiah 40:29).

Do you feel drained? Exhausted? Ask God for help. Depend on Him for the power to go on and the strength to make it up the mountain.

Dennis Fisher

God Promises

To Help Us When We Can't See

WHEN MORNING COMES
HEBREWS 11:1-8

*Faith is confidence in what we hope for
and assurance about what we do not see.*

Hebrews 11:1

It was very late when we stopped for the night at a country inn outside of the Bavarian city of Munich in Germany.

We were delighted to see that our cozy room had a balcony, although an oppressive fog made it impossible to see into the darkness. But when the sun rose a few hours later, the haze began to fade. Then we could see what had been grimly shrouded the night before—a completely idyllic scene—peaceful and lush green meadow, sheep grazing with tiny tinkling bells about their necks, and big white clouds in the sky that looked exactly like more sheep—huge, fluffy sheep!

Sometimes life can get clouded over by a heavy fog of despair. Our situation may look so dark that we begin to lose hope. But just as the sun burns away a fog, our faith in God can burn away the haze of doubt. Hebrews 11 defines faith as "confidence in what we hope for and assurance about what we do not see" (v. 1). The passage goes on to remind us of the faith of Noah, who was "warned about things not yet seen," yet obeyed God (v. 7). And Abraham who went where God directed—even though he didn't know where that would be (v. 8).

Though we have not seen Him and cannot always feel His presence, God is always present and will help us through our darkest nights.

Cindy Hess Kasper

God Promises
His Presence

WHY AM I AFRAID?
2 KINGS 6:8–17

*"Don't be afraid," the prophet answered. "Those who
are with us are more than those who are with them."*

2 Kings 6:16

Columnist George Cantor told how he dealt with a childhood fear. Almost every night he was awakened by something, and he imagined scary creatures lurking outside his room. Often he would be too scared to go back to sleep. Sometimes he would go and lie down by his parents' bedroom door, figuring that as long as he was near them, nothing would hurt him.

That child's need for some physical evidence of his parents' presence reminds me of the young servant of Elisha who woke up early one morning and found that the Syrian army had surrounded the city. Alarmed and afraid, he cried out to Elisha, "Oh no, my lord! What shall we do?" (2 Kings 6:15). After Elisha prayed, the Lord opened the young servant's eyes. What he saw must have filled him with awe and wonder. The Bible says that he saw "the hills full of horses and chariots of fire all around Elisha" (v. 17).

We too at times long for God to give us some kind of reassurance that He is near, and sometimes He does. But that's the exception. He wants us to learn to trust His promise that He is with us. No matter how frightening the situation, God's people always have more on their side than the enemy has on his.

Mart DeHaan

God Promises

That Jesus Provides a Better World

MAKING PEACE WITH TROUBLE
JOHN 16:22-33

In this world you will have trouble.
But take heart! I have overcome the world.

John 16:33

We were almost home when I noticed it: the needle of our car's temperature gauge was rocketing up. As we pulled in, I killed the engine and hopped out. Smoke wafted from the hood. The engine sizzled like bacon. I backed the car up a few feet and found a puddle beneath: oil. Instantly, I knew what had happened: The head gasket had blown.

I groaned. We'd just sunk money into other expensive repairs. Why can't things just work? I grumbled bitterly. Why can't things just stop breaking?

Can you relate? Sometimes we avert one crisis, solve one problem, pay off one big bill, only to face another. Sometimes those troubles are much bigger than an engine self-destructing: an unexpected diagnosis, an untimely death, a terrible loss.

In those moments, we yearn for a world less broken, less full of trouble. That world, Jesus promised, is coming. But not yet: "In this world you will have trouble," He reminded His disciples in John 16. "But take heart! I have overcome the world" (v. 33). Jesus spoke in that chapter about grave troubles, such as persecution for the believer's faith. But such trouble, He taught, would never have the last word for those who hope in Him.

Troubles both small and large may dog our days. But Jesus's promise of a better tomorrow with Him encourages us not to let our troubles define our lives today.

Adam Holz

God Promises
Peace

QUAKING ASPENS
PHILIPPIANS 4:6–9

*Now may the Lord of peace himself give
you peace at all times and in every way.*
2 Thessalonians 3:16

While I was visiting Michigan's Upper Peninsula, two trees caught my attention. Though the leaves on the surrounding trees were not moving, the leaves of these trees were fluttering with just the slightest hint of a breeze. I pointed them out to my wife, and she told me they were called quaking aspens. I was struck by the visual effect of those shaking leaves. While all the other trees appeared calm and steady, the quaking aspen leaves shook, even with only the faintest breeze.

Sometimes I feel like a quaking aspen. People around me seem to be moving through life without issues or concerns, apparently steady and secure, while even the slightest issue can unsettle my heart. I see others and marvel at their calm and wonder why my own life can so easily be filled with turbulence. Thankfully, the Scriptures remind me that genuine, steadying calm can be found in the presence of God. Paul wrote, "Now may the Lord of peace himself give you peace at all times and in every way. The Lord be with all of you" (2 Thessalonians 3:16). Not only does God offer peace but He himself is the Lord of peace.

When we enter the disturbing, unsettling seasons of life, it is good to know that real peace is available in the God of all peace.

Bill Crowder

God Promises
The Spirit's Help

THE ADVOCATE
JOHN 16:7–15

When he, the Spirit of truth, comes,
he will guide you into all the truth.
John 16:13

As I boarded the airplane to study in a city a thousand miles from home, I felt nervous and alone. But during the flight, I remembered how Jesus promised His disciples the comforting presence of the Holy Spirit.

Jesus's friends must have felt bewildered when He told them, "It is for your good that I am going away" (John 16:7). How could they who witnessed His miracles and learned from His teaching be better off without Him? But Jesus told them that if He left, then the Advocate—the Holy Spirit—would come.

Jesus, nearing His last hours on earth, shared with His disciples (in John 14–17, today known as the Farewell Discourse) to help them understand His death and ascension. Central in this conversation was the coming Holy Spirit, an advocate who would be with them (14:16–17), teaching (v. 26), testifying (v. 26), and guiding them (16:13).

We who have accepted God's offer of new life have been given this gift of His Spirit living within us. From Him we receive so much: He convicts us of our sins and helps us to repent. He brings us comfort when we ache, strength to bear hardships, wisdom to understand God's teaching, hope and faith to believe, love to share.

We can rejoice that Jesus sent us the Advocate.

Amy Boucher Pye

God Promises

A Future with No Curse

WHAT WILL BE
REVELATION 22:1–5

No longer will there be any curse.
Revelation 22:3

You and I have something in common. We live in a mixed-up, tarnished world, and we have never known anything different. Adam and Eve, however, could remember what life was like before the curse. They could recall the world as God intended it to be—free of death, hardship, and pain (Genesis 3:16–19). In pre-fall Eden, hunger, unemployment, and illness did not exist. No one questioned God's creative power or His plan for human relationships.

The world we have inherited resembles God's perfect garden only slightly. To quote C. S. Lewis, "This is a good world gone wrong, but [it] still retains the memory of what ought to have been." Fortunately, the cloudy memory of what the earth should have been is also a prophetic glimpse into eternity. There, just as Adam and Eve walked and talked with God, believers will see His face and serve Him directly. There will be nothing between God and us. "No longer will there be any curse" (Revelation 22:3). There will be no sin, no fear, and no shame.

The past and its consequences may cast a shadow on today, but a believer's destiny carries the promise of something better—life in a place as perfect as Eden.

Jennifer Benson Schuldt

God Promises
His Presence in Our Lives

ARE YOU THERE?
EXODUS 3:11–14

I will be with you.
Exodus 3:12

When his wife contracted a terminal illness, Michael longed for her to experience the peace he had through his relationship with God. He had shared his faith with her, but she wasn't interested. One day, as he walked through a local bookstore, a title caught his eye: *God, Are You There?* Unsure how his wife would respond to the book, he walked in and out of the store several times before finally buying it. To his surprise, she accepted it.

The book touched her, and she began to read the Bible too. Two weeks later, Michael's wife passed away—at peace with God and resting in the assurance that He would never leave or forsake her.

When God called Moses to lead His people out of Egypt, He didn't promise him power. Instead, He promised His presence: "I will be with you" (Exodus 3:12). In Jesus's last words to His disciples before His crucifixion, He also promised God's eternal presence, which they would receive through the Holy Spirit (John 15:26).

There are many things God could give us to help us through life's challenges, such as material comfort, healing, or immediate solutions to our problems. Sometimes He does. But the best gift He gives is himself. This is the greatest comfort we have: whatever happens in life, He will be with us; He will never leave nor forsake us.

Leslie Koh

God Promises
To Strengthen Us

SOMEONE IS WITH YOU
ISAIAH 41:8–10

*Do not fear, for I am with you; do not be dismayed,
for I am your God. I will strengthen you and help you;
I will uphold you with my righteous right hand.*

Isaiah 41:10

Every night a boy had to walk past what he believed was a haunted house. A friend gave him a good-luck charm to give him courage. An adult said, "It's sinful to be afraid. Trust God! Be brave!" But he was still afraid. Then someone said with compassion, "I know what it is to be afraid. I will walk with you past the house." That's all the boy needed to quell his fears.

Several years ago, I was asked to conduct a funeral. I had spoken at many similar occasions as a pastor, but this one was different. Physical and emotional exhaustion had depleted my inner reserves, causing me to lose all confidence in myself. But as the hour approached, I held to the promise of Isaiah 41:10 and did what I knew I had to do.

Looking back, I've concluded that it wasn't simply using a Bible verse or telling myself to trust God that helped me through. Instead, it was because Someone was at that funeral, not only comforting the grieving but also lifting my fears. That Someone was Jesus Christ, who himself had endured intense sorrow and grief. He was there in the person of the Holy Spirit.

Are you facing fear today? Let the words of Isaiah 41:10 remind you that the Lord is with you.

Dennis DeHaan

God Promises

To Forgive and Bless His People

WHO IS LIKE HIM?
MICAH 7:14–20

Who is a God like you, who pardons sin?
Micah 7:18

I know a young woman who refuses to believe that she can be forgiven of her sins because, as she says, "God wouldn't want someone like me." She recognizes the stain of her immoral conduct, but she doesn't realize the wonder of God's grace!

Actually, no one can fully comprehend God's grace, but like the prophet Micah we can marvel at it and rejoice. Although he sorrowfully recounted the sins of his people, Micah went on to acknowledge the Lord's goodness (7:1–20). And he expressed confidence in God's promise to forgive and bless His people (vv. 18–20).

God's people today have even more reason to praise Him. Micah didn't realize that God's Son would one day become a human being, live a sinless life, and pay the price for our sins on the cross. He didn't know that Jesus would break the power of death and live in heaven as our Advocate until we join Him there. And Micah couldn't read Paul's yet unwritten exclamation, "If God is for us, who can be against us? He who did not spare His own Son, but gave him up for us all—how will he not also, along with him, graciously give us all things?" (Romans 8:31–32).

In the words of Micah, we can say with confidence and adoration, "Who is a God like you?"

Herb Vander Lugt

God Promises

To Restore Us

RESTORED
JOEL 2:18–27

I will repay you for the years the locusts have eaten.

Joel 2:25

An infestation of Mormon crickets caused more than $25 million in lost crops in a couple of western US states. The crickets came in such numbers that people couldn't so much as take a step without finding one underfoot. The grasshopper-like insect, named for attacking the crops of the Utah pioneers in 1848, can eat an astounding thirty-eight pounds of plant material in their lifetimes, despite being merely two to three inches long. The impact of infestations on farmers' livelihoods—and the overall economy of a state or country—can be devastating.

The Old Testament prophet Joel described a horde of similar insects ravaging the entire nation of Judah as a consequence of their collective disobedience. He foretold an invasion of locusts (a metaphor for a foreign army, in the minds of some Bible scholars) like nothing previous generations had seen (Joel 1:2). The locusts would lay waste to everything in their path, driving the people into famine and poverty. If, however, the people would turn from their sinful ways and ask God for forgiveness, Joel says the Lord would "repay [them] for the years the locusts have eaten" (2:25).

We too can learn from Judah's lesson: Like insects, our wrongdoings eat away at the fruitful, fragrant life God intended for us. When we turn toward Him and away from our past choices, He promises to remove our shame and restore us to an abundant life in Him.

Kirsten Holmberg

God Promises
A Great Reunion

SNAPSHOTS OF HEAVEN
1 THESSALONIANS 4:13–18

After that, we who are still alive and are left will be caught up together with them in the clouds to meet the Lord in the air. And so we will be with the Lord forever.

1 Thessalonians 4:17

When my son was ten, I asked him, "Why do you want to go to heaven?" I expected to hear something about streets of gold or not having to go to school or something similar. Instead, Steve said, "Because I want to see Grandpa."

It's been many years now since my dad, Steve's grandpa, went to be with the Lord. But I don't think time will ever diminish how much Steve admires and misses his World War II veteran grandfather. That's why the fact that Steve will see him again in heaven was so important to him.

The prospect of heaven is one of the most comforting truths in the Bible. Not only can we find hope in knowing that we will someday be in Jesus's presence but we can also anticipate seeing loved ones who are waiting for us on the other side (1 Thessalonians 4:14, 17).

Imagine a grieving widow who has the assurance of being reunited with her husband of fifty years. Imagine sorrowing parents knowing that their child who succumbed to disease will be reunited with them. What a wonderful hope!

The promise of reunion in heaven gives us a brief glimpse of what our eternal home will be like. The prospect of seeing the people we love gives us snapshots of heaven in an album of hope.

Dave Branon

God Promises
A Crown

THE PROMISED PRIZE
2 TIMOTHY 4:1–8

---

*Now there is in store for me the crown of righteousness, which
the Lord, the righteous Judge, will award to me on that day.*

2 Timothy 4:8

I received a magazine sweepstakes letter that addressed me by name and repeatedly mentioned a $500,000 prize. It spoke of instant wealth and a lifetime of leisure. Finally, at the bottom of page two, in very small print, I found the part I was looking for. As required by law, the letter told me that the approximate numerical odds of my winning the prize were one in eighty million. Now, that's a slim chance if there ever was one!

Contrast that with Paul's anticipation of what awaited him in heaven: "Now there is in store for me the crown of righteousness, which the Lord, the righteous Judge, will award to me on that day" (2 Timothy 4:8). Note his assurance: "There is in store for me." Not "there might be" or "there's a slim chance." It's "there is."

J. Oswald Sanders writes, "This crown is awarded to those who have completed the Christian race with integrity, with eyes fixed on the coming Lord. It is the reward for fulfilling the ministry entrusted to one."

If you have welcomed Christ into your life, long for His appearing, and are faithfully running your race, then the same prize awaits you. Count on it, plan on it, anticipate it! It's a promise from God.

David McCasland

God Promises
To Reward Our Waiting for Him

GOD WILL MAKE A WAY
PSALM 27

Wait for the LORD; be strong and take heart and wait for the LORD.
Psalm 27:14

Rebecca was at her lowest as she drove her aging car to the day care center to pick up her daughter. Her boss was making life difficult again. The landlord was raising the rent. And as a single mom, she felt all alone. "I'm trying my best," she told God. "Please help me."

Just then a song by Don Moen came on the radio. The title? "God Will Make a Way." Moen's song explains that when we have no idea how to get through our circumstance, God will "make a way" that we can't figure out on our own.

"Please do that for me, God," Rebecca pleaded as she listened. "I can't go any further."

The psalmist David too called out to the Lord when he was in desperate straits. He prayed, "Hear my voice when I call, LORD; be merciful to me and answer me" (Psalm 27:7). Then David testified expectantly, "Wait for the LORD; be strong and take heart and wait for the LORD" (v. 14).

God specializes in showing His power in hopeless situations. Israel was in just such a place when God parted the sea before them (Exodus 13:17–14:31). Daniel was protected in the lions' den (Daniel 6:10–23). Paul and Silas were delivered from prison (Acts 16:25–40).

God made a way for Rebecca too. A better job she had applied for months earlier suddenly opened up. The increase in her income would cover the rent. Then a family in her church made a newer car available to her.

If life seems to be closing in on you, don't despair! Trust God. He has promised to make a way.

David Egner

God Promises
Heaven

ASTONISHED JOY!
PHILIPPIANS 3:20–41

They will see his face, and his name will be on their foreheads.
Revelation 22:4

Do you sometimes wonder what heaven will be like? All of us do, I suppose. I confess, however, that the nearer I come to the end of earth's journey the more often I indulge in "sanctified curiosity" about the home Jesus has promised to believers. What will be my reaction when I cross the river and enter into glory?

British theologian Stephen Neill asked himself the same question. At first he was inclined to think his emotion would be astonishment. But then he decided that his emotion, "to put it a little more precisely," would be "astonished joy."

Yes, astonished joy indeed! The apostle Paul called believers in Christ citizens of heaven, and wrote, "We eagerly await a Savior from there, . . . who . . . will transform our lowly bodies so that they will be like his glorious body" (Philippians 3:20–21). Paul looked forward to a day when sin and pain and grief would be gone forever.

What a soul-thrilling vision that will be when we see our Lord! What indescribable ecstasy we will experience! Fully aware at last of the sheer marvel of redemptive grace that has brought us into the presence of unparalleled beauty, we will be filled with astonished joy!

Vernon Grounds

God Promises
Courage

WHEN LIFE GOES BAD
1 SAMUEL 30:1–6

David found strength in the LORD his God.

1 Samuel 30:6

Everything looked bleak to David and his men when they arrived at Ziklag (1 Samuel 30:1–6). The Amalekites had attacked the city and taken their wives and children captive. The men were so discouraged that they wept until they had no more energy. And David, their leader, was "greatly distressed" because the people were contemplating stoning him (v. 6).

In the end, David's army rescued their families and defeated the Amalekites. But the story takes a great turn even before that when "David found strength in the LORD his God" (v. 6). Other translations use the words *encouraged* or *refreshed*.

The text doesn't say exactly how David did this. But it makes me wonder, In what ways can we strengthen, encourage, or refresh ourselves in the Lord when we're feeling discouraged?

First, we can remember what God has done. We can list the ways He has cared for us in the past and how He has provided for us or answered a prayer request.

Second, we can remember what God has promised. "Be strong and courageous . . . for the LORD your God will be with you wherever you go" (Joshua 1:9).

Like David, let's learn to strengthen ourselves in the Lord, and then let's leave the rest with Him.

Anne Cetas

God Promises
To Carry Us

ON HIS SHOULDERS
LUKE 15:3–7

The one the LORD loves rests between his shoulders.
Deuteronomy 33:12

Our family likes to hike, and we've had some grand adventures together. But when our boys were young, our enthusiasm caused us to walk too fast and too far, and their legs often grew weary. They couldn't keep up the pace, despite their determined efforts and our assurance that the end of the trail was just over the next hill.

"Dad," would come the plaintive request, accompanied by upraised arms, "will you carry me?" "Of course," I would reply, and hoist the child on my shoulders. He was not a burden, for he was little and light.

How often, like my children, I've grown weary, and the end of my efforts is not even in sight. I can no longer keep up or accomplish the task. But I am learning that I can turn with arms upraised to my heavenly Father, who walks beside me, and I can ask Him to carry me.

I know He will lay me on His shoulder as a shepherd carries the lamb that was lost (Luke 15:5). There He will joyfully carry me all day long, for I am little and light—no burden to Him. There I find rest. "Let the beloved of the LORD rest secure in him, for he shields him all day long, and the one the LORD loves rests between his shoulders" (Deuteronomy 33:12).

David Roper

God Promises
That His Word Stands Forever

GOD'S ENDURING WORD
PSALM 119:89–96

Heaven and earth will pass away, but my words will never pass away.
Matthew 24:35

At the beginning of World War II, aerial bombings flattened much of Warsaw, Poland. Cement blocks, ruptured plumbing, and shards of glass lay strewn across the great city. In the downtown area, however, most of one damaged building still stubbornly stood. It was the Polish headquarters for the British and Foreign Bible Society. Still legible on a surviving wall were these words: "Heaven and earth shall pass away, but my words shall not pass away" (Matthew 24:35 KJV).

Jesus made that statement to encourage His disciples when they asked Him about the "end of the age" (v. 3). But His words also give us courage in the midst of our embattled situation today. Standing in the rubble of our shattered dreams, we can still find confidence in God's indestructible character, sovereignty, and promises.

The psalmist wrote: "Your word, LORD, is eternal; it stands firm in the heavens" (Psalm 119:89). But it is more than the word of the Lord; it is His very character. That is why the psalmist could also say, "Your faithfulness continues through all generations" (v. 90).

As we face devastating experiences, we can define them in terms either of despair or of hope. Because God will not abandon us to our circumstances, we can confidently choose hope. His enduring Word assures us of His unfailing love.

Dennis Fisher

God Promises
Wisdom

WISE AS SERPENTS
MATTHEW 10:16–20

For it will not be you speaking, but the
Spirit of your Father speaking through you.
Matthew 10:20

A young man got into a financial tangle by loaning $500 to a friend who lived in another city without the benefit of a written note. He didn't even ask for a receipt indicating the amount loaned.

When the young man needed his money, he realized he had nothing to document his claim. In desperation he consulted his father. After a moment of consideration, the father said, "Oh, that's easy. Text him and say you need the $1,000 you loaned him." The young man said, "You mean $500." "No," said the father. "You say $1,000, and he will immediately write back that he owes you only $500. Then you will have it in writing."

If an earthly father can be clever enough to devise such a plan, imagine the possibilities available from the heavenly Father. God is the source of all true wisdom. To the disciples who would face hostile authorities, Jesus said the Father would give them the words to say (Matthew 10:19–20). The promise of such help was not given to all. But as we choose to live for Him, He will give us wisdom in those crucial moments when we face hostility.

Father, help us to believe that as we live for you, you will be our source of wisdom when we go through times of crisis.

Mart DeHaan

God Promises
To Dwell with Us

WITH US AND IN US
JOHN 14:15–21

*I will ask the Father, and he will give you another
advocate to help you and be with you forever.*

John 14:16

My son had just started nursery school. The first day he cried and declared, "I don't like school." My husband and I talked to him about it. "We may not be physically there, but we are praying for you. Besides, Jesus is with you always."

"But I can't see Him!" he reasoned. My husband hugged him and said, "He lives in you. And He won't leave you alone." My son touched his heart and said, "Yes, Jesus lives in me."

Kids are not the only ones who suffer from separation anxiety. In every stage of life we face times of separation from those we love, sometimes because of geographical distance and sometimes because of death. However, we need to remember that even if we feel forsaken by others, God hasn't forsaken us. He has promised to be with us always. God sent the Spirit of truth—our Advocate and Helper—to dwell with us and in us forever (John 14:15–18). We are His beloved children.

My son is learning to trust, but so am I. Like my son, I can't see the Spirit, but I feel His power as each day He encourages me and guides me as I read God's Word. Let us thank God for His wonderful provision, the Spirit of Christ who is with us and in us. We are certainly not alone!

Keila Ochoa

God Promises
To Provide for Us

THE LITTLE THINGS TOO
2 KINGS 6:1–7

*My God will meet all your needs according
to the riches of his glory in Christ Jesus.*

Philippians 4:19

Pastor Harold Springstead was driving along on his way to preach at a little country church when he felt a sudden vibration. A tire had gone flat. As the seventy-eight-year-old pastor maneuvered his car to a stop, a trucker pulled up behind him. A young man jumped out, assessed the situation, and cheerfully changed the tire. Pastor Springstead got to the service in plenty of time, and it was not until later that he realized his car didn't even have a jack!

It was a minor problem. He was a retired faithful servant of God. It was a tiny congregation. We might think God would be too busy with larger and more important needs than to be concerned about a flat tire. But His promise to provide for the needs of His people covers little things as well as big ones.

The same God who helped Elisha retrieve the borrowed ax head (2 Kings 6:5–7), who supplied food for a faithful widow (1 Kings 17:8–16), and who provided wine at a small-town wedding (John 2:1–10) meets our needs as well.

Think back over the past few days. Has the Lord taken care of some minor needs in your life? Has He solved some nagging problem? Thank Him! As today unfolds, remember that He provides the little things too.

David Egner

God Promises
To Stand By You

TRIUMPH IN TRAGEDY
HEBREWS 11:35–40

My comfort in my suffering is this: Your promise preserves my life.
Psalm 119:50

Patricia St. John, who has been described as an ordinary woman with an extraordinary faith, poured out her life ministering to people in the neediest places on our planet. She was in Sudan when war refugees flooded that country. They had suffered terribly and had lost everything, yet those among them who were Christians still gave thanks to God.

Patricia said that she stood one night in a small, crowded Sudanese church listening to those uprooted believers singing joyfully. Suddenly a life-changing insight burned its way into her mind. "We would have changed their circumstances," she said, "but we would not have changed them." She realized that God "does not always lift people out of the situation. He himself comes into the situation. . . . He does not pluck them out of the darkness. He becomes the light in the darkness."

Does Patricia's insight apply to your life? What if, despite your fervent prayer, God doesn't see fit to deliver you from terrible circumstances? God's Word tells us that believers often suffer (Hebrews 11:35–38). What then?

God promises to stand by you. He'll strengthen you and give you the grace to rejoice—even in the face of suffering and loss. That's real triumph in tragedy.

Vernon Grounds

God Promises

To Etch Us in His Memory

NEVER FORGOTTEN
ISAIAH 49:8–16

I will not forget you!
Isaiah 49:15

Egged on by my children to prove that I had endured years mastering the basics of piano, I sat down and started playing the C Major scale. Having played very little piano in nearly two decades, I was surprised I remembered! Feeling brave, I proceeded to play seven different scales by heart one right after the other. I was shocked! Years of practicing had imprinted the notes and technique so deeply in my fingers' "memory" that they instantly knew what to do.

There are some things that can never be forgotten. But God's love for His children is far more deeply imprinted than any of our fading memories—in fact, God can't forget us. This is what the Israelites needed to hear when the exile left them feeling abandoned by Him (Isaiah 49:14). His response through Isaiah was unequivocal: "I will not forget you!" (v. 15). God's promise to care for His people was more certain than a mother's love for her child.

To assure them of His unchanging love, He gave them a picture of His commitment: "See, I have engraved you on the palms of my hands" (v. 16). It's a beautiful image of God's constant awareness of His children, their names and faces always before Him.

Still today, we can easily feel overlooked and forgotten. How comforting to remember that we're "etched" on God's hands—always remembered, cared for, and loved by our Father.

Lisa Samra

God Promises
To Clean Us Up

TOTALLY GREEN
1 JOHN 1:1–10

---

*If we confess our sins, he is faithful and just and will
forgive us our sins and purify us from all unrighteousness.*
1 John 1:9

A friend was updating me on his past year—a year in which he had been receiving ongoing medical treatment for cancer. The smile on his face was a powerful testimony to the good news he had just received. He said that at his one-year checkup the doctor announced that the test results all pointed to one thing: "You are totally clean!" What a difference two words can make! To my friend, totally clean meant every trace of the disease that had threatened his life only months before had been wiped from his body. We rejoiced to hear that he was totally clean!

King David, after his moral failure with Bathsheba, longed for a similar thing to happen in his heart. Hoping for the stains of his sin to be washed away, he cried out, "Create in me a pure heart, O God, and renew a steadfast spirit within me" (Psalm 51:10). The good news for him and for us is that our sins can be taken care of. When we need cleansing, John's familiar words bring hope: "If we confess our sins, he is faithful and just and will forgive us our sins and purify us from all unrighteousness" (1 John 1:9).

We can't cleanse our own hearts; only God can do that. If we confess our sins to Him, He promises to make us totally clean!

Bill Crowder

God Promises

The Resurrection of Christians

SUNRISE HOPE
1 CORINTHIANS 15:20–28

*Very early on the first day of the week, just
after sunrise, they were on their way to the tomb.*

Mark 16:2

Think of what it would be like if we went to bed some night knowing that the sun would not rise again the next morning. Think of the coldness, the unending darkness, the inescapable fingers of death that would gradually move across the earth. Plants would wither, flowers would wilt, trees would die, and all of life would perish for lack of sunlight.

But praise God, the sun does rise every day. Its warm, life-giving light floods the earth. The "death" of a sunset each day is followed by the "resurrection" of a sunrise the next day— and our hope is renewed. Every morning the rays of the sun remind us that the long night of sin and darkness will give way to eternal day in heaven.

Even more sure than the rising of the morning sun is the certainty of our resurrection in Jesus Christ. The dark night of death came upon Him, and His lifeless body was laid in the tomb. But He arose! And in His resurrection is the promise of our own resurrection to life. The apostle Paul declared, "So in Christ all will be made alive" (1 Corinthians 15:22).

The next time you see the sun rise and watch its rays brighten the morning sky, let hope fill your heart. It is a reminder of your own sure resurrection!

David Egner

God Promises

To Be an Ever-Present Part of Our Lives

THE DAILY PRAYER
EPHESIANS 6:18–19

Pray in the Spirit on all occasions with all kinds of prayers and requests. With this in mind, be alert and always keep on praying for all the Lord's people.

Ephesians 6:18

Singer/songwriter Robert Hamlet wrote "Lady Who Prays for Me" as a tribute to his mother, who made a point of praying for her boys each morning before they went to the bus stop. After a young mom heard Hamlet sing his song, she committed to praying with her own little boy. The result was heartwarming! Just before her son went out the door, his mother prayed for him. Five minutes later he returned—bringing kids from the bus stop with him! His mom was taken aback and asked what was going on. The boy responded, "Their moms didn't pray with them."

In the book of Ephesians, Paul urges us to pray "on all occasions with all kinds of prayers" (6:18). Demonstrating our daily dependence on God is essential in a family since many children first learn to trust God as they observe genuine faith in the people closest to them (2 Timothy 1:5). There is no better way to teach the utmost importance of prayer than by praying for and with our children. It is one of the ways they begin to sense a compelling need to reach out personally to God in faith.

When we "start children off" by modeling a "sincere faith" in God (Proverbs 22:6; 2 Timothy 1:5), we give them a special gift, an assurance that God is an ever-present part of our lives—continually loving, guiding, and protecting us.

Cindy Hess Kasper

God Promises
That He Provides What We Desire

THE HOPE OF THE HEART
ROMANS 4:13–25

*Yet he did not waver through unbelief regarding
the promise of God, but was strengthened in his faith.*

Romans 4:20

Promises are the hope of our heart. A child's security depends on a parent's promise to keep him or her safe. A spouse can live with confidence because of a mate's promise of fidelity, loyalty, and love. Businesses depend on promises from employees, vendors, and clients. Countries remain safe when neighbors keep their promise to honor their borders.

Unfortunately, hearts and relationships are broken in all of those situations by unkept promises. There is one Promise Maker, though, who can be trusted completely and without fear. That one is God. He has given us hundreds of promises in His Word, and He keeps every one of them.

If anyone had reason to wonder if God could or would keep His promises, it was Abraham. But "against all hope, Abraham in hope believed" (Romans 4:18). We know that what God had promised him—that he and his wife would have a child when they were both past ninety years old—could not have happened without divine intervention.

Are you looking for hope? Then search the Scriptures diligently and claim the promises of God that apply to you. Promises truly are the hope of the heart, and God always keeps His word.

Dave Branon

God Promises

To Make All Things New

SOUNDS OF SIRENS
REVELATION 21:1–5

*He who was seated on the throne said,
"I am making everything new!"*
Revelation 21:5

I was enjoying my son's high school soccer game when the relative calm and normalcy of that warm September afternoon was shattered by a sound both distinctive and alarming—the sound of sirens. The shrill whine seemed out of place at such a pleasant moment, and it demanded my attention. According to singer Don Henley, a siren usually means that "somebody's going to emergency" or "somebody's going to jail." He's right. In either case, someone's day, perhaps including the law enforcement or rescue personnel, just took a turn for the worse.

As I lost my attention on the game and thought about the siren fading into the distance, it occurred to me that sirens are a reminder of a powerful reality: Our world is sadly broken. Whether the siren is the result of criminal activity or personal tragedy, it reminds us that something is desperately wrong and needs to be made right.

At such times, it helps to remember that God sees our world in its brokenness and has pledged that one day He will wipe away the old and make "everything new" (Revelation 21:5). That promise encourages us in the hardships of life, and it provides the whisper of His comfort—a whisper that can drown out even the sound of sirens.

Bill Crowder

SEPTEMBER 12

God Promises
Rewards

FAITHFULNESS REQUIRED
1 CORINTHIANS 4:1–5; 14–20

*It is required that those who have been
given a trust must prove faithful.*

1 Corinthians 4:2

Much of our attention and praise is directed toward highly visible and successful people. But occasionally we read about an ordinary, obscure person being honored for many years of faithful service. It may be a school custodian, a cafeteria worker, a handyman, or a clerk in a store who has served others in a dependable and unselfish way.

That kind of reliability often goes unnoticed, but I believe it's a powerful picture of how we are to live. Although consistency may not be flashy, days add up to a life of great significance to God.

Paul wrote, "It is required that those who have been given a trust must prove faithful" (1 Corinthians 4:2). If we live faithfully for Christ, God has promised to reward us at His appointed time. When the Lord comes, He "will bring to light what is hidden in darkness and will expose the motives of the heart. At that time each will receive their praise from God" (v. 5).

When we long for success, God says, "I will reward you."

When we ache for recognition, God says, "I see you."

When we are ready to quit, God says, "I will help you."

Whether our service is public or private, our responsibility is the same—to be faithful.

David McCasland

God Promises
That We Can Hold Loosely to This World

HEAVENLY COUNTRY
HEBREWS 11:8–16

Our citizenship is in heaven.
Philippians 3:20

During high school, my closest friend and I took a pair of horses out for an afternoon ride. We slowly roamed through fields of wildflowers and wooded groves. But when we nosed the horses in the direction of the barn, they took off toward home like twin rockets. Our equine friends knew that it was time for dinner and a good brushing, and they could hardly wait.

As Christians, our true home is heaven (Philippians 3:20). Yet sometimes our desires tether us to the here and now. We enjoy God's good gifts—marriage, children, grandchildren, travel, careers, friends. At the same time, the Bible challenges us to focus on "things above" (Colossians 3:1–2). Things above may include the unseen benefits of heaven: God's enduring presence (Revelation 22:3–5), unending rest (Hebrews 4:9), and an everlasting inheritance (1 Peter 1:4).

Recently I read, "Believers desire the heavenly inheritance; and the stronger the faith is, the more fervent [the desire]." Several Old Testament believers mentioned in Hebrews 11 had strong faith in God that enabled them to embrace His promises before receiving them (v.13). One such promise was heaven. If we too put our faith in God, He will give us a desire for that "heavenly country" (v. 16 NKJV) and will loosen our grip on this world.

Jennifer Benson Schuldt

God Promises
To Honor His Promises

LOOK TO THE STARS
PSALM 46

No matter how many promises
God has made, they are "Yes" in Christ.
2 Corinthians 1:20

The devastating storms of trial can leave our lives in shambles. Former securities vanish in a whirlwind of personal tragedy and loss. The death of a loved one, the trauma of divorce, the loss of position, the anguish of incurable disease, or even our own sins can tear us loose from all that once gave us purpose, meaning, and identity. The hurricane force of any one of these tragedies can so overwhelm us that we wonder if we will ever recover. So, how do we weather such events? By refocusing our lives on the unchanging promises of God.

One afternoon a frightening storm forced two prospectors to seek shelter in a cave. When it had passed, they emerged to a disheartening sight. Trees had been uprooted; familiar landmarks were gone. All of the notations and observations they had made to guide them out of the forest were useless. One man sat down in despair. But the other said, "We are not lost. Night is soon coming, and when the stars shine again, we'll get our bearings. The stars are still up there in the sky, and we can find our way home by looking at them."

Believer, your life is "hidden with Christ in God" (Colossian 3:3). He loves you; He is in control; He is with you. These promises will never change. If your life is in turmoil, don't fix your eyes on relationships that can be broken and securities that can vanish. Look instead to the stars of God's unfailing promises and begin anew. Because they are always shining, life is never hopeless.

Dennis DeHaan

SEPTEMBER 15

God Promises
To Be There!

HE'S NEAR TO HEAR
PSALM 145:17–21

The LORD is near to all who call on him,
to all who call on him in truth.

Psalm 145:18

When I was seven years old, my grandfather was caretaker of a wooded estate. One fall evening I took my toy gun, called for my dog Pal, and headed down a path into the forest. I walked bravely into the woods. Soon, though, it began to get dark and I panicked. "Grandpa!" I shouted.

"I'm right here," he said calmly, only a few yards away. He had seen me go into the woods and had followed me to make sure I was okay. Talk about being relieved!

As followers of Christ, we sometimes venture into unfamiliar territory. We try new things. We take on responsibilities in the work of the Lord that are bigger than we've ever attempted before. We risk rejection when we witness to friends about Christ. It can get pretty scary.

But wherever we go, God is there. His pledge to be near is backed up by His omnipresence. His promise to help us is backed up by His mighty power. He will hear the cries of those who fear Him (Psalm 145:19–20).

So take some risks in your walk with God. Venture out into the scary unknown in your service or giving or witnessing. God is nearer to you than Grandpa Hayes was to me in the darkening woods. He will always hear your cry.

David Egner

SEPTEMBER 16

God Promises
To Sustain and Carry Us

NO LINE TO LOVE
ISAIAH 46:3–10

I have made you and I will carry you.
Isaiah 46:4

Sometimes when my Labrador retriever wants attention, he'll take something of mine and parade it in front of me. One morning as I was writing at the desk with my back turned, Max snatched my wallet and ran off. But realizing I hadn't seen him do it, he returned and nudged me with his nose—wallet in mouth, eyes dancing, tail wagging, taunting me to play.

Max's antics made me laugh, but they also reminded me of my limitations when it comes to being attentive to others. So often I've intended to spend time with family or friends, but other things occupy my time and awareness. Before I know it, the day slips away and love is left undone.

How comforting to know that our heavenly Father is so great that He's able to attend to each of us in the most intimate ways—even sustaining every breath in our lungs for as long as we live. He promises His people, "Even to your old age and gray hairs I am he, I am he who will sustain you. I have made you and I will carry you" (Isaiah 46:4).

God always has time for us. He understands every detail of our circumstances—no matter how complex or difficult—and He is there whenever we call on Him in prayer. We never have to play a trick to get our Savior's unlimited love.

James Banks

God Promises
That All Who Seek Him Find Him

MAGIC EYE
HEBREWS 11:1–10

[God] rewards those who earnestly seek him.
Hebrews 11:6

One of my nephews brought a book of Magic Eye images to a family gathering. Magic Eye images look like ordinary two-dimensional patterns, but when they are viewed in a certain way, the flat surface appears three-dimensional.

We took turns trying to train our eyes to make the three-dimensional image pop out. One family member had trouble seeing the extra dimension. Several times I noticed he had the book open, looking at it from all different distances and directions. But even though he couldn't see the hidden image, he believed it was there because others had seen it.

His persistence made me think about the importance of having the same tenacity in matters of faith. The danger for those who doubt is that they stop looking for God because they believe He can't be found. Moses warned the Israelites that future generations would wander from God. He promised, however, that those who seek God with all their heart and soul will find Him (Deuteronomy 4:29). The book of Hebrews confirms that God rewards those who diligently seek Him (11:6).

If you struggle to believe, remember: Just because you don't see God doesn't mean He doesn't exist. He promises to be found by those who seek Him.

Julie Ackerman Link

God Promises

That Jesus Will Return

SONGBIRD IN THE DARK
LUKE 1:67–80

The Dayspring from on high has visited us.
Luke 1:78 NKJV

Just before the sunrise, we often hear songbirds welcoming the dawn. Despite the darkness, we know that the radiant light of the sun will soon appear.

Fanny Crosby has been called "The Songbird in the Dark." Though blinded in infancy, she wrote hymns that inspirationally envision our future reunion with Christ. Early in her life, Fanny had a dream in which she saw the panorama of a glorious heaven, and many of her songs reflect that theme. By the time of her death, she had penned at least eight thousand hymns. Songs such as "Tell Me the Story of Jesus" and "To God Be the Glory" are still popular today.

When Zacharias praised God in anticipation of the Messiah, he also looked forward to a spiritual sunrise. With a clear reference to the words of Malachi 4:2, he proclaimed: "The Dayspring [sunrise] from on high has visited us; to give light to those who sit in darkness" (Luke 1:78–79 NKJV). That Messiah came to earth, died for our sins, rose again, ascended, and promised to return for us.

Do you feel surrounded by dark and confusing circumstances? You can still lift your praise to God for the bright future you will share with His Son. The words of Fanny Crosby's beloved hymn "Blessed Assurance" encourage us as we anticipate this glorious reunion with Christ.

Dennis Fisher

God Promises
To Be Faithful

CONSISTENT FATHER
2 TIMOTHY 2:3-13

*If we endure, we will also reign with him. If we disown him,
he will also disown us; . . . he cannot disown himself.*

2 Timothy 2:12–13

I once knew a father who displayed an alarming lack of consistency. When he was in a happy frame of mind, he allowed his children to get away with anything short of complete mayhem. But when he was in a foul mood, the slightest provocation could ignite a severe reaction from him. His children learned to take a quick look at Dad when he walked in the door. Then they made themselves scarce or greeted him enthusiastically, depending on what they saw. Even the dog seemed to notice the difference.

God is not like such a father. He is thoroughly consistent and just. This is the theme of the "trustworthy saying" Paul quoted in 2 Timothy 2:11–13.

God always rewards faith and perseverance. Likewise, He always punishes faithlessness and disobedience. The words "If we are faithless, He remains faithful" are a warning against presumption, not a reassuring word to the faithless. God's faithfulness means that He follows through on His threats as well as His promises.

The one thing God cannot do is act contrary to His nature. Although He will fulfill His threats to those who continue to deny Him, He will also fulfill His promises to the faithful.

What a warning this is to the faithless! But what a comfort to those who put their faith in Christ!

Herb Vander Lugt

God Promises
Great Peace and Joy

THE FACTORY OF SADNESS
JOHN 16:28–33

[God] will wipe every tear from their eyes.
Revelation 21:4

As a lifelong Cleveland Browns football fan, I grew up knowing my share of disappointment. Despite being one of only four current teams to have never appeared in a Super Bowl championship game, the Browns have a loyal fan base that sticks with the team year in and year out. But because the fans usually end up disappointed, many of them now refer to the home stadium as the "Factory of Sadness."

The broken world we live in can be a "factory of sadness" too. There seems to be an endless supply of heartache and disappointment, whether from our own choices or from things beyond our control.

Yet the follower of Christ has hope—not only in the life to come but also for this very day. Jesus said, "I have told you these things, so that in me you may have peace. In this world you will have trouble. But take heart! I have overcome the world" (John 16:33). Notice that without minimizing the struggles or sadness we may experience, Christ counters them with His promises of peace, joy, and ultimate victory.

Great peace is available in Christ, and it's more than enough to help us navigate whatever life throws at us.

Bill Crowder

God Promises
To Rescue His Flock

GOD OUR RESCUER
EZEKIEL 34:5–12

I will rescue them from all the places where they were scattered.
Ezekiel 34:12

In the open sea, a rescuer positioned her kayak to assist panicked swimmers competing in a triathlon. "Don't grab the middle of the boat!" she called to swimmers, knowing such a move would capsize her craft. Instead, she directed weary swimmers to the bow, or front, of the kayak. There they could grab a loop, allowing the safety kayaker to help rescue them.

Whenever life or people threaten to pull us under, as believers in Jesus we know we have a Rescuer. "For this is what the Sovereign LORD says: I myself will search for my sheep. . . . I will rescue them from all the places where they were scattered" (Ezekiel 34:11–12).

This was the prophet Ezekiel's assurance to God's people when they were in exile. Their leaders had neglected and exploited them, plundering their lives and caring "for themselves rather than for [God's] flock" (v. 8). As a result, the people "were scattered over the whole earth, and no one searched or looked for them" (v. 6).

But "I will rescue my flock," declared the Lord (v. 10), and His promise still holds.

What do we need to do? Hold fast to almighty God and His promises. "I myself will search for my sheep and look after them," He says (v. 11). That's a saving promise worth holding tightly.

Patricia Raybon

God Promises
A Way to Overcome Temptation

LEAST POWERFUL PEOPLE
1 CORINTHIANS 10:1–13

If you think you are standing firm, be careful that you don't fall!
1 Corinthians 10:12

An unusual list called The 100 Least Powerful People in the World appeared in the online publication *24/7 Wall St.* Among those selected were corporate executives, sports figures, politicians, and celebrities who shared one common characteristic—they used to be powerful. Some were victims of circumstances, others made poor business decisions, while others lost their influence because of moral failure.

In 1 Corinthians 10, Paul draws a somber lesson from Old Testament history. The people Moses led from slavery in Egypt toward freedom in the promised land kept turning their backs on God who had delivered them (vv. 1–5). Idolatry, immorality, and grumbling were among the things that brought them down (vv. 6–10). Paul points to their collapse as an example to us, and he sounds this warning: "Let him who thinks he stands take heed lest he fall" (v. 12 NKJV).

Every follower of Jesus can stand firm on God's promise: "He will see to it that every temptation has a way out, so that it will never be impossible for you to bear it" (v. 13 Phillips). All of us have power to influence others in their faith. How tragic to squander it by yielding to a temptation that God has empowered us to resist.

David McCasland

Help in Times of Trouble

A GOOD GOD
PSALM 46

---

*The LORD is a refuge for the oppressed,
a stronghold in times of trouble.*

Psalm 9:9

When my brother-in-law was a missionary in Mali, West Africa, he was involved in a traffic accident. A man had wandered into the road in front of Chuck's motorcycle. The cycle struck the man and sent Chuck and the bike sliding along the ground for more than two hundred feet. Shortly after Chuck regained consciousness in the hospital, his doctor told him he had been "really lucky." Chuck smiled and replied, "God is good."

Later he thought about the day's events. The man who was struck hadn't received any permanent injuries, and Chuck would also recover from his injuries. But what if one of them had been killed? He thought, God would be no less good.

When we experience tragedy, we may wonder about God's goodness. Is God always good? Yes, He is. He doesn't promise that bad things will never happen to us, but He does promise to be "our refuge and strength" (Psalm 46:1). He doesn't promise that we will never walk through heart-wrenching circumstances, but He promises that we won't be alone (23:4).

God is good—no matter what suffering we are experiencing. Even when we don't understand, we can say with Habakkuk, "Yet I will rejoice in the LORD, I will be joyful in God my Savior" (3:18).

Cindy Hess Kasper

God Promises

A Multitude of Ways He Guides

DRIVING IN THE DARK
PSALM 119:105–112

Your word is a lamp for my feet, a light on my path.
Psalm 119:105

I've always thought that I could get through just about anything if the Lord would tell me what the outcome would be. I believe that "in all things God works together for the good of those who love him" in the end (Romans 8:28), but I'd do a lot better in dark times if I knew exactly what the "good" would look like.

But God usually doesn't show us where He is taking us. He just asks us to trust Him. It's like driving a car at night. Our headlights never shine all the way to our destination; they illuminate only about 200 feet ahead. But that doesn't deter us from moving forward. We trust our headlights. All we really need is enough light to keep moving forward.

God's Word is like headlights in dark times. It is full of promises we need to keep us from driving our lives into the ditch of bitterness and despair. His Word promises that He will never leave us nor forsake us (Hebrews 13:5). Scripture assures us that He knows the plans He has for us, plans for wholeness and not for evil, to give us "hope and a future" (Jeremiah 29:11). And He tells us that our trials are there to make us better, not bitter (James 1:2–4).

So the next time you feel as if you're driving in the dark, remember to trust your "headlights"—God's Word will light your way.

Joe Stowell

SEPTEMBER 25

God Promises
Things Are Dependable

YOU CAN COUNT ON IT
1 KINGS 8:54–61

Not one word has failed of all the good promises he gave.
1 Kings 8:56

A man who lived in northern Michigan went for a walk in a densely forested area. When darkness began to settle in, he decided it was time to head for home. He was familiar with hiking in the woods and felt he had a keen sense of direction, so he didn't bother to look at his compass.

After walking for a long time, though, he decided he'd better check it. He was surprised to see that the compass indicated he was going west—not east as he had thought. But he was so sure of his own sense of direction that he concluded there must be something wrong with the compass. He was about to throw it away in disgust when this thought came to him: My compass has never lied to me yet—maybe I should believe it. He chose to follow its direction and soon found his way out of the woods and back home.

There is One who never leads us astray. His instructions are always trustworthy. What God promises, He performs. In 1 Kings 8:56, Solomon told the congregation of Israel that "not one word has failed of all the good promises he gave." If we think so highly of our own judgment that we refuse to rely on God's Word, we are asking for trouble and will only become more confused. His words have never failed, and they never will. You can count on it!

Richard DeHaan

God Promises

That Our Faith Gives Us a Forward View

SEEING BACKWARDS
HEBREWS 11:13–16, 23–27

All these people were still living by faith when they died.
They did not receive the things promised; they
only saw them and welcomed them from a distance.

Hebrews 11:13

My husband and I rode the train backward from Grand Rapids to Chicago one summer. Sitting in seats that faced the rear of the train, all we could see was where we had been, not where we were going. Buildings, lakes, and trees flew by the window after we had passed them.

I didn't like it. I'd rather see where I'm going.

Sometimes we may feel that way about life too—wishing we could see ahead. We'd like to know how certain situations are going to turn out, how God is going to answer our prayers. But all we can know is where we've been. That is, if it were not for faith.

The "faith chapter" of the Bible, Hebrews 11, tells us about two realities that some people in Old Testament times could see by faith. It speaks of Noah, Abraham, and Sarah, who all died in faith. "They did not receive the things promised; they only saw them and welcomed them from a distance." They were longing for "a better country—a heavenly one" (vv. 13, 16). Besides the promise of heaven, verse 27 tells us that by faith Moses could also see "him who is invisible," meaning God.

While we don't know the outcome of today's struggles, believers in Jesus can by faith see forward to where we're going: We will have a heavenly home where we will live with Jesus forever.

Anne Cetas

SEPTEMBER 27

God Promises
To Be Dependable

GOD'S GUARANTEE
ROMANS 4:16–25

*In the hope of eternal life, which God, who does
not lie, promised before the beginning of time.*

Titus 1:2

The dependability of God's Word rests entirely upon His unchanging character. He is not only the God of truth but He is also truth itself. Therefore, we can rely with complete confidence on whatever He says. Balaam spoke of God's trustworthiness when he said, "God is not human, that he should lie" (Numbers 23:19). Abraham also found this to be so, "being fully persuaded that God had power to do what he had promised" (Romans 4:21). Looking at God's promise from a human point of view, we might say that He has more at stake than we do. We stand to lose our soul; He stands to lose His character.

This reminds me of a story I read in a Christian magazine. A boy went to a lady's house to sell some berries he had picked. "Yes, I'll buy some," said the lady as she took the pail and went inside. Without concern for the berries, the boy stayed at the door, whistling to some birds perched in a cage. "Don't you want to come in and see that I don't take more than I should? How do you know I won't cheat you?" she asked. The boy responded from the porch, "I'm not worried. Besides, you'd get the worst of it." "Get the worst of it," said the lady. "What do you mean by that?" "Oh, I would only lose a few berries, but you would make yourself a thief." That boy had keen insight.

God must be true to himself. Nothing can possibly prevent Him from fulfilling His word. His character secures it. He cannot lie! Bound up in every one of His promises is His impeccable, holy character, which guarantees what He has said.

Paul Van Gorder

God Promises

A Transcendent Peacefulness

FLOWING PEACE
JOHN 14:16–27

Peace I leave with you; my peace I give you.
John 14:27

"I'm not surprised you lead retreats," said an acquaintance in my exercise class. "You have a good aura." I was jolted but pleased by her comment, because I realized that what she saw as an "aura" in me, I understood to be the peace of Christ. As we follow Jesus, He gives us the peace that transcends understanding (Philippians 4:7) and radiates from within—though we may not even be aware of it.

Jesus promised His followers this peace when, after their last supper together, He prepared them for His death and resurrection. He told them that though they would have trouble in the world, the Father would send them the Spirit of truth to live with them and be in them (John 14:16–17). The Spirit would teach them, bringing to mind His truths; the Spirit would comfort them, bestowing on them His peace. Though soon they would face trials—including fierce opposition from the religious leaders and seeing Jesus executed—He told them not to be afraid. The Holy Spirit's presence would never leave them.

Although as God's children we experience hardship, we too have His Spirit living within and flowing out of us. God's peace can be His witness to everyone we meet—whether at a local market, at school or work, or in the gym.

Amy Boucher Pye

God Promises

The Lord's Presence

SOULS AND WALLETS
HEBREWS 13:5-6

Be content with what you have.

Hebrews 13:5

The book of Hebrews strikes a strange note for men and women living with the values of the twenty-first century. "Keep your lives free from the love of money," the writer urged, "and be content with what you have" (13:5). He wasn't saying that having money is a sin, but it can be a problem. Our world has bought into the myth that riches and contentment go together—that they're almost the same thing. Yet many wealthy people who boast large bank accounts are not content. Sometimes they are not content with how much they have, and many live in dread that they will lose what they have.

"Be content with what you have." Well, what do you have? Do you immediately think of what's in your savings account or stock portfolio? That's the wrong place to look. The writer of Hebrews said that if you live with faith in the Lord of eternity, you have Him. He has promised, "Never will I leave you; never will I forsake you" (13:5). You have Him, so you can say with confidence, "The Lord is my helper; I will not be afraid. What can mere mortals do to me?" (v. 6).

If you have everything else but the Lord, you don't have much at all. If you have the Lord's presence and little else, you can be content. Better to have a satisfied soul than a thick wallet.

Haddon Robinson

God Promises
To Give Us Eternal Life

WITH HIM FOREVER
JAMES 4:11–17

*What is your life? You are a mist that
appears for a little while and then vanishes.*

James 4:14

In 1859, during the turbulent years prior to America's Civil War, Abraham Lincoln had the opportunity to speak to the Agricultural Society in Milwaukee, Wisconsin. As he spoke, he shared with his listeners the story of an ancient monarch's search for a sentence that was "true and appropriate in all times and situations." His wise men, faced with this heady challenge, gave him the sentence, "And this too shall pass away."

This is certainly true of our present world—it is constantly in the process of deterioration. And it's not happening just to the world; we also face the reality in our own lives that our days are numbered. James wrote, "What is your life? You are a mist that appears for a little while and then vanishes" (James 4:14).

Although our current life is temporary and will pass away, the God we worship and serve is eternal. He has shared that eternity with us through the gift of His Son, Jesus Christ. He promises us a life that will never pass away: "For God so loved the world that he gave his one and only Son, that whoever believes in him shall not perish but have eternal life" (John 3:16).

When Christ returns, He will take us home to be with Him forever!

Bill Crowder

God Promises
Strength for Now

ENOUGH FOR TODAY
MATTHEW 6:25-34

Do not worry about tomorrow, for tomorrow will worry about itself.
Matthew 6:34

Life can be monotonous. The road that lies before us seems to stretch mile after mile across a flat, barren desert with no oasis in sight. How then are we to handle wearisome responsibilities when there's no foreseeable relief from our burdens?

Oliver de Vinck, severely disabled from birth, lay helplessly on his bed for all of his thirty years, unable to care for himself. Day after day and year after year his parents put every spoonful of food into his mouth, changed his diapers, and still maintained a happy home.

One day Oliver's brother Christopher asked his father how they managed. He explained that they didn't worry about the long succession of tomorrows that might lie before them. They lived a day at a time, asking, "Can I feed Oliver today?" And the answer always was, "Yes, today I can do it."

Jesus taught us how we can handle life's routine: "Do not worry about tomorrow, for tomorrow will worry about itself. Each day has enough trouble of its own" (6:34). In faith—and with prayer—we can break life and its often wearisome tasks into bite-size pieces, entrusting the unpredictable future to the grace of Him who promises that "your strength will equal your days" (Deuteronomy 33:25).

Vernon Grounds

God Promises

The Joy of Eternal Life

A FLY'S REMINDER
ECCLESIASTES 9:4–12

Anyone who is among the living has hope.

Ecclesiastes 9:4

When I first began working in the small office I now rent, the only inhabitants were a few mopey flies. Several of them had gone the way of all flesh, and their bodies littered the floor and windowsills. I disposed of all but one, which I left in plain sight.

That fly carcass reminds me to live each day well. Death is an excellent reminder of life, and life is a gift. Solomon said, "Anyone who is among the living has hope" (Ecclesiastes 9:4). Life on earth gives us the chance to influence and enjoy the world around us. We can eat and drink happily and relish our relationships (vv. 7, 9).

We can also enjoy our work. Solomon advised, "Whatever your hand finds to do, do it with all your might" (v. 10). Whatever our vocation or job or role in life, we can still do things that matter, and do them well. We can encourage people, pray, and express love with sincerity each day.

The writer of Ecclesiastes says, "Time and chance happen to them all. . . . No one knows when their hour will come" (vv. 11–12). It's impossible to know when our lives on earth will end, but gladness and purpose can be found in this day by relying on God's strength and depending on Jesus's promise of eternal life (John 6:47).

Jennifer Benson Schuldt

God Promises

To Protect Us in Various Ways

KEPT!
PSALM 25:14-20

*Guard my life and rescue me; do not let me
be put to shame, for I take refuge in you.*
Psalm 25:20

A little girl named Gloria was quite shy and always stayed close to her mother. If a crisis arose or something made her fearful, however, she'd immediately run to her daddy. He would hold her and assure her that she had nothing to fear. In her eyes, Daddy had great strength, and she knew that he would take care of her at any cost. In much the same way, the believer can run to the Lord and find shelter and perfect safety in times of trial and anxiety. The Scripture says that the name of the Lord is a strong tower in which to hide (Proverbs 18:10).

Here are some comforting biblical promises, assuring you as God's child that you will not be disappointed when you turn to Him in times of distress: He will "keep" you as the apple of His eye (Psalm 17:8). He will "keep you in all your ways" (Psalm 91:11 NKJV). He will "keep" you as a shepherd cares for his flock of sheep (Jeremiah 31:10 NKJV). He will "keep" you "in perfect peace" (Isaiah 26:3). He will "keep" you from the hour of temptation and support you in the time of trial (Revelation 3:10). He will "keep you from stumbling" (Jude v. 24). He will "keep" you from the evil one (John 17:15).

Have you turned to the Lord Jesus Christ in your time of need? Are you enjoying the protection of His loving care? Enjoy the amazing security of being "kept" by God!

Henry Bosch

God Promises
Rewards for Faithfulness

FOR HIS EYES ONLY
MATTHEW 6:1–8, 16–18

Your Father, who sees what is done in secret, will reward you.
Matthew 6:18

Typically, as we age we lose our prominence and our positions of influence. Even those of us who have never sought the limelight seem increasingly to fade into the shadows.

Obscurity and anonymity are good, however, for it is difficult to perform in public without wondering what impression we're making on others. We fret over the extent that our reputations are being enhanced or damaged. And therein lies our peril: To the degree that we seek human recognition, we forfeit God's approval. On the other hand, to lose the admiration of men and women may turn us to seek God's approval only.

Here is a test for our gifts, our prayers, our fasts: Are they done for God's eyes only? If so, though overlooked and unnoticed by others, we have our Father's acknowledgment and reward.

Three times Jesus repeated to His disciples: "Your Father, who sees what is done in secret, will reward you" (Matthew 6:4, 6, 18). This is our assurance as well. Every unobserved gift of time, energy, and love; every petition we whisper in our Father's ears; every secret, inward struggle against sin and self-indulgence will be fully rewarded in due time. In the end, His "Well done, good and faithful servant!" is all that will matter (Matthew 25:21).

David Roper

God Promises

To Give Strength, Even in the Bad Times

WORST POSSIBLE SCENARIOS
JOB 1:13–22

When he has tested me, I will come forth as gold.
Job 23:10

When I used to teach at a Bible college in a large city, I sometimes graded papers at a food court while waiting for a commuter train. One day, I accidentally bumped my large cup of coffee. Its entire contents emptied into my open briefcase.

In most cities, there is a quiet reserve on the part of fellow commuters. However, the coffee splash was so dramatic that it could not be ignored. A man sitting nearby said aloud, "Worst possible scenario!"

That comment was obviously an overstatement. But each of us dreads the thought of something in particular: financial loss, the death of a child or spouse, cancer, or another loss or hardship.

The book of Job is a case study in worst possible scenarios. Yet Job wisely assessed God's role in trying circumstances of loss and poor health: "He knows the way that I take; when he has tested me, I will come forth as gold" (Job 23:10). From this wise statement we can learn two valuable lessons: One is that what we dread most can be used to test our character and make us stronger. The other is that God will provide the strength and comfort to see us through.

Cling to God. He has promised to work on our behalf, even in the worst possible scenario.

Dennis Fisher

God Promises
His Power for Our Needs

I KNOW I CAN
EPHESIANS 3:14–21

[God] is able to do immeasurably more than we ask or imagine, according to his power that is at work within us.

Ephesians 3:20

Remember the story of *The Little Engine That Could*? That determined little train climbed the steep hill by chanting positively, "I think I can. I think I can." And then, as it gained more resolve, it declared, "I know I can. I know I can."

No one would disagree that followers of Christ should think and live in a positive way. But do you ever find yourself depending too much on your own abilities rather than on the power of the indwelling Holy Spirit?

In John 15, Jesus explained our need for complete dependence on Him when He said, "If you remain in me and I in you, you will bear much fruit; apart from me you can do nothing" (v. 5). Paul reminded us that we "can do all this through him who gives [us] strength" (Philippians 4:13), that "this all-surpassing power is from God and not from us" (2 Corinthians 4:7), and that we are strengthened "with power through his Spirit" (Ephesians 3:16).

Because of God's power, we can do whatever He asks of us—through Him. We can base our confidence not in our own abilities, but in God's absolute promises.

So today, with exceedingly more power than the little engine could ever muster, we can say, "I know I can. I know I can—because of Jesus."

Cindy Hess Kasper

God Promises
To Provide for Us

EVERYTHING WE NEED
2 PETER 1:1–11

His divine power has given us everything we need for
a godly life through our knowledge of him
who called us by his own glory and goodness.

2 Peter 1:3

I often feel completely inadequate for the tasks I face. Whether it's teaching Sunday school, advising a friend, or writing articles for this publication, the challenge often seems larger than my ability. Like Peter, I have a lot to learn.

The New Testament reveals Peter's shortcomings as he tried to follow the Lord. While walking on water to Jesus, Peter began to sink (Matthew 14:25–31). When Jesus was arrested, Peter swore he didn't know Him (Mark 14:66–72). But Peter's encounter with the risen Christ and the power of the Holy Spirit changed his life.

Peter came to understand that God's "divine power has given us everything we need for a godly life through our knowledge of him who called us by his own glory and goodness" (2 Peter 1:3). An amazing statement from a man who had many flaws!

"[God] has given us his very great and precious promises, so that through them you may participate in the divine nature, having escaped the corruption in the world caused by evil desires" (v. 4).

Our relationship with the Lord Jesus Christ is the source of the wisdom, patience, and power we need to honor God, help others, and meet the challenges of today. Through Him, we can overcome our hesitations and feelings of inadequacy.

In every situation, He has given us everything we need to serve and honor Him.

David McCasland

God Promises
Peace in a Chaotic World

TRUST IN CRISIS
JOHN 14:19–27

Peace I leave with you.
John 14:27

Ted, one of the elders in our church, used to be a police officer. One day after responding to a report of violence, he said the situation turned life-threatening. A man had stabbed someone and then menacingly turned the blade toward Ted. A fellow officer had taken a position and fired his weapon at the assailant as he attacked Ted. The criminal was subdued, but Ted was shot in the crossfire. As he was driven by ambulance to the hospital, he felt deep waves of peace flowing over his soul from the Holy Spirit. Ted felt so tranquil that he was able to offer words of comfort to the law enforcement officer who was emotionally distraught over the crisis.

The Lord Jesus promised us peace in crisis. Just hours before His own crucifixion, Christ comforted His disciples with these words: "Peace I leave with you; my peace I give you. I do not give to you as the world gives. Do not let your heart be troubled and do not be afraid" (John 14:27).

What is your worst fear? If you should have to face it, Christ will be there with you. Trusting Him through prayer makes available the "peace of God, which transcends all understanding," and it "will guard your hearts and your minds in Christ Jesus" (Philippians 4:7).

Dennis Fisher

God Promises

A Reward for Trusting Him

PERFECT PEACE IS POSSIBLE
ISAIAH 26:1–9

You will keep in perfect peace those whose minds
are steadfast, because they trust in you.

Isaiah 26:3

Few things (if anything at all) in this fallen world can be called perfect. But God promises to keep us in "perfect peace" if we keep our minds focused on Him and continue trusting Him (Isaiah 26:3).

So why do we find it so difficult to trust Him? Often, it's because we're afraid that things won't go as we want them to unless we control them ourselves. The less we are in control, the more anxious and worried we become.

Author Hannah Whitall Smith wrote, "It is not hard, you find, to trust the management of the universe, and of all the outward creation, to the Lord. Can your case then be so much more complex and difficult than these, that you need to be anxious or troubled about His management of you?"

Yet we often think our situation is too difficult for God. If we can't solve things ourselves, we doubt that He can. We have our Christian beliefs, yes—but that isn't the same as believing God. Believing God is a personal response that grows out of our Christian faith and is expressed by our increasing trust in Him and His promises.

As our mind remains on Him, He keeps us in perfect peace. This has been the experience of countless believers, and you can experience it too.

Joanie Yoder

God Promises
To Take Us Home

DO YOU HAVE HOPE?
1 THESSALONIANS 1

*They tell how you turned to God from idols to serve the living
and true God, and to wait for his Son from heaven.*
1 Thessalonians 1:9–10

Several years ago, millionaire Eugene Lang was asked to speak to a class of sixth graders from East Harlem, New York. What could he say to inspire these students, most of whom would drop out of school? Scrapping his notes, he decided to speak to them from his heart. "Stay in school," he admonished, "and I'll help pay the college tuitions for every one of you."

That was a turning point. For the first time in their lives, these students had hope. One said, "I had something to look forward to, something waiting for me. It was a golden feeling." Nearly ninety percent of that class went on to graduate from high school.

People without hope are people without a future. But when hope is restored, life is restored. This is especially true for those who come to know Christ. He gives a sure basis for hope. He has promised to return to earth to take us to our eternal home (John 14:3; 1 Thessalonians 4:17). Till then, there is help through the power of the Holy Spirit (1 Thessalonians 1:5). The believer experiences a new kind of life now and anticipates its fulfillment when Jesus returns.

Is that hope alive in your heart? If not, admit that you are a sinner. Trust Christ as your Savior. And He'll give you a hope that makes life worth living.

Mart DeHaan

God Promises

That His Promises Are Trustworthy

WHOM CAN WE BELIEVE?
PSALM 12

The words of the LORD are flawless.
Psalm 12:6

You may have had a coworker say to you, "I need to borrow some money so I can go out for lunch. I'll pay you back after my next paycheck." But two months and several hints later, you still don't have your money back.

Or maybe a friend has told you, "Thanks for letting me use your car. I'll have it back early enough for you to get to church on time tonight." But you end up waiting and then hurrying into church a half hour late.

Or a husband or wife has said, "I promise, dear, we'll talk about it tonight." But it never happens, and the issue that is harming the marriage keeps growing.

Many people give their word, but sometimes we can't rely on what they say. After we get burned a few times, we begin to feel that we can't trust anybody.

David, who wrote Psalm 12, felt the same way. We don't know the specific situations that prompted his words, but he felt surrounded by untrustworthy people. He lamented, "Everyone lies" (v. 2).

Everyone, that is, except God. His words are pure and flawless, like silver that has been through a refiner's fire seven times (v. 6). We can believe God. His promises stand. He cannot lie.

David Egner

God Promises
To Be Found by All Who Seek Him

RING IN THE DUMPSTER
MATTHEW 13:44–46

Seek and you will find; knock and the door will be opened to you.

Matthew 7:7

In college, I woke up one morning to find Carol, my roommate, in a panic. Her signet ring was missing. We searched everywhere. The next morning we found ourselves picking through a dumpster.

I ripped open a trash bag. "You're so dedicated to finding this!"

"I'm not losing a two-hundred-dollar ring!" she exclaimed.

Carol's determination reminds me of the parable Jesus told about the kingdom of heaven, which "is like treasure hidden in a field. When a man found it, he hid it again, and then in his joy went and sold all he had and bought that field" (Matthew 13:44). Certain things are worth going great lengths to find.

Throughout the Bible, God promises that those who seek Him will find Him. In Deuteronomy, He explained to the Israelites that they would find Him when they turned from their sin and sought Him with all their hearts (4:28–29). In the book of 2 Chronicles, King Asa gained encouragement from a similar promise (15:2). And in Jeremiah, God gave the same promise to the exiles, saying He would bring them back from captivity (29:13–14).

If we seek God, through His Word, worship, and in our daily lives, we will find Him. Over time, we'll know Him on a deeper level. That will be even better than the sweet moment when Carol pulled her ring out of that trash bag!

Julie Schwab

God Promises

To Carry Us Safely at Death

DYING WITH CERTAINTY
2 TIMOTHY 4:6–18

The Spirit himself testifies with our spirit that we are God's children.
Romans 8:16

Over a period of a few months, I visited two dying people—a man of eighty-two and a woman of fifty-two. Neither wanted to die. Both were greatly loved by their families. Each had many reasons for wanting to keep on living. Along with many others, I prayed earnestly for their healing, but God had other plans.

As soon as these two people realized that God wasn't going to heal them, I saw an amazing transformation in them. They both displayed a calm acceptance of death. Their faces took on a new glow, and from their lips came words of testimony and praise. They knew they were God's children and had the assurance that they would soon be with Jesus in heaven. The peace and joy they radiated brought comfort to their loved ones and friends.

What was the source of such absolute certainty in the face of dying? It wasn't what any of those who ministered to them said or did. It was supernatural grace imparted by the indwelling Holy Spirit. Paul put it like this: "The Spirit himself testifies with our spirit that we are God's children" (Romans 8:16).

Praise God! All who trust Christ and who walk in fellowship with Him need not dread the hour of death.

Herb Vander Lugt

God Promises
You Can't Go Where God Isn't

WE'RE NEVER ALONE
PSALM 139:1–12

Jesus replied, "Anyone who loves me will obey my teaching."
John 14:23

Have you ever been alone—really alone?

Many people can answer yes because they feel that way every day. I'm not referring to people who live in a remote cabin on a mountaintop far from civilization. I'm talking about those who feel alone in a crowded mall or in a church full of people.

I'm referring to people who simply cannot find anyone to connect with. Perhaps they are new to a community. Maybe they have lost a spouse. It could be that they simply feel alone because they think of themselves as different, unusual, and left out of normal communication with others.

Have you ever been alone, really alone? If so, there's good news. If you have invited Christ into your life as Savior and Lord, you're never alone. You have His constant presence. Here is His promise: "I am with you always, to the very end of the age" (Matthew 28:20). And from God the Father: "Never will I leave you; never will I forsake you" (Hebrews 13:5). Recognize with the psalmist that there's no place you can go where God is not with you (Psalm 139:7).

Sure, we all need flesh-and-blood companions, but let's not overlook the reality of the Lord's presence. We can depend on it. With Him by our side, we're never alone.

Dave Branon

OCTOBER 15

God Promises
Eternal Life

LIFE BEYOND THE GRAVE
JOHN 11:1–44

Whoever lives by believing in me will never die. Do you believe this?
John 11:26

My beloved husband Bill died of cancer at the age of forty-eight. One tearful morning I read John 11, the story about Jesus raising Lazarus from the dead. I was reassured by two truths I found in Jesus's words to His disciples on their way to Lazarus's grave.

The first truth was revealed when Jesus said that Lazarus was asleep and that He would wake him (vv. 11–14). His disciples responded, "Lord, if he sleeps he will get better." Jesus replied, "Lazarus is dead." Saying that He would waken Lazarus, I believe, was His gentle way to teach them that they didn't need to dread death any more than sleep. Because of His power, resurrecting someone from the grave was like waking someone from sleep.

I saw a second truth in Jesus's statement to Martha: "The one who believes in me will live, even though they die; and whoever lives by believing in me will never die" (vv. 25–26). Of course, believers aren't exempt from dying physically, but Jesus promised that they will live eternally. As the resurrection and the life, He will "waken" their bodies someday. His power to do this was demonstrated when He raised Lazarus (vv. 43–44).

When someone we love goes to be with Jesus, these promises give us comfort and assurance.

Joanie Yoder

God Promises
Two Very Important Things

CLAIM THE PROMISE
PSALM 29

The LORD gives strength to his people;
the LORD blesses his people with peace.

Psalm 29:11

Psalm 29 has been called the "stormy psalm." It describes turbulent waters, rolling thunders, roaring fires, and the crashing cedars of Lebanon. Then there's verse 11. It's like a rainbow in the cloud, a calm in the storm—offering strength and peace to God's people. Its truth can become a reality in life's great crises.

In 1555, Nicholas Ridley was burned at the stake because of his witness for Christ. On the night before Ridley's execution, his brother offered to remain with him in the prison chamber to be of assistance and comfort. Nicholas declined the offer and replied that he meant to go to bed and sleep as quietly as ever he did in his life. Because he knew the peace of God, he could rest in the strength of the everlasting arms of his Lord to meet his need.

God gives us strength for those times when we are weak and fearful. He provides it for each day and for every difficulty. God also gives us peace that guards the door of our heart in the midst of great peril and trials. As Paul said in Philippians 4:7, it's a peace that goes beyond our ability to understand it.

Are you facing a difficulty—divorce, the loss of a loved one, a severe physical or emotional crisis? Turn it over to God. You'll have many trying days, but He'll give you the strength to go on and His peace to comfort your soul. Claim the double promise of Psalm 29:11 as your own.

Paul Van Gorder

God Promises
To Be Present with Us

BURNING QUESTION
EXODUS 3:1–6, 10–14

I AM WHO I AM.

Exodus 3:14

An old Native American story tells of a young boy who was sent into the woods alone on an autumn night to prove his courage. Soon the sky darkened and the sounds of night filled the air. Trees creaked and groaned, an owl screeched, and a coyote howled. Even though he was frightened, the boy remained in the woods all night, as the test of courage required. Finally morning came, and he saw a solitary figure nearby. It was his grandfather, who had been watching over him all night long.

When Moses went deep into the desert, he saw a burning bush that didn't burn up. Then God began talking to him from the bush, commissioning him to go back to Egypt and lead the Israelites out of cruel slavery to freedom. A reluctant Moses began to ask questions: "Who am I that I should go?"

God simply answered, "I will be with you."

"Suppose I . . . say to them, 'The God of your fathers has sent me to you,' and they ask me, 'What is his name?' Then what shall I tell them?" God said to Moses, "I AM WHO I AM. . . . [Say to them,] I AM has sent me to you'" (Exodus 3:11–14). The phrase "I AM WHO I AM" can be interpreted, "I will be who I will be," and it reveals God's eternal and all-sufficient character.

God has promised always to be present with those who believe in Jesus. No matter how dark the night, the unseen God is ready to respond appropriately to our need.

David Egner

═══════ *God Promises* ═══════
Courage Despite Problems

BAD NEWS?
PSALM 112:1–10

They will have no fear of bad news;
their hearts are steadfast, trusting in the LORD.
Psalm 112:7

Several years ago, before cell phones became common, a seminar leader asked the audience, "If someone came into this meeting, called your name, and said, 'You have a phone call,' would you assume that it was good news or bad news?" Most of us admitted we would think it was bad news, but we weren't sure why.

It points out a common burden many people carry—the fear of bad news. It may be a natural concern for the safety of those we love, but it can become an irrational dread of tragedy.

When we are most afraid, we most need confidence in God. Psalm 112 speaks of a person who fears the Lord, delights in His commandments, and is gracious to others (vv. 1, 4–5). But perhaps most striking is those who fear the Lord "will have no fear of bad news; their hearts are steadfast, trusting in the LORD" (v. 7).

A hymn by Frances Havergal reminds us that a trusting heart is the answer for a worried mind: "Stayed upon Jehovah, hearts are fully blest; finding, as He promised, perfect peace and rest."

The Bible doesn't promise that we will never receive bad news. But it does assure us that we don't have to live each day in gnawing fear of what might happen. "[Our] hearts are secure, [we] will have no fear" (v. 8).

David McCasland

God Promises

To Cast Aside No Seekers

THE BLACKNESS OF MIDNIGHT
REVELATION 20

They are . . . wandering stars, for whom
blackest darkness has been reserved forever.

Jude vv. 12–13

When I was a young boy, our family visited an old abandoned copper mine. After we descended into the mine, our guide suddenly turned off his flashlight and we were enveloped by an oppressive blackness. It seemed as though we could feel the darkness.

Through the years, the memory of our descent into that pit has reminded me again and again of Jesus's words concerning the lost, who are "cast out into outer darkness" (Matthew 8:12 NKJV). As terrifying as it was to be in that cave for just a few moments, imagine what it would be like for eternity!

We don't hear much about hell these days. But that doesn't mean there is no such place.

Have you ever thought about where you will spend eternity? According to the Scriptures, you will spend it in one of two places—either heaven or hell.

If you have never made sure of heaven, why not pray something like this right now: "Lord Jesus, I believe that you died on the cross for my sins and rose again from the dead. I now receive you as my Savior. I don't want to be lost. I want to go to heaven. Save me!"

Jesus promised, "Whoever comes to me I will never drive away" (John 6:37).

Richard DeHaan

God Promises

That Jesus Christ Is Coming Back

"I SHALL RETURN!"
JOHN 14:1–6

"Men of Galilee," they said, "why do you stand here looking into the sky? This same Jesus, who has been taken from you into heaven, will come back in the same way you have seen him go into heaven."

Acts 1:11

When General Douglas MacArthur left the Philippines in the early months of World War II, he fled Corregidor Island off the coast of Manila in apparent defeat. Upon reaching Australia, he sent back this now famous declaration: "I shall return!" And he kept his promise, for three years later he stood on Philippine soil and proclaimed, "I have returned!"

This suggests another scene, one of far greater significance for mankind. Two thousand years ago, Jesus Christ came to this earth, stayed for a short time, and then returned to heaven. Just before He went to the cross and suffered what appeared to be a tragic end to His brief life, He said to His disciples, "I will come back" (John 14:3). He was not referring to His resurrection, but to a later event, the hour of which is known only to the Father. After He ascended on high, the first message sent back to earth was the promise, "This same Jesus . . . will come back in the same way" (Acts 1:11). And the closing statement of the Bible is an affirmation of this sacred pledge (Revelation 22:20).

The second coming of Christ is called "the blessed hope" (Titus 2:13). Indeed, it is the only hope for this old world with all its problems. Every effort of man to bring about a golden age of universal peace and prosperity is doomed to failure. That day will come only when Jesus Christ, the Prince of Peace, returns to this earth to rule and reign in perfect righteousness! We know not when that day will be, but He will return—perhaps today!

M. R. DeHaan

God Promises
To Preserve the Bible

THE LOST LIBRARY
ISAIAH 40:6–8

The grass withers and the flowers fall,
but the word of our God endures forever.
Isaiah 40:8

My favorite sections of the local library are history and the periodicals. What about you? Imagine if one Saturday morning you showed up at the library, only to find your favorite books reduced to a pile of ashes.

Centuries ago, that is what happened when thousands of books at the Library of Alexandria caught fire. Alexandria was the place to do research in the ancient world. Then on a fateful day in 47 BC, Julius Caesar set fire to his ships in the Alexandrian harbor to prevent them from falling into enemy hands. The fire soon spread to the docks and the naval arsenal, ultimately destroying 400,000 of the library's precious scrolls.

Such a tragedy shows just how perishable written materials can be. This makes the preservation of our Bible such a marvel. The Word of God has survived book burnings, riots, revolutions, persecutions, and catastrophes. Yet scholars tell us that the manuscripts have been accurately preserved through millennia of careful, meticulous copying.

God inspired the writing of Scripture (2 Timothy 3:16), and He has promised to preserve it through the centuries (Isaiah 40:8). Next time you open your Bible, take a moment to reflect on how precious it is, and thank God for keeping it safe for you.

Dennis Fisher

God Promises
That We Are Connected to Jesus, the Vine

A WORK IN PROGRESS
JOHN 15:9–17

*Grow in the grace and knowledge of
our Lord and Savior Jesus Christ.*

2 Peter 3:18

Pablo Casals was considered to be the preeminent cellist of the first half of the twentieth century. When he was still playing his cello in the middle of his tenth decade of life, a young reporter asked, "Mr. Casals, you are ninety-five years old and the greatest cellist that ever lived. Why do you still practice six hours a day?"

Mr. Casals answered, "Because I think I'm making progress."

What a great attitude! As believers in Christ, we should never be satisfied to think we have reached some self-proclaimed pinnacle of spiritual success, but rather continue to "grow in the grace and knowledge of our Lord and Savior Jesus Christ" (2 Peter 3:18). Jesus reminds us in John 15:16 that He chose us to "go and bear fruit." The result of healthy growth is continuing to bear spiritual fruit throughout our lives. Our Lord promises: "I am the vine; you are the branches. If you remain in me and I in you, you will bear much fruit" (v. 5).

In a steady and faithful progression to become more and more like the One we love and serve, we can be confident that He who began "a good work" in us will continue it until it is finally finished on the day when He returns (Philippians 1:6).

Cindy Hess Kasper

God Promises

To Forgive Confessed Sin

WHY CAN'T I FEEL FORGIVEN?
1 JOHN 1:5–27

*If we confess our sins, he is faithful
and just and will forgive us our sins.*

1 John 1:9

The anguish in the caller's voice revealed her pain. It wasn't the first time she had called me. The reason was always the same. She had said and done some things that hurt her sister badly, and now she was having trouble feeling forgiven.

Oh, it's not that she hadn't done everything the Bible tells us to do. She had. She had confessed her sin to the Lord—repeatedly—and went several times to her sister to ask for complete forgiveness. But this woman could not accept it. She simply could not believe that she was truly forgiven.

Why can't some people accept God's forgiveness? The cause is often their unbelief. God has promised to forgive us when we confess our sins (1 John 1:9). To doubt His forgiveness is to doubt His integrity. We are forgiven because He declared it, not because we feel it. We have no reason to let unbelief block the joy and peace and freedom that we have every right to experience.

Perhaps you are feeling unforgiven. Ask God to help you accept His forgiveness. Believe His truth and reject the lies your feelings are telling you. Your trust will glorify Him, and your inner joy and peace will return.

God keeps His word. So when we ask Him to forgive us, we can be confident that we are forgiven.

David Egner

God Promises

Hope for the Future

GAZING AT THE HORIZON
HEBREWS 11:8–16

We are looking for the city that is to come.

Hebrews 13:14

Almost as soon as the ferryboat started to move, my little daughter said she felt ill. Seasickness had already begun to affect her. Soon I was feeling queasy myself. "Just stare at the horizon," I reminded myself. Sailors say this helps to regain a sense of perspective.

The Maker of the horizon (Job 26:10) knows that sometimes in life we may become fearful and restless. We can regain perspective by focusing on the distant but steady point of our destiny.

The writer of Hebrews understood this. He sensed discouragement in his readers. Persecution had driven many of them from their homes. So he reminded them that other people of faith had endured extreme trials and had been left homeless. They endured it all because they anticipated something better.

As exiles, these readers could look forward to the city whose architect is God, the heavenly country, the city God prepared for them (Hebrews 11:10, 14, 16). So in his final exhortations, the writer asked his readers to focus on God's promises. "For here we do not have an enduring city, but we are looking for the city that is to come" (13:14).

Our present troubles are temporary. We are "foreigners and strangers on earth" (11:13), but gazing at the horizon of God's promises provides the point of reference we need.

Keila Ochoa

God Promises
Fulfillment

JOYFUL LIVING
1 TIMOTHY 6:17–19

Command those who are rich in this present world . . .
to put their hope in God, who richly
provides us with everything for our enjoyment.
1 Timothy 6:17

Our search for joy takes us many different directions—dream holidays, shopping, food, clothes, friends, cars—the list is almost endless.

My guess is that if you perked up at the mention of shopping, holidays, or cars, you might have felt a twinge of guilt. We often view the joy of temporal things as less than spiritual and show our discomfort by apologizing for nice things: "I wouldn't have bought this, but someone gave me a wonderful deal." As if real Christians never eat at nice restaurants, drive cool cars, or wear designer clothes!

No doubt God's greatest gift to us is our relationship with His Son Jesus. It's a gift beyond comparison. Jesus promised that when we abide in Him we will experience the fulfillment of His joy (John 15:11), and without that kind of deep, abiding joy the rest of life is mundane at best.

But Scripture also casts the joy of the Lord in terms of temporal things. The enjoyment of "things" can be a positive spiritual experience. When we recognize that He "richly provides us with everything for our enjoyment" (1 Timothy 6:17) and that "every good and perfect gift is from above" (James 1:17), our hearts should be full of thankfulness and praise. This, in and of itself, is an act of worship! Enjoy the Giver and the gifts.

Joe Stowell

God Promises
Our Good in Life or in Death

ALL-TIME PROTECTION
PSALM 121

The LORD will keep you from all harm—he will watch over your life.
Psalm 121:7

A rather feisty, older woman told one of my pastor friends, "I don't need Christ in the daytime. When I'm awake, I can take care of myself. But I do pray at night when I am going to sleep. In fact, I've said bedtime prayers since I was a child." Apparently, that woman felt she was more than adequate to take care of herself when she was awake but could use a little divine help when she was asleep.

The writer of Psalm 121 recognized his need for God's protecting mercy at all times. He portrayed the Lord watching over us during the light of day and the dark of night. He pictured God keeping us safe from dangers seen and unseen, at home and away, through time and eternity.

I often quote this psalm to people before they undergo surgery. God has seen most of them safely through the operation. Recently, however, three friends died on the operating table. Did God fail in His promise to protect them? Indeed not! He saw them safely into His presence, where He will care for them forever and ever.

Give thanks to God for watching over you all the days and nights of your life until now. Trust Him for your future. God protects us at all times, even when He decides to lead us home.

Herb Vander Lugt

OCTOBER 27

God Promises

Help for the Weary

PROMISED STRENGTH
ISAIAH 40:10–11, 28–31

[God] gives strength to the weary and increases the power of the weak.

Isaiah 40:29

Jonah Sorrentino was deeply hurt at age six when his parents separated. As a result, he held a lot of anger and bitterness inside. At fifteen, Jonah learned of God's love for him and became a believer in Jesus Christ.

Jonah, also known as recording artist KJ-52, admits that he used to live like a victim of circumstances. In an interview with *Christianity Today*, he explained how he began to experience healing: "You definitely have to acknowledge that, no, you're not okay."

He added, "You also have to reach a point of saying, 'I'm not going to dwell on everything of the past . . . on anger or bitterness or hurt. I'm going to move forward because God is going to give me the strength to do that.'" God helped him to forgive his parents.

In one of his songs, the recording artist expressed that he had discovered the following truths: Strength is available in Christ, the Lord has life mapped out for you, and while it is sometimes hard to accept, He is ready to care for you.

If we've been hurt badly, we may wonder how we can live with a painful past. God could take away our pain instantly and forever, if He chooses to. Often, though, He heals us slowly, and scars remain. He carries us—gently leading us as a shepherd cares for His flock (Isaiah 40:11).

We may not be healed completely in this life, but we can count on God's promises. He gives "strength to the weary" and increases their power (v. 29).

Anne Cetas

God Promises
To Keep Us Safe

LOOKING AHEAD
PSALM 125

The LORD surrounds his people both now and forevermore.
Psalm 125:2

I recall talking with a man who expressed his apprehension about the future. He was certain the stock market was going to crash. He was afraid our country was being taken over by evil forces and the church was overrun with worldliness. And even though he professed faith in Jesus Christ, he was afraid that by some quirk or oversight he will end up in hell.

Psalm 125 reminds us that we do not need to fear the future. The psalmist praises God because He has promised to protect and preserve His people. As the mountains around Jerusalem will not be moved, the psalmist sang, so the Lord surrounds His people forever (vv. 1–2).

God promises to provide us with His grace. We are safe for all eternity because He said so. Jesus said that not one of His own will be snatched from His Father's hand (John 10:28). And Paul wrote that nothing can separate us from the love of God (Romans 8:38–39).

This does not mean we are free to go out and sin. Paul wrote emphatically about the inconsistency of practicing a sinful lifestyle when we have "died to sin" (Romans 6:1–4).

We who know the Lord and walk in His ways have every assurance that our future is as secure as the unchanging character of God.

David Egner

God Promises

His Peace in Life's Storms

LIGHT IN THE DARK
PSALM 18:28–36, 46–49

You, LORD, keep my lamp burning;
my God turns my darkness into light.

Psalm 18:28

A severe thunderstorm passed through our new town, leaving high humidity and dark skies in its wake. I took our dog, Callie, for an evening stroll. The mounting challenges of my family's cross-country move grew heavier on my mind. Frustrated by the countless ways things had strayed so far from our high hopes and expectations, I slowed to let Callie sniff the grass. I listened to the creek that runs beside our house. Tiny lights flashed on and off while hovering over the patches of wildflowers climbing up the creek's bank. Fireflies.

The Lord wrapped me in peace as I watched the blinking lights cutting through the darkness. I thought of the psalmist David singing, "You, LORD, keep my lamp burning" (Psalm 18:28). Proclaiming that God turns his darkness into light, David demonstrated confident faith in the Lord's provision and protection (vv. 29–30). With God's strength, he could handle anything that came his way (vv. 32–35). Trusting the living Lord to be with him through all circumstances, David promised to praise Him among the nations and sing the praises of His name (vv. 36–49).

Whether we're enduring the unpredictable storms in life or enjoying the stillness after the rains have passed, the peace of God's constant presence lights our way through the darkness. Our living God will always be our strength, our refuge, our sustainer, and our deliverer.

Xochitl Dixon

God Promises

That in the End, We Win

WHEN LIFE SEEMS UNFAIR
PSALM 73

I envied the arrogant when I saw the prosperity of the wicked.

Psalm 73:3

Have you ever felt that life is unfair? For those of us who are committed to following the will and ways of Jesus, it's easy to get frustrated when people who don't care about Him seem to do well in life. A businessman cheats yet wins a large contract, and the guy who parties all the time is robust and healthy—while you or your loved ones struggle with finances or medical issues. It makes us feel cheated, like maybe we've been good for nothing.

If you've ever felt that way, you're in good company. The writer of Psalm 73 goes through a whole list of how the wicked prosper, and then he says, "Surely in vain I have kept my heart pure" (v. 13). But the tide of his thoughts turns when he recalls his time in God's presence: "Then I understood their final destiny" (v.17).

When we spend time with God and see things from His point of view, it changes our perspective completely. We may be jealous of the nonbelievers now, but we won't be at judgment time. As the saying goes, what difference does it make if you win the battle but lose the war?

Like the psalmist, let's praise God for His presence in this life and His promise of the life to come (vv. 25–28). He is all you need, even when life seems unfair.

Joe Stowell

God Promises

To Help Us in Our Troubles

GOD'S TENDER CARE
PSALM 31:1–14

You saw my affliction and knew the anguish of my soul.
Psalm 31:7

During a time of grief, C. S. Lewis observed that his neighbors walked across the street to avoid him when they saw him approaching.

David too knew a time of grief when he said, "I am the utter contempt of my neighbors and an object of dread to my closest friends. . . . I am forgotten as though I were dead" (Psalm 31:11–12).

Perhaps you've known times when friends seem to forget you in your sorrow. They fail to call, or write, or promise to pray.

But those are the times when we can sense God's tenderness most deeply. When the days are long and lonely and no one seems to care, He seeks us out and surrounds us with lovingkindness. Our sorrow, far from burdening Him, draws out His tender compassion. He knows the troubles of our soul (v. 7). And He cares. Thus we can commit our spirit into His hand (v. 5), as our Lord Jesus did when all forsook Him and fled.

Poet Frank Graeff asks, "Does Jesus care when my heart is pained too deeply for mirth and song; as the burdens press, and the cares distress, and the way grows weary and long?" The answer? Yes! He invites us to give our burdens and cares to Him, because He cares for us (1 Peter 5:7).

Trust God to care for you today.

David Roper

God Promises

To Hear Our Petitions

GOD'S MERCIES
GENESIS 32:3–13

*I am unworthy of all the kindness and
faithfulness you have shown your servant.*

Genesis 32:10

"Less than the least of all God's mercies." This was the motto seventeenth-century English poet and clergyman George Herbert engraved on his signet ring, and it was the phrase with which he signed his letters and books. The Old Testament patriarch Jacob had spoken these words when he pondered God's goodness despite his own sin and shame: "I am unworthy of all the kindness and faithfulness you have shown your servant" (Genesis 32:10).

The word *mercies* is from the Hebrew word *chesed*, meaning "God's enduring love." I think it is significant that it rose from the heart of one who saw himself as utterly unworthy.

Relying solely on God's faithful love, Jacob cries out: "Save me!" What an odd combination of thoughts: "I am unworthy. . . . Save me" (vv. 10–11). Unlike some who seem to have it all together, Jacob knew that everything he brought to God had been ruined by sin. He thought of himself as a man undeserving of God's grace. His hope lay not in his worth but in the promise of God to look with favor on those who throw themselves on His mercy. Humility and contrition are the keys that open the heart of God.

As He did with Jacob, God hears us when we humbly cry out to Him for mercy.

David Roper

God Promises
The Return of Jesus

ARE YOU READY?
MATTHEW 24:36–46

You also must be ready, because the Son of Man
will come at an hour when you do not expect him.
Matthew 24:44

When Jesus promised His disciples that He would one day return to earth, He said He would come at a time they did not expect (Matthew 24:44). Therefore, people today who set dates for Christ's second coming are wasting their time. Jesus never told His followers how to calculate the day of His return. Rather, He emphasized that our main priority is to make sure we're ready for Him, and that we are occupied in His service when He comes (vv. 45–46).

A woman who lived by this teaching was shopping in a small country store. Several young people were just standing around doing nothing. Knowing she was a Christian, they began ridiculing her. "We hear you're expecting Jesus to come back," they jeered. "That's right," she replied brightly. "Do you really believe He's coming?" they asked. "Absolutely," she answered. They said, "Well, you'd better hurry home and get ready. He might be on the way!" Facing them, she said, "I don't have to get ready—I keep ready!"

Are you ready for the arrival of God's Son? Will you be glad to see Jesus when He returns? If not, get ready now. Without delay, turn away from your sin and trust Jesus Christ as your Lord and Savior. Then keep ready by walking in His will by the power of the Holy Spirit every day.

Joanie Yoder

God Promises
Wisdom and a Crown

JOYFUL TRIALS
JAMES 1:1–12

Consider it pure joy, my brothers and sisters,
whenever you face trials of many kinds.

James 1:2

The Bible tells us to respond to difficult circumstances in a way that is directly opposed to our natural tendency. One of the most challenging of those commands is this: "Consider it pure joy . . . whenever you face trials of many kinds" (James 1:2).

It seems unusual to see the term "pure joy" associated with trials. We are to consider ourselves happy—not resisting trials and temptations as intruders but welcoming them as friends. I don't know about you, but that's not the first thing that pops into my mind.

This outlook would seem absurd and unattainable if not for the reason behind it: "the testing of your faith produces perseverance" (v. 3). An attitude of joy is not based on what we feel but on what we know of God and His work in our lives. Therefore, a painful process that yields a desired goal can be welcomed as a friend.

It's not the testing of our strength but the trying of our faith in almighty God that develops our endurance. Through it all, the Lord promises wisdom for today (v. 5) and a crown of life for those who persevere (v. 12).

My natural response to difficult circumstances is "Oh, no!" The Lord wants me to see what He can accomplish through them and say, "Oh, yes!"

David McCasland

God Promises

Everlasting Mercy and Forgiveness

THANKS IN EVERYTHING
1 CHRONICLES 16:8–34

Give thanks to the LORD, for he is good; his love endures forever.
1 Chronicles 16:34

Scottish minister Alexander Whyte (1836–1921) was known for his uplifting prayers in the pulpit. He always found something for which to be grateful.

One Sunday morning the weather was so gloomy that one church member thought to himself, "Certainly the preacher won't think of anything for which to thank the Lord on a wretched day like this." Much to his surprise, however, Whyte began by praying, "We thank Thee, O God, that it is not always like this." True to form, Whyte found cause for thanksgiving.

Because of a detached retina, my sight in one eye became severely impaired. Shortly after heart bypass surgery, I suffered the complete blockage of an artery and the collapse of its replacement. Later, I was diagnosed as having Parkinson's disease, which made it impossible for me to continue teaching on radio and television.

Now, I can imagine some people saying, "Certainly no one can think of anything for which to thank the Lord in circumstances like that!" But they're wrong. I have countless blessings—so many that I can echo the words of David, "Give thanks to the Lord, for He is good!" Can you?

Richard DeHaan

God Promises

To Be with Us

PRACTICING CHRIST'S PRESENCE
MATTHEW 28:16–20

My Presence will go with you.

Exodus 33:14

I am with you always.

Matthew 28:20

Israel was given this precious promise from God, "My Presence will go with you." It was meant to strengthen and encourage the Israelite people on the long and tiresome journey to the promised land. Likewise, today we are assured that Jesus walks with us through the spiritual wastelands of this world, and we must learn to count on this daily.

A preacher once counseled with a member of his church who found it difficult to sense God's presence when praying. The man had always thought of Him as being far away and unreachable. After trying several approaches, the pastor said, "Think of the Lord riding beside you in the car, or sitting next to you in an empty chair at the table." Taking this advice, the man soon learned to converse with Christ as "friend with Friend." Later, when he became terminally ill, he always wanted an empty chair beside his bed. He would turn that way whenever he talked with the Savior. One morning his wife came into his room and found that he had died during the night. His hand lay palm up on the chair as if he had rested it in the hand of the Lord in his final moments.

Because of Christ's promise to be with us, we too can have a warm and personal contact with Him daily. You may not need to put a chair by your bed to make Christ seem near. But one thing is sure—practicing the presence of Christ will revolutionize your life.

Henry Bosch

God Promises
His Strength for Our Needs

IF ONLY WE COULD . . .
PSALM 28

The LORD is the strength of his people.
Psalm 28:8

The weeping Alaskan cedar tree whipped from side to side in the storm's strong winds. Regie loved the tree, which not only had provided shelter from the summer sun but also had given her family privacy. But now the fierce storm was tearing the roots from the ground. Quickly, Regie, with her fifteen-year-old son in tow, ran to try to rescue the tree. With her hands and ninety-pound frame firmly planted against it, she and her son tried to keep it from falling over. But they weren't strong enough.

God was King David's strength when he called out to Him in another kind of storm (Psalm 28:8). Some commentators say he wrote this during a time when his world was falling apart. His own son had risen in rebellion against him and was trying to take the throne (2 Samuel 15). He felt so vulnerable and weak that he feared God might remain silent and he would die (Psalm 28:1). "Hear my cry for mercy as I call to you for help," he said to God (v. 2). God gave David strength to go on, even though his relationship with his son never mended.

How we long to prevent bad things from happening! If only we could. But in our weakness, God promises we can always call to Him to be our Rock (vv. 1–2). When we don't have the strength, He's our shepherd and will carry us forever (vv. 8–9).

Anne Cetas

God Promises
Help Along the Way

BUMPS ARE FOR CLIMBING ON
GENESIS 45:1–8

You intended to harm me, but God intended it for good.
Genesis 50:20

Bible teacher Warren Wiersbe told the story of a little boy who was leading his younger sister up a steep mountain path. There were many rocks in the way, so the climbing was tough. Finally, the little girl, exasperated by the hard climb, said to her brother, "This isn't a path at all. It's all rocky and bumpy." "Sure," her brother replied, "but the bumps are what you climb on."

If anyone ever faced obstacles, Joseph did. His brothers hated him. He was sold into slavery. He was falsely accused and thrown into an Egyptian prison. Yet he continued to trust in the Lord and walk by faith. Rather than causing him to stumble, these hardships were steppingstones in his service for the Lord.

Others in the Bible also displayed this attitude of trust: Abraham, Moses, Samuel, Gideon, and even Jesus himself. For each of them, the way of doing the will of God was marked with opposition, hardship, and difficulty. Yet they didn't let these things stop them.

What about you? Obstacles in your way? Rocks in the path? Do you feel like quitting? Turn to the Lord for the strength, the grace, and the direction that come only from Him. Take your eyes off the difficulties and keep them steadfast on the goal of being prepared for greater usefulness. God did not promise to remove all the stones from your path, but He has promised to help you every step of the way.

Remember, "Bumps are what you climb on."

David Egner

God Promises
To Be Our Companion

TEMPORARY TEARS
1 PETER 5:6–11

And the God of all grace, . . . after you have suffered a little while, will himself restore you and make you strong, firm and steadfast.
1 Peter 5:10

Author George MacDonald (1824–1905) wrote, "God has come to wipe away our tears. He is doing it; He will have it done as soon as He can; and until He can He would have them flow without bitterness; to which end He tells us it is a blessed thing to mourn because of the comfort that is on its way."

While we wait for that comfort, we can be assured that God will not allow us to be tested beyond our ability to bear the trial. Every difficult circumstance is timed with exact precision. Every hard situation is screened through His perfect love. We will not suffer one moment more, nor will we suffer more intensely than is necessary. "To a close-shorn sheep God gives wind by measure" goes an old Basque saying. In other words, God will not allow those most vulnerable to life's difficulties to be overtaken by them.

There may be deep waters through which you must wade; there may be fires through which the ore of your character must pass. But in the midst of them God promises to be your partner, companion, and faithful friend. He will "perfect, establish, strengthen, and settle you" (1 Peter 5:10 NKJV).

And then, when He has finished His work, He will take you home to heaven and wipe away all your tears—forever (Revelation 21:4).

David Roper

God Promises

To Care Even If We Forget

GOD REMEMBERS
2 TIMOTHY 4:9–22

*When you come, bring the cloak that I left with
Carpus at Troas, and my scrolls, especially the parchments.*

2 Timothy 4:13

Confined to prison and nearing life's end, the apostle Paul made an unusual threefold request—a visit from Timothy, a cloak, and some books and parchments. Although Bible scholars can't say positively what was on these papyri and skins, they are quite sure they were portions of Scripture. Paul was looking for a loving relationship, basic material needs, and God's Word as he contemplated eternity.

A ninety-one-year-old woman wrote, "I spend about one hour each day with my Lord, reading my Bible and Christian literature. When people ask what good all my reading does if I can't remember what I've read, my answer is always the same. I'm in pretty good health, have a roof over my head, and have plenty of food to eat. . . . I also have two sons and one grandson who love me dearly. My cup runneth over. I am not concerned about my memory. I just do my reading and God does the remembering."

Does the way look dark? Keep reading God's Word. If you can no longer read, listen to it online (biblegateway.com) or on a CD. Thank the Lord daily for meeting your physical needs. Draw on the support of other Christians.

Even if you forget God's promises, you'll discover that He never forgets them. He'll strengthen you and stand with you.

Dennis DeHaan

God Promises
To Be with Us Even in Death

"NOTHING IS EVER SURE!"
JAMES 4:13–17

Why, you do not even know what will happen tomorrow. What is your life? You are a mist that appears for a little while and then vanishes.

James 4:14

In November 1975, the huge freighter *SS Edmund Fitzgerald* sank in the cold waters of Lake Superior during a fierce storm. Only a week before the tragedy, chief steward Robert Rafferty had sent a postcard to his wife. It said, "I may be home by November 8. However nothing is ever sure." The irony of his words was noted in a *Detroit Free Press* article listing the names of the twenty-eight other crew members who perished in the disaster.

Not a day passes without a reminder that our earthly life can come to an end at any moment. Whether it's a report of a tragic plane crash, a car accident on a local highway, or the mute testimony of obituary notices, one message comes through loud and clear: We are here today, but we may be gone tomorrow! James expressed this truth when he wrote, "What is your life? It is even a mist that appears for a little time and then vanishes."

Is our only certainty, then, the sobering prospect that at any moment we may be thrust into eternity? No indeed! Christ is the anchor of the soul. He paid the penalty for our sins on the cross, and if we admit our guilt before God, we will receive forgiveness and eternal life by trusting Him. He has promised to remain with us, even in the hour of death.

Does your brief earthly life seem futile because "nothing is ever sure"? Then trust Christ! He provides a joyous certainty that can be yours right now!

Dennis DeHaan

God Promises

That He Will Be with Us

STRONG AND COURAGEOUS
JOSHUA 1:1–9

As I was with Moses, so I will be with you;
I will never leave you nor forsake you.

Joshua 1:5

Each night, as young Caleb closed his eyes, he felt the darkness envelop him. The silence of his room was regularly suspended by the creaking of the wooden house in Costa Rica. Then the bats in the attic became more active. His mother had put a nightlight in his room, but the young boy still feared the dark. One night Caleb's dad posted a Bible verse on the footboard of his bed. It read: "Be strong and courageous. Do not be afraid; . . . for the LORD your God will be with you" (Joshua 1:9). Caleb began to read those words each night—and he left that promise from God on his footboard until he went away to college.

In Joshua 1, we read of the transition of leadership to Joshua after Moses died. The command to "be strong and courageous" was repeated several times to Joshua and the Israelites to emphasize its importance (vv. 6–7, 9). Surely, they felt trepidation as they faced an uncertain future, but God reassuringly said, "As I was with Moses, so I will be with you; I will never leave you nor forsake you" (v. 5).

It's natural to have fears, but it's detrimental to our physical and spiritual health to live in a state of constant fear. Just as God's encouragement helped His servants of old, we too can be strong and courageous because of the One who promises to always be with us.

Cindy Hess Kasper

God Promises

To Keep His Word; We Need to Obey

PROMISES AND COMMANDS
GENESIS 15:4–6; 22:1-19

Take now your son. . . . Sacrifice him . . . as a burnt offering.
Genesis 22:2

Author and pastor Steve Lawson says he often hears a disturbing statement from people involved in a lifestyle that directly contradicts a command of Scripture. In order to justify their actions, they say, "Hey! God wants me to be happy, and this will make me happy." Apparently these people want to believe God's promises to bless them, but they ignore His commands to be holy.

Consider Abraham's response to a difficult situation. He had been promised that he would father a nation of innumerable people. What joy this must have held out for him! Then God commanded that Abraham sacrifice his only son. In the patriarch's mind, the command was in obvious conflict with the promise (Genesis 15:5; 22:2).

How could God's promise be fulfilled if Abraham obeyed the command? If he would have reacted like the people Steve Lawson was talking about, he would have told God to forget it. Yet he didn't. He obeyed God's command, and he saw God provide a substitute sacrifice. Abraham obeyed God and the promise was kept.

We need to remember that our duty is to obey God's commands. His duty is to keep His promises. In God's way of doing things, those two things never conflict.

Dave Branon

God Promises

To Meet Our Needs

HE WILL PROVIDE
GENESIS 22:1–14

*Abraham answered, "God himself will provide
the lamb for the burnt offering, my son."*
Genesis 22:8

Pastor Roy S. Nicholson told of a time when he had no money to buy food. Determined to trust God for his needs and not tell anyone, he and his wife presented their case to the Lord in prayer.

The next morning he set the table for breakfast, confident that the Lord would provide something to eat. Just then a boy from their Sunday school came to the house with a sack of flour and some milk. Tears welled up in the pastor's eyes. No sooner had he left than Granny Turner appeared at the door carrying a large serving tray loaded with Virginia ham, eggs, grits and gravy, hot biscuits, butter, jelly, and coffee. Nicholson was filled with praise to God

Abraham faced an even more serious test of faith. God had told him he would become the father of a great nation, but then God asked him to sacrifice his promised son Isaac on the altar. How could Abraham do such a thing? Many years of trusting God for his long-awaited son had taught him that his confidence in God would be fully rewarded. "God himself will provide the lamb," he told Isaac.

Faith like that is not born in a day. It's the result of continually seeing God's faithfulness to His promises, and it grows as we daily choose to believe what He says.

Dennis DeHaan

God Promises
To Renew Our Strength

TESTED YOUR TIREDNESS
ISAIAH 40:18–31

Those who hope in the LORD will renew their strength.
Isaiah 40:31

Someone confided in me that she was feeling guilty. She said, "Even though I'm a Christian, I still get so tired!" As I searched the Scriptures, I found that God's people sometimes suffered fatigue and even exhaustion. Today's church seems unwilling to acknowledge this, however. In the name of victorious Christian living, some view all weariness as a failure to trust and obey God.

But according to Isaiah, our Creator anticipates weariness in His finite creatures. He promises to renew our strength if we wait on Him (40:30–31). He also understands that our need for strength, like our need for food, isn't a once-for-all provision.

Our choice is not whether we will experience weariness but what we will be weary about. In my own life, I suffered exhaustion during a long period of time because of worry, fear, and bitterness. Thanks to the Lord, these negative feelings no longer dominate me. But I still get very tired because of my involvement in worthy causes and my desire to live faithfully as a servant of Christ.

Give yourself a "tiredness test." If you are tired for the wrong reasons, humbly seek God's loving correction. If you are tired for the right reasons, seek God's renewing strength. You don't need to feel guilty about feeling weary.

Joanie Yoder

God Promises

To Carry Us Forever

HE WILL NEVER LET YOU FALL
PSALM 55:16–22

Cast your cares on the LORD and he will sustain you.

Psalm 55:22

When the elevated railroad was introduced in New York City in the late 1800s, some people worried that it might collapse under the weight of its passengers. Francis L. Patton, former president of Princeton Theological Seminary, said that "the proprietors of the road took great pleasure in notifying the public of the fact that this road had been subjected to a most abnormal and enormous tonnage, and that consequently people of ordinary weight might deem themselves quite safe."

The professor then drew this spiritual analogy: "I feel the same way about the Christ." Patton was sure he could travel the road to heaven "above the din and dust of daily life, because this elevated road . . . has given no sign of instability."

The same heavenly Father who promised to carry His people Israel all the way from birth to old age (Isaiah 46:3–4) promises never to leave us (Hebrews 13:5). His redemptive grace in Jesus Christ can never be overloaded, His strength never exhausted. Our heavenly Father's almighty arms have the capacity to safely carry all who come to Him.

In childlike faith, let's respond to the words of the psalmist and cast all our cares on the Lord (Psalm 55:22), knowing that He will never let us fall.

Vernon Grounds

God Promises
Unbreakable Truths

PEOPLE OF INTEGRITY
PSALM 119:153–160

For the word of the LORD is right and true;
he is faithful in all he does.

Psalm 33:4

Part of the unspoken code among the settlers of the American West was that a man always kept his word. That explains why Andrew Garcia made a 1,300-mile trek in 1879 to pay a debt. In September of the previous year, he had bought supplies in Bozeman, Montana, to hunt buffalo. The ten pack-mules, ammunition, food, and gear cost him $300 more than he had, so a merchant loaned him the rest. He promised to pay it back by January 1.

The winter snows came early that year, however, and Garcia couldn't get back to Bozeman. His travels took him through Colorado and down into New Mexico. Finally, a year later, he headed back to Bozeman. "Don't bother," his buddies told him. But Garcia believed in keeping his word, so he returned and paid the debt.

Followers of Christ should also be known as people of integrity. If we say we'll help with a Sunday school class, or assist in the nursery, or spend time with a family member, or complete a job as agreed, do we keep our word even if something better comes along. Are we true to our word?

God's promises are never broken (Psalm 119:160), and what He does, He does in truth (Psalm 33:4). As His followers, our words are to be as true as His Word.

Herb Vander Lugt

God Promises
To Forgive Us

HIDDEN SIN
1 JOHN 1:5–10

You, God, know my folly; my guilt is not hidden from you.
Psalm 69:5

Chuck had slowed to a stop when his car was hit from behind and was pushed into the vehicle ahead of him. A sickening, crunching sound indicated that additional vehicles had collided behind them.

As Chuck sat quietly for a moment, he observed that the vehicle directly behind him was pulling out into traffic. Obviously hoping to avoid an encounter with police, the escaping driver neglected to notice he had left something behind. When the police arrived, an officer picked up the hit-and-run driver's license plate from the ground and said to Chuck, "Someone will be waiting for him when he arrives home. He won't get away with this."

Scripture tells us: "You may be sure that your sin will find you out" (Numbers 32:23), as this man who fled the accident would discover. We may sometimes be able to hide our sin from the people around us, but nothing is ever "hidden from God's sight" (Hebrews 4:13). He sees each of our failures, thoughts, and motivations (1 Samuel 16:7; Luke 12:2–3).

Believers are given a wonderful promise: "If we confess our sins, [God] is faithful and just and will forgive us our sins and purify us from all unrighteousness" (1 John 1:9). So don't let unconfessed, so-called "hidden" sins come between you and God (vv. 6–7).

Cindy Hess Kasper

God Promises

To Sustain the Universe

ORDINANCES OF HEAVEN
PSALM 19:1–7

*If I have not made my covenant with day and night
and established the laws of heaven and earth,
then I will reject the descendants of Jacob and David.*
Jeremiah 33:25–26

Mark your calendar now if you want to see the next celestial convergence of Venus, Jupiter, and the moon. On November 18, 2052, you'll be able to peer through the evening darkness as those solar system neighbors "gather" in a tiny area of the sky. That remarkable juxtaposition of reflective spheres last sparkled the night sky on December 1, 2008, and it will happen again at mid-century.

This predictability, as well as things such as eclipses and the return of Halley's Comet (July 28, 2061), proves the orderliness of the universe. If no fixed set of laws governed the movement of everything in the universe, such predictions could not be made.

Are these set rules more than random standards? Can we see God's hand in these celestial certainties? Look at Jeremiah 33:25–26. God has in view the covenantal relationship between himself and His people, and He uses a scientific fact in the analogy. In effect, God says that His fixed universal laws, "the ordinances of heaven and earth" (NKJV), have the same certainty as His promises to His covenant people.

God's laws have governed the universe since its creation—and continue to do so with astounding predictability. So mark your calendar, and be amazed by God's unchanging control.

Dave Branon

God Promises

Never to Leave Us Unattended

THE MENTION OF HIS NAME
JOHN 16:17–24

*I will see you again and you will rejoice,
and no one will take away your joy.*

John 16:22

When the soloist began to sing during our Sunday worship service, the congregation gave him full, hushed attention. His mellow bass-baritone voice brought them the soul-touching words of an old song by Gordon Jensen. The song's title expresses a truth that grows more precious the older we become: "He's as Close as the Mention of His Name."

We've all experienced times of separation from our loved ones. A child marries and moves far away. Parents are separated from us because of career or health. A child goes off to school in another state or country. True, we have texting, FaceTime, and Zoom. But we are here and they are there. And then there is the separation of death.

But as believers in Christ, we have His promise that we are never alone. Though we may feel alone, He hasn't gone anywhere. He's right here, right now, always and forever. When He left this earth, He told His followers, "Surely I am with you always, to the very end of the age" (Matthew 28:20). He also promised us, "Never will I leave you; never will I forsake you" (Hebrews 13:5).

The silent plea, the whispered mention of His name, even the very thought of Him brings us solace and reassurance. "He's as close as the mention of His name."

David Egner

God Promises

Peace

PRAYER WITH THANKSGIVING
PHILIPPIANS 4:6–13

Do not be anxious about anything, but in every situation, by prayer and petition, with thanksgiving, present your requests to God.

Philippians 4:6

Judy's rare brain condition required delicate surgery. The risky procedure took place in the operating theater at a research hospital with many doctors and medical students observing.

Just before the operation was to begin, the surgeon asked, "Do you have any questions?" Judy replied, "May I pray for you?" With many looking on, she thanked God for the surgeon's great skill, asked wisdom for him, and committed the surgery into the Lord's hands.

How it must delight God's heart when we unashamedly bring our cares to Him with thanksgiving! Judy didn't ask God to spare her life. She was sure that her heavenly Father knew how much she longed to live. She simply thanked Him for the surgeon's knowledge and skill, and she entrusted herself to the Great Physician's special care.

Judy got a new lease on life that day. And those doctors got a firsthand look at faith in the true and living God. Paul said, "In every situation, by prayer and petition, with thanksgiving, present your requests to God" (Philippians 4:6). Notice that God does not promise to give you all you want, but rather, "the peace of God, which transcends all understanding, will guard your hearts and your minds in Christ Jesus" (v. 7). What a gift!

Dennis DeHaan

God Promises

Wisdom and Understanding

BEYOND INFORMATION
PROVERBS 1

---

*The LORD gives wisdom; from his mouth
come knowledge and understanding.*

Proverbs 2:6

An investment company's full-page ad in *The Wall Street Journal* began with these words: "Information is everywhere. Insight is all too rare. For insight goes beyond information to discern underlying truths."

Today, we are long on information and short on insight. Television offers scores of channels. Siri and "Hey, Google" give us instant access to endless information. Other online sources give us the temperature in Timbuktu and the baseball score in Baltimore. We're wired and tired from trying to grasp the meaning of all we know.

Years ago, a friend encouraged me to read a chapter from Proverbs each day. One chapter each day takes me through this marvelous book of God's wisdom every month. "You can get knowledge in college," my friend said, "but wisdom comes from God."

Here's what almighty God promises when we seek His wisdom: "If you call out for insight and cry aloud for understanding, . . . then you will . . . find the knowledge of God. For the LORD gives wisdom; from his mouth come knowledge and understanding" (Proverbs 2:3–6).

One chapter of Proverbs every day. Try it for a month and see how God's Word will give you the wisdom to transform information into insight.

David McCasland

God Promises
Jesus Will Return

FIRE MOUNTAIN
MATTHEW 24:36–44

---

*Be ready, because the Son of Man will come
at an hour when you do not expect him.*

Matthew 24:44

Rising 2,900 meters (9,600 feet) above the rainforest in Indonesia's southern Java, Mount Merapi (the Fire Mountain) is one of the world's most dangerous volcanoes.

As the Fire Mountain showed signs of renewed activity, authorities tried to evacuate local residents. Then, several years ago, Merapi spewed a gray plume of sulfurous smoke that resembled a flock of sheep leaving the crater. Amazingly, villagers ignored the signs and returned to tending their livestock, apparently forgetting that in 1994 Merapi had killed sixty people. It's our human tendency to ignore signs.

When Jesus left the temple at Jerusalem for the last time, His disciples asked what would signal His return to earth (Matthew 24:3). He told them many things to watch for, but He also warned that people would still be unprepared.

The apostle Peter told us that in the last days scoffers would say of Jesus's return: "Where is this 'coming' he promised? Ever since our ancestors died, everything goes on as it has since the beginning of creation" (2 Peter 3:4).

Scoffers are with us today, just as Peter warned. Are you among them? Or are you ready for the Lord Jesus to return? Ignoring these signs is even more dangerous than living in the shadow of the Fire Mountain.

C. P. Hia

God Promises
To Deal with Injustice

POETIC JUSTICE
ESTHER 3:2–11; 7:1–10

"It is mine to avenge; I will repay," says the Lord.
Romans 12:19

For nearly a year, a former publishing colleague lived under a cloud of fear that he would be fired. A new boss in the department, for reasons unknown, began filling his personnel file with negative comments. Then on the day my friend expected to lose his job, the new boss was fired instead.

When the Israelites were taken as captives to Babylon, a Jew named Mordecai found himself in this kind of situation. Haman, the highest noble of King Xerxes, expected every royal official to kneel down and honor him, but Mordecai refused to bow to anyone but God (Esther 3:1–2). This outraged Haman, and he set out to destroy not only Mordecai but also every Jew in the whole Persian empire (vv. 5–6). Haman convinced Xerxes to sign a decree authorizing the destruction of all Jews and started building a gallows for the execution of Mordecai (5:14). But in a startling turn of events, Haman was executed on the gallows he had built for Mordecai, and the Jewish people were spared (7:9–10; 8).

In literature, this is called poetic justice. Not everyone gets justice in such dramatic fashion, but Scripture promises that God will one day avenge all injustice (Romans 12:19). While we wait, we are to do what we can to work for justice and leave the results in God's hands.

Julie Ackerman Link

God Promises

Holy Spirit Power

SCATTERED
ACTS 8:1-4

Those who had been scattered preached the word wherever they went.

Acts 8:4

If I had been among the early Christians forced to leave Jerusalem because of persecution (Acts 8:1), what would I have said to my new neighbors? Would I have reminisced about how much I missed my home church? Would I have complained about how hard it was on the kids to start over in a new place? Probably!

But there's no hint of complaint among those displaced believers—only an enthusiastic witness to Christ the risen Lord. After being "scattered throughout Judea and Samaria" they "preached the word wherever they went" (Acts 8:1, 4).

What began in Jerusalem on the Day of Pentecost was not tied to geography, peace, or prosperity. It was the Spirit in them fulfilling Jesus's promise in Acts 1:8, "You will receive power when the Holy Spirit comes on you; and you will be my witnesses in Jerusalem, and in all Judea and Samaria, and to the ends of the earth."

When God allows difficult circumstances in our lives—a lost job; a demanding family need; a relocation to another city, state, or country—can we see His hand and sense His power? May we be like those early Christians, accepting the Lord's leading and joyfully proclaiming His Word wherever we are.

David McCasland

God Promises

To Come Alongside Us

ON OUR SIDE
ROMANS 8:31–39

If God is for us, who can be against us?

Romans 8:31

A young Christian was working at his first job, the night shift at a refrigerator assembly plant, trying to earn money for Bible college. The people he worked with were pretty rough, and he was laughed at for being a Christian. The harassment occurred at every break and gradually became more and more vulgar.

One night was worse than the others. They were laughing at him, swearing, and mocking Jesus. He was about ready to quit. Then an older man sitting at the back of the room said, "That's enough! Find someone else to pick on." They immediately backed off. Later the older fellow said to the young man, "I saw that you were having a difficult time, and I wanted to let you know I'm on your side."

Maybe you're a Christian and are standing alone against others who do not know God. It seems as if Satan is winning. The Lord may send a fellow believer to stand with you. But even if He doesn't, you can be confident that He is on your side. He demonstrated that by sending His Son Jesus to die in your place on the cross. You can never be separated from His love and care (Romans 8:38–39).

With assurance you can now say, "If God is for us, who can be against us?" (v. 31).

David Egner

God Promises
Sufficient Grace

THE STRONG WEAK PEOPLE
2 CORINTHIANS 12:1–10

I will boast all the more gladly about my weaknesses,
so that Christ's power may rest on me.

2 Corinthians 12:9

If there is anything we love to hate more than the arrogance of others, it would have to be the awareness of our own weakness. We detest it so much that we invent ways to cover our personal inadequacy.

Even the apostle Paul needed to be reminded of his own frailty. He was jabbed time and again by what he called "a thorn in my flesh" (2 Corinthians 12:7). He didn't name his thorn, but J. Oswald Sanders reminds us that whatever it was, "it hurt, humiliated, and restricted Paul." Three times he begged the Lord to take it away, but his request was not granted. Instead, he used his thorn to tap into God's all-sufficient grace. The Lord promised, "My grace is sufficient for you, for my power is made perfect in weakness" (v. 9).

Courageously, Paul began to "own" his weakness and put the Lord's grace to the test, a pathway that Sanders calls "a gradual educative process" in the apostle's life. Sanders notes that eventually Paul no longer regarded his thorn as a "limiting handicap" but as a "heavenly advantage." And his advantage was this: When he was weak in himself, he was strong in the Lord.

As we accept our weaknesses, in Christ we can be strong weak people.

Joanie Yoder

God Promises
Love and Faithfulness

ANGRY FLOODS
PSALM 93

---

*The seas have lifted up, LORD, the seas have lifted up their voice;
the seas have lifted up their pounding waves.*
Psalm 93:3

Trouble comes our way, according to Psalm 93, in relentless waves that surge and pound against our souls and break upon them with furious force. "The seas have lifted up, LORD, the seas have lifted up their voice" and they are deafening (v. 3).

Yet above the tempest we hear the psalmist's refrain: "Mightier than the thunder of the great waters, mightier than the breakers of the sea—the LORD on high is mighty" (v. 4).

Indeed, "the Lord reigns"! He is clothed with majesty and strength. He sits as King, exalted higher than the waves that rise above us, deeper than their immeasurable depths, greater than their strongest surge. The storm is in His all-powerful hands: "The world is established, firm and secure," for His rule over it was established long ago (v. 1). He rules the raging of the sea; "even the wind and the waves obey him" (Mark 4:41). He speaks and they are still.

The storm will not last forever. Yet, while it rages, you can cling to the Lord's promises of love and faithfulness, for His "statutes . . . stand firm" (Psalm 93:5). Waves of trouble and grief may sweep over you, but you will not be swept away. He "is able to keep you from stumbling" (Jude v. 24). Our Father in heaven is holding your hand.

David Roper

God Promises

And We Remain Patient

INSTANT NOTHING
HEBREWS 6:9-20

*We do not want you to become lazy, but to imitate those who
through faith and patience inherit what has been promised.*

Hebrews 6:12

In a lighthearted *Time* magazine essay, Sarah Vowell tells that she signed
up for a three-hour, $39 course called "Instant Piano for Hopelessly Busy
People." Regretting that she hadn't stuck with music lessons as a child, she
made it her goal to learn to play one piece by memory. What she found was
that even this seemingly simple task required hours of practice. There is no
such thing as "instant" piano. But as she continued to practice, a recognizable melody began to emerge from her fingers.

Her experience is a good reminder that though we often desire
immediate results in our walk of faith, this too is a matter of patient
practice. The writer of Hebrews encouraged Christians to be spiritually
diligent throughout their lives. He urged them not to become sluggish
but to "imitate those who through faith and patience inherit what has
been promised" (Hebrews 6:12).

Our efforts do not make God's promises come true. But like Abraham,
who patiently endured, we focus on the power and integrity of the
living God, whose promises give us hope, "this hope as an anchor for
the soul" (v. 19).

Since there are no instant results, let's keep practicing the Lord's
instructions as we walk patiently by faith toward the fulfillment of all He
has promised.

David McCasland

God Promises
An Abundance of Things

SOMETHING FOR THE SOUL
PSALM 119:9–16

I have hidden your word in my heart
that I might not sin against you.

Psalm 119:11

Filled to the brim with inspiring anecdotes and stories, the books in the series *Chicken Soup for the Soul* quickly became bestsellers. It's no wonder. A title that includes "chicken soup" brings back memories of childhood, stuffed-up noses, and scratchy throats—a time when only a warm blanket and Mom's steaming chicken and rice soup will bring about relief.

Scientific evidence now indicates that Mom was pretty smart. Chicken soup is beneficial for fighting colds. It's also one of the foods that people describe as "comfort food."

When it's not my body but my heart that is aching, I long for the comfort of God's Word: soothing words like "Cast all your anxiety on him because he cares for you" (1 Peter 5:7); assuring words that nothing can "separate us from the love of God that is in Christ Jesus our Lord" (Romans 8:38–39).

The Bible—the world's all-time bestseller—is filled with promises, reminders, challenges, and knowledge of God. When you're feeling discouraged, try ladling up a big serving of God's Word. Having a Bible within reach (or better yet, Scripture hidden in your heart) infinitely trumps a bowl of Mom's chicken soup. It will warm your heart and begin your healing.

Cindy Hess Kasper

God Promises
That He'll Help Us Resist Temptation

GOD'S RESTRAINT
PSALM 76:1–12

*Surely your wrath against mankind brings you praise,
and the survivors of your wrath are restrained.*

Psalm 76:10

Augustine said that God "judged it better to bring good out of evil, than not to permit any evil to exist." Thus God takes the worst evil that men and women can do to us and turns it into good. Even the wrath of ungodly men brings praise to Him (Psalm 76:10).

God has not promised that your life will be easy—indeed it may not be. But He has promised to sustain you in your struggle and uphold you with His mighty arm. If you trust Him, He will empower you to make your way bravely through extraordinary difficulty with faith, hope, and love. The trials God permits in your life will lead to His praise and glory, if only you will abide in Him.

Furthermore, there will be a restraint and a respite. The Hebrew text is somewhat obscure in Psalm 76:10. Literally it reads, "Surely the wrath of man will praise You; the remnant of wrath [God] will bind." God will use men's wrath to bring glory and praise to himself, but when that purpose is fulfilled He will then restrain it.

God will not allow you to be pressed beyond endurance. That is His sure promise. When the lesson has been learned, when the revelation of God's glory is complete and your soul has been tried and proven—then God will raise His hand and save you. He will say, "No more."

David Roper

God Promises

To Remember Our Sorrows

THE GIFT OF TEARS
JOHN 11:32-44

Jesus wept.
John 11:35

I called a longtime friend when his mother died. She had been a close friend of my mother, and now both had passed on. As we spoke, our conversation slipped easily into a cycle of emotion—tears of sorrow now that Beth was gone and tears of laughter as we recalled the caring and fun person she had been.

Many of us have experienced that strange crossover from crying one moment and laughing the next. It's an amazing gift that emotions of both sorrow and joy can provide a physical release in this way.

Since we are made in God's image (Genesis 1:26) and humor is such an integral part of almost every culture, I imagine that Jesus must have had a wonderful sense of humor. But we know that He also knew the pain of grief. When his friend Lazarus died, Jesus saw Mary weeping, and "he was deeply moved in spirit and troubled." A short time later, He too began to weep (John 11:33–35).

Our ability to express our emotions with tears is a gift, and God keeps track of each tear we cry. Psalm 56:8 says, "You keep track of all my sorrows. You have collected all my tears in your bottle. You have recorded each one in your book" (NLT). But one day—we are promised (Revelation 7:17)—"God will wipe away every tear from [our] eyes."

Cindy Hess Kasper

God Promises
To Teach and Instruct

INSTINCTS
PSALM 32

I will instruct you and teach you in the way you should go;
I will counsel you with my loving eye on you.

Psalm 32:8

Flying into a storm is a dangerous experience. The temptation is to fly by your instincts, or, as aviators say, "by the seat of your pants." But as any pilot will tell you, that's a prescription for disaster. If you rely on your feelings and instincts, you become disoriented, thinking the plane is going up when it's actually going down. Thankfully, the instrument panel is set to magnetic north and can be trusted every time. Letting your instruments guide you, even when it feels like they're wrong, helps ensure safety in the storm.

We all face storms that threaten to confuse and disorient us. It may be a call from the doctor's office, a friend who has betrayed you, or a shattered dream. Those are the times to be especially careful. When you are blinded by life's disappointments, don't trust your instincts. Flying by the seat of your pants in the storms of life can lead to despair, confusion, and vengeful responses that make matters worse. God wants to guide you, and His Word is packed with wisdom and insights for living. His "word is a lamp for my feet, a light on my path" (Psalm 119:105). Where He leads is always right!

Go to your Bible, and trust God to guide you. He promises, "I will instruct you and teach you in the way you should go" (Psalm 32:8).

Joe Stowell

God Promises
Wisdom

WISE BEHAVIOR
1 SAMUEL 18:1–5

*Whatever mission Saul sent him on, David was so
successful that Saul gave him a high rank in the army.*

1 Samuel 18:5

Four times in 1 Samuel 18, the writer tells us that David "behaved wisely" (vv. 5, 14, 15, 30 NKJV). In fact, he behaved "more wisely than all the servants of Saul, so that his name became highly esteemed" (v. 30 NKJV).

The phrase "highly esteemed" suggests an unusual respect. David was honored by all the people, but more significantly he was highly respected by those in Saul's court who were impressed by his noble character.

As Christians come to know Jesus better through obedience to His Word, they will begin to display qualities of character that set them apart from others, for true wisdom is to live in a Christlike way. It is more than common sense; it is uncommon behavior.

James said, "The wisdom that comes from heaven is first of all pure; then peace-loving, considerate, submissive, full of mercy and good fruit, impartial and sincere" (3:17). This gracious way of making our way through the world can come only "from heaven."

David's experience can be our experience. God's promise to him is also true for believers today. He said, "I will instruct you [cause you to be wise] and teach you in the way you should go" (Psalm 32:8).

Are we learning to behave wisely?

David Roper

God Promises

A Surprising Visit by Jesus

I'M READY
LUKE 12:22-40

*Be ready, because the Son of Man will come
at an hour when you do not expect him.*

Luke 12:40

A friend of mine who has lived all her life in California goes to sleep every night with her shoes and a flashlight under the bed. When she was a child, her father required every family member to be ready to leave the house if an earthquake were to come during the night.

"During a tremor," my friend says, "windows shatter and electricity is lost. With shoes I can walk on broken glass and with a light I can find my way in the dark. I never go to bed without them. I'm ready."

When Jesus spoke to His followers about His return, He said, "Be ready, because the Son of Man will come at an hour when you do not expect him" (Luke 12:40).

What does it mean for a Christian to be ready for Christ's return? Jesus said that instead of worrying about material things, we are to trust God's provision and make His kingdom our priority (vv. 22–31). Instead of fear that grasps, we are to demonstrate faith that gives (vv. 32–34). Like faithful servants, we should expect our Master at any time, because He will return at an unexpected hour (vv. 35–40).

Jesus promised to return, and He told us how to live as we wait for His coming. Our lives, more than our lips, are to say, "I'm ready!"

David McCasland

That He Works All Things Out in His Way

NO EXPLANATION NEEDED
JOB 42

You asked, "Who is this that obscures my plans without knowledge?" Surely I spoke of things I did not understand, things too wonderful for me to know.

Job 42:3

A Christian who believed God had led him to take a daring step of faith remarked, "If God doesn't give me success in this matter, He'll certainly have a lot of explaining to do!"

It's easy to judge this man's words, but have you ever said, "When I get to heaven, I certainly expect God to explain why some of my prayers were not answered and why tragedies were not always prevented!"

In Romans 8:28, Paul didn't promise that all circumstances and events would be explained—if, indeed, we could comprehend the explanation! Instead, he promised that "in all things God works for the good of those who love him, who have been called according to his purpose."

The story of Job reassures us that questioning God is common to human experience. Yet, when Job demanded that God justify His lack of intervention in his trials, He didn't comply. Instead, He bombarded Job with His own searching questions (Job 38–41). The Almighty does not have to explain himself, nor is He required to reveal His grand design. He reveals himself and His plans, in His way and in His time.

Thoroughly humbled, Job admitted, "I spoke if things I did not understand, things to wonderful for me to know." Like Job, will you now trust God—no explanation required?

Joanie Yoder

God Promises
Future Glory

TOO MUCH WITH US
ROMANS 8:14-25

*The Spirit you received brought about your adoption
to sonship. And by him we cry, "Abba, Father."*

Romans 8:15

William Wordsworth wrote, "The world is too much with us." He meant that too often we get caught up in the world's mad rush and fail to appreciate God's creation. But it's also easy to feel that the world is too much with us when we see people suffer for their faith in God.

The world is too much with us when we read the tragic story of a missionary family in India devastated by the murder of the father and two sons at the hands of people who hate Christians. And this world can overwhelm us when we think of three missionary families in Colombia whose fathers and husbands were kidnapped and held for years. Added to these stories could be your own account of unjust treatment because of your faith. It happens in every country of the world.

Despite these sad situations, though, we have hope. We have the hope that comes from being God's children (Romans 8:16–17). We can call our Creator, "Abba, Father" (v. 15). We have His promise of future glory—a glory that far overshadows "our present sufferings" (v. 18).

Are the burdens of this world too much with you? Look to your heavenly Father. He lovingly offers help and hope to His struggling children.

Dave Branon

God Promises

Power in Crisis

GOD'S STRENGTH, NOT OURS
PSALM 46

God is our refuge and strength, an ever-present help in trouble.

Psalm 46:1

The truth that God supplies all our needs stands as a fitting motto for every believer in Jesus Christ. Even in severe trial, saints of all ages have found comfort and support in the assurance that God's strength is more than adequate for every adversity.

An American ocean liner encountered a severe storm while crossing the Atlantic. One of the sailors was tending his duties on deck when he was washed into the sea. Instantly the cry went up, "Man overboard!" A crewman quickly grabbed a life preserver and threw it over the stern. In a few moments he felt a tug on the lifeline. Peering into the darkness, he shouted to the man in the water, "Have you got the line?" A faint reply came back, "No, but the line has me!" The exhausted sailor had slipped the lifesaver over his shoulders and under his arms, realizing he didn't have enough strength to hold on to it.

As Christians, we experience storms and trials in life that sometimes overwhelm us. We come to the end of our own strength. Even though our faith may be weak or we feel we have no faith left, He supports us and lifts us out of despair.

We can praise the Lord that we do not have to hang on when the waves of distress and sorrow roll over us! He holds us! By leaning on God and trusting the promises of His Word, we can survive every crisis.

Henry Bosch

God Promises
To Be with Us in Sorrow

UNIMAGINABLE
PSALM 23

Even though I walk through the darkest valley,
I will fear no evil, for you are with me.
Psalm 23:4

Bart Millard penned a megahit in 2001 when he wrote, "I Can Only Imagine." The song pictures how amazing it will be to be in Christ's presence. Millard's lyrics offered comfort to our family the next year when our seventeen-year-old daughter, Melissa, died in a car accident, and we imagined what it was like for her to be with the Lord.

But the word *imagine* spoke to me in a different way in the days following Mell's death. As fathers of Melissa's friends approached me, full of concern and pain, they said, "I can't imagine what you're going through."

Their expressions were helpful, showing that they were grappling with our loss in an empathetic way—finding it unimaginable.

David pinpointed the depth of great loss when he described walking through "the darkest valley" (Psalm 23:4). The death of a loved one certainly is that, and we sometimes have no idea how we're going to navigate the darkness. We can't imagine ever being able to come out on the other side.

But as God promised to be with us in our darkest valley now, He also provides great hope for the future by assuring us that beyond the valley we'll be in His presence. For the believer, to be "away from the body" means being present with Him (2 Corinthians 5:8). That can help us navigate the unimaginable as we imagine our future reunion with Him and our loved ones.

Dave Branon

God Promises
To Provide Forgiveness

WAITING GAME
ISAIAH 30:12–19

How gracious he will be when you cry for help!
As soon as he hears, he will answer you.

Isaiah 30:19

We are sometimes slow to go to God for forgiveness. We carry our guilt around for days, weeks, or even longer before dealing with our sin. Why do we wait so long?

Some of us may feel that going to God immediately makes forgiveness cheap. Others may consider it arrogant to expect God to forgive.

In Isaiah 30:18–19, the Lord told stubborn, unrepentant Israel that He was waiting to be gracious to them. He promised that the moment He heard their cry He would be merciful and answer them.

God's eagerness to forgive sin became most clear through Christ's suffering on the cross. His death was sufficient to pay the penalty for sin so He could offer forgiveness to everyone in the whole world (1 John 2:2). Therefore, we can "approach God's throne of grace with confidence, so that we may receive mercy and find grace to help us in our time of need" (Hebrews 4:16). The phrase "in our time of need" means "without delay."

Do you need forgiveness? God is waiting for you to receive it. If you'll repent and come boldly to Him without delay, He won't keep you waiting. At the sound of your voice, He'll be very gracious to you.

Joanie Yoder

God Promises
That His Word Is Eternal

THE BOOK THAT ENDURES
ISAIAH 40:1-8

The grass withers and the flowers fall,
but the word of our God endures forever.

Isaiah 40:8

The Bible, God's written Word, has withstood the passing of the centuries and the criticism of its detractors. Inspired by the Holy Spirit, it is the rev elation of truth and tells how man can have eternal life. Other books may quickly rise to popularity, but they soon disappear from the bookshelves and are replaced by new titles. Authors with great insight strive to make their works last for centuries, but there is no guarantee that what they say is truth and will endure. The Bible, however, will stand forever.

In 1874 the Scriptures were under severe attack by critics, and John W. Haley published a defense entitled *Alleged Discrepancies of the Bible*. In the preface he wrote, "Finally, let it be remembered that the Bible is neither dependent upon nor affected by the success or failure of my book. Whatever may become of the latter, whatever may be the verdict passed upon it by an intelligent public, the Bible will stand. In the ages yet to be, when its present assailants and defenders are moldering in the dust, and when our very names are forgotten, [God's Word] will be, as it has been during the centuries past, the guide and solace of millions." How true!

In the unsure world in which we live, we sometimes wonder if anything we read—whether in print or online—can be believed. Then turn to the Bible. Behind it stands God's guarantee that it will outlast the passing of time and the attacks of its critics. It has already endured for thousands of years; and we have the promise that it will "stand forever." Put your trust in the message of the Book that endures.

David Egner

DECEMBER 11

God Promises
That He Will Give Us Guidance

GUIDANCE FROM ABOVE
PSALM 25:4–15

Show me your ways, LORD, teach me your paths.
Psalm 25:4

The Global Positioning System (GPS) is changing the way we work, travel, and play. Using the signals from multiple satellites, an inexpensive GPS receiver can compute your location anywhere in the world. Using the information can help a lost hiker return to camp, enable a driver to locate a house in a strange city, or guide commercial fishermen back to the place of a big catch. In a very real sense, it is "guidance from above."

But it helps only the person who believes the information and acts on it. What if a person viewed the GPS readout and said, "I can't possibly be where this says I am"? What good would it be if a person turned off the unit, jammed it in a pocket, and headed out on his own, saying, "I know I'm going east, even if this thing says I'm going south"?

In a similar way, God's guidance through the Bible benefits us only when we trust His Word and obey it. "He guides the humble in what is right," the psalmist wrote, "and teaches them his way. All the ways of the LORD are loving and faithful toward those who keep the demands of his covenant" (Psalm 25:9–10).

Remember, guidance from above is promised to all who will accept God's Word and follow His directions.

David McCasland

God Promises

Mountain Peaks of Assurance

BEYOND THE SHADOWS
PSALM 121

I lift up my eyes to the mountains—where does my help come from? My help comes from the LORD, the Maker of heaven and earth.

Psalm 121:1–2

I love the view of the Rockies from Denver. In the foreground are the foothills, and behind them are the high mountains. On a clear day, one can see Long's Peak, Mount Evans, and others reaching altitudes of 14,000 feet, their tops covered with snow.

Early one morning, as I looked west to the mountains, I saw a sight that filled me with wonder. Because of a layer of low, gray clouds, the foothills lay in heavy shadows. Snow was probably falling. The foothills were dark and ominous, enough to discourage any potential traveler. But beyond them, the white, snow-capped peaks of the high mountains were glistening in the bright sunlight. They seemed to say, "Once you get through the shadows, you'll be all right."

As I looked at that sight, I thought how much it is like our spiritual journey. We are pilgrim followers of Christ. Ahead we may be able to see only the foothill shadows of hardship, illness, disappointment, trouble. The way appears foreboding and difficult. But then we lift our eyes higher. There, gleaming afar in the sunlight, are the glorious mountain peaks of God's promises.

Where are you right now? In gloomy foothills, clouded in darkness? Don't despair. Keep moving upward. Sunlit mountain peaks lie just beyond.

David Egner

DECEMBER 13

God Promises

His Continual Care and Concern

NOT ABANDONED
ISAIAH 49:13–16

*I will not forget you! See, I have
engraved you on the palms of my hands.*
Isaiah 49:15–16

Years ago, while my husband and I were visiting the Smithsonian Air and Space Museum in Washington, DC, we noticed a baby stroller by itself with no one nearby. We assumed that the parents had left it there because it was too bulky and were now carrying their child. But as we approached, we saw a sleeping baby inside. Where was a parent . . . a sibling . . . a babysitter? We hung around for quite some time before hailing a museum official. No one had shown up to claim that precious child! The last we saw of him, he was being wheeled away to a safe place.

That experience made me think about what it's like to be abandoned. It's an overwhelming feeling that no one cares anything about you. It's a real and excruciatingly painful feeling. But even though people may abandon us, God's love and presence are assured. The Lord promises that He will never leave us (Deuteronomy 31:8). He will be with us wherever we go, "always, to the very end of the age" (Matthew 28:20).

The Lord will never falter in His commitment to His children. Even if we have been abandoned by others, we can find confidence in His promise that nothing will ever "separate us from the love of God that is in Christ Jesus our Lord" (Romans 8:35–39).

Cindy Hess Kasper

DECEMBER 14

God Promises
That the Godly Will Flourish

OF TIME AND TREES
PSALM 1

*That person is like a tree planted by streams of water,
which yields its fruit in season and whose leaf
does not wither—whatever they do prospers.*

Psalm 1:3

People who don't want to wait four decades for a globe Norway maple to grow in their front yard can buy a thirty-foot specimen from a New York nursery for $42,000. A fifty-foot European beech is a "bargain" for only $20,000. In spite of the prices, the country's leading nurseries report soaring sales of mature trees.

As one customer put it: "I can't wait for a banana to ripen. I only buy them bright yellow. There's no patience for watching a tree grow."

We humans are always in a hurry, looking for shortcuts to skirt the process and grasp the product. And sometimes we expect instant maturity in our Christian walk and growth in faith. What a contrast to the enormous leisure of God in His dealings with us!

The psalmist affirmed God's promise that the person who delights in His Word will "be like a tree planted by streams of water, which yields its fruit in season" (Psalm 1:2–3). A growing Christian, whether a new believer or a seasoned saint, is like a healthy tree—planted, nourished, and fruitful.

If our roots are in God's Word and our hearts are drawing sustenance from Him, we will flourish. And growth toward maturity brings joy to the God of patience.

David McCasland

God Promises

That Joy Will Replace Our Sorrow

WAITING FOR JOY
2 CORINTHIANS 4:8–18

Weeping may stay for the night, but rejoicing comes in the morning.
Psalm 30:5

A large part of life centers around anticipation. How much we would lose if we were to wake up one day to the unexpected announcement: "Christmas in ten minutes!" The enjoyment in many of life's events is built on the fact that we have time to anticipate them.

Christmas, vacations, mission trips, sporting events. They all grow in value because of the hours we spend looking forward to them—eagerly running through our minds the fun, challenges, and excitement they'll bring.

I think about the value of anticipation and the thrill it can bring to the human heart when I read Psalm 30:5, "Weeping may stay for the night, but rejoicing comes in the morning." The psalmist is declaring the comforting idea that our earthly sorrow lasts but a short time when compared with the anticipated joy that will begin in heaven and last forever. Paul pens a similar idea in 2 Corinthians 4:17, where we discover that our "light and momentary troubles" lead to a glory of eternal value.

For now, those of us who weep can dwell on hope instead of hopelessness and anticipation instead of sorrow. It may be nighttime in our hearts, but just ahead lies the dawn of eternity. And with it, God promises the endless joy of heavenly morning.

Dave Branon

God Promises

A Secure Future

AS GOOD AS HIS WORD
HEBREWS 10:19–25

He who promised is faithful.
Hebrews 10:23

Insurance agent Ken Specht had called on Medicus Robertson at the electronics store where he worked. Robertson agreed to purchase a $5,000 life insurance policy, which would double in value in case of his accidental death. Mr. Specht said that his company would cover the client until the formal policy application could be issued.

Just then an irate customer burst through the door and shot Robertson, killing him instantly. The insurance company later paid the widow $10,000, minus the $10.50 premium Robinson had not paid. Instead of seeking a legal loophole, the agent kept his word.

We who have put our trust in Jesus Christ for our salvation can be sure that God will keep His word. Because "he who promised is faithful" (Hebrews 10:23), the author of Hebrews encouraged believers to boldly "draw near to God," confident that He has accepted us and our sins have been forgiven (v. 22). And we are to encourage one another to be faithful to Him because we know that He will one day return for us (vv. 24–25).

We have a hope that is based on the trustworthy promises of God. Our future is secure. God has always proven himself to be as good as His word.

David Egner

DECEMBER 17

God Promises

Tranquility

PEACE IN THE STORM
JOHN 14:21–27

You will keep in perfect peace those whose
minds are steadfast, because they trust in you.

Isaiah 26:3

How do you face emergencies? If you keep your mind centered on the Lord, you can have a deep, settled peace whatever the problem. Late nineteenth-century preacher A. B. Simpson, commenting on Isaiah 26:3, remarked, "The Christian's rest is not the result of passive inaction. Rather, it is an active reliance on the mighty and everlasting arms of God." In other words, being content depends on more than good feelings or a trouble-free environment. Peace comes as we build our lives on God's promises despite the intensity of outward conflicts.

A contest was held in which artists were invited to paint a picture of perfect peace. The judges eventually narrowed the number of competitors to two. The first had created a scene of a quiet mountain lake. The second depicted a thundering waterfall with the branch of a birch tree bending over the foam. On the fork of that limb, wet with spray, a robin sat undisturbed on her nest. The first picture spoke of tranquility, but the second won the prize because it showed in dramatic detail that absolute calmness can be found in the midst of turbulent surroundings. Yes, it is easy to remain unruffled when everything is quiet and serene. But to rest while the storm is raging—that is "perfect peace."

As you face the trials and testings of life, turn your anxieties over to the Lord. Center your thoughts on Him and the precious promises of His Word, and you'll experience a peace that transcends all understanding (Philippians 4:7).

Henry Bosch

DECEMBER 18

God Promises

Light in the Darkness

EVERLASTING HOPE
PSALM 146

*Blessed are those whose help is the God of Jacob,
whose hope is in the LORD their God.*

Psalm 146:5

The week before Christmas, two months after my mom died, holiday shopping and decorating sat at the bottom of my priority list. I resisted my husband's attempts to comfort me as I grieved the loss of our family's faith-filled matriarch. I sulked as our son, Xavier, stretched and stapled strands of Christmas lights onto the inside walls of our home. Without a word, he plugged in the cord before he and his dad left for work.

As the colorful bulbs blinked, God gently drew me out of my darkness. No matter how painful the circumstances, my hope remained secure in the light of God's truth, which always reveals His unchanging character.

Psalm 146 affirms what God reminded me on that difficult morning: My endless "hope is in the LORD," my helper, my mighty and merciful God (v. 5). As Creator of all, He "remains faithful forever" (v. 6). He "upholds the cause of the oppressed," protecting us and providing for us (v. 7). "The LORD lifts up those who are bowed down" (v. 8). He "watches over" us, "sustains" us, and will always be King (vv. 9–10).

Sometimes, when Christmas rolls around, our days will overflow with joyful moments. But sometimes, we'll face loss, experience hurt, or feel alone. At all times, though, God promises to be our light in the darkness, offering us tangible help and everlasting hope.

Xochitl Dixon

God Promises

Responsibilities in His Future Kingdom

PAPER CROWNS
1 CORINTHIANS 6:1–6

The Lord's people will judge the world.

1 Corinthians 6:2

After a holiday meal at my house, everyone opened party favors filled with candy, small toys, and confetti. But there was something else in the favors—a paper crown for each of us. We couldn't resist trying them on, and we smiled at each other as we sat around the table. For just a moment, we were kings and queens, even if our kingdom was a dining room littered with the remnants of our dinner.

This sparked a memory of a Bible promise I don't often think about. In the next life, all believers will share ruling authority with Jesus. Paul mentions this in 1 Corinthians 6 where he asks, "Do you not know that the Lord's people will judge the world?" (v. 2). Paul referenced this future privilege because he wanted to inspire believers to settle disputes peacefully on earth. They had been suing each other and consequently harming the reputation of other believers in their community.

We become better at resolving conflict as the Holy Spirit produces self-control, gentleness, and patience within us. By the time Jesus returns and completes the Spirit's work in our lives (1 John 3:2–3), we'll be ready for our eventual role as "a kingdom and priests to serve our God, and . . . reign on the earth" (Revelation 5:10). Let's hold on to this promise that glitters in Scripture like a diamond set in a crown of gold.

Jennifer Benson Schuldt

God Promises

Love Made Complete

THE BIRTH OF CHRISTMAS
LUKE 1:26–38

---

*When Joseph woke up, he did what the angel of the
Lord commanded him and took Mary home as his wife.*

Matthew 1:24

When the angel Gabriel appeared to Mary and then to shepherds with
good news for the world (Luke 1:26–27; 2:10), was it good news to this
teenage girl? Perhaps Mary was thinking: How do I explain my pregnancy
to my family? Will my fiancé, Joseph, call off the betrothal? What will the
townspeople say? Even if my life is spared, how will I survive as a mother
all alone?

When Joseph learned about Mary's pregnancy, he was troubled. He
had three options. Go ahead with the marriage, divorce her publicly and
allow her to be scorned by friends and family, or break off the engagement
quietly. Joseph chose option three (Matthew 1:19), but God intervened.
He told Joseph in a dream, "Do not be afraid to take Mary home as your
wife, because what is conceived in her is from the Holy Spirit" (v. 20).

For Mary and Joseph, Christmas began with submitting themselves
to God in spite of the unthinkable emotional challenges before them.
They entrusted themselves to God and in doing so demonstrated for us
the promise of 1 John 2:5: "If anyone obeys his word, love for God is truly
made complete in them."

May God's love fill our hearts this Christmas season—and every
day—as we walk with Him in obedience.

Albert Lee

DECEMBER 21

God Promises
Joy to the Whole World

HEART OF JOY
JOHN 15:1–11

*I have told you this so that my joy may be in you
and that your joy may be complete.*

John 15:11

While waiting in the gate area of Singapore's Changi Airport to board my flight, I noticed a young family—mom, dad, and son. The area was crowded, and they were looking for a place to sit. Suddenly, the little boy began loudly singing "Joy to the World." He was about six years old, so I was pretty impressed that he knew all the words.

What captured my attention even more was the look on the boy's face—his beaming smile matched the words he was singing as he proclaimed to everyone at the gate the joy of the Christ who has come.

This joy is not limited to exuberant children nor should it be confined to the Christmas season. The overflowing joy of knowing Christ's presence in our lives was one of the themes of Jesus's final teaching with His disciples the night before He died on the cross. He told them of His extravagant love for them—that He loved them as the Father loved Him (John 15:9). After sharing what this eternal relationship looks like, Jesus said, "I have told you this so that my joy may be in you and that your joy may be complete" (v. 11).

What a promise! Through Jesus Christ our hearts can be filled with joy—real joy!

Bill Crowder

God Promises

Joy Forevermore

JOY

LUKE 2:8–12

I bring you good news that will cause great joy for all the people.

Luke 2:10

After Adam and Eve disobeyed God, joy was lost. God expelled them from their garden home to prevent something worse from happening. If they had eaten from the tree of life after eating from the tree of the knowledge of good and evil, they would have lived forever in their misery.

Life outside the garden was not easy. Adam and Eve had to work hard for their food. The reality of death was everywhere, and animals preyed on one another. Even worse, the couple's firstborn son murdered his younger brother. What could be worse? Sin had pierced their lives, and the couple could not stop joy from draining out.

But God had a plan to restore joy. Joy was lost in the garden of Eden when death came, but joy returned through birth—the birth of God's own Son. "I bring you good news that will cause great joy for all the people" (Luke 2:10). Jesus grew up to heal the sick, give sight to the blind, and raise the dead. But this was just a taste of things to come. God entered our world, experienced our sorrow, and conquered death, giving us hope that He will keep His promise to end pain and eliminate sorrow and death (John 11:25–26; 1 Corinthians 15:3–4; Revelation 21:4). No wonder Christmas is the season of joy!

Julie Ackerman Link

God Promises

Jesus and Salvation

A PROMISE FULFILLED
MATTHEW 1:18–25

*She will give birth to a son, and you are to give him the
name Jesus, because he will save his people from their sins.*

Matthew 1:21

In baseball's off-season, teams' general managers concentrate on trading
players to set themselves up for a winning season the next year. But if you
are a fan of teams that have losing records year after year, you don't expect
much. So, when your sad-sack team makes grand promises about a newly
acquired player, you have your doubts. Some team official might confidently suggest that the team is now headed for the World Series, but you
are skeptical. It sounds like a promise that most likely he can't deliver on.

No doubt the Jews of Jesus's day, who were living under the oppressive
thumb of Rome, had to wonder if God would ever make good on His
promise to send a Deliverer to forgive sin and restore the glory of Israel
(Isaiah 1:26; 53:12; 61). God had long ago promised one, but the people
hadn't heard a word from Him in four hundred years. But then, at just the
right moment, the angel announced to Joseph that Mary would give birth
to a Son who would "save his people from their sins" (Matthew 1:21).

Christmas proves that God is a promise-keeping God! He said that
He would send a Deliverer, and He did. Your sin is not beyond the reach
of this promise. He is ready and waiting to forgive your sins—all of them.

Joe Stowell

God Promises
He'll be with Us Always

IMMANUEL
ISAIAH 8:1-10

The virgin will conceive and give birth to a son, and they
will call him Immanuel (which means "God with us").

Matthew 1:23

Since that first Christmas day two thousand years ago, the assurance that God is with His people has taken on new meaning. Before Jesus was born, the Israelites were assured that even in judgment they could have hope because God was with them (Isaiah 8:8, 10). Yet they didn't know God as fully as we can today.

We have a great advantage because through reading the New Testament we can see the glory of God "in the face of Christ" (2 Corinthians 4:6). And we can sense His presence in all situations of life because He is made real to us by the Holy Spirit (Romans 8:10–16).

When I need to be reassured that God is with me, I think about Jesus as He is revealed in the New Testament. I recall how He took little children in His arms and blessed them (Matthew 19:13–15). Then I think of His crucifixion, which reminds me of all He endured to be my Savior (27:27–54). Finally, I reflect on His promise, "I am with you always, to the very end of the age" (28:20).

The birth of Jesus gave new significance to the name Immanuel, which means "God with us" (1:23). Because He lived among us, died for us, and sent His Spirit to indwell us, we can rejoice!

Herb Vander Lugt

The Help of the Holy Spirit

UNOPENED GIFTS
JOHN 14:12-31

*I will ask the Father, and he will give you
another advocate to help you and be with you forever.*
John 14:16

Can you imagine a child on Christmas morning leaving his presents unopened? Yet millions of people are doing something like that by ignoring or rejecting Jesus Christ as their Savior. Everyone has a gift with a tag that reads: TO: (your name) FROM: God. But it can be opened only by repentance and faith.

God hasn't given us just one gift, however. He singled out a second gift-giving occasion. At Christmastime, we celebrate God's gift of His Son to the world. But on the Day of Pentecost, He and His Son together gave to believers another gift—the Holy Spirit (John 14:16; 16:7).

Again, imagine a child at Christmas who opens just one package but leaves all the others tightly wrapped. Today the Holy Spirit indwells every believer, yet we often fail to make full use of all that He has given to us. If we ask Him, the Holy Spirit will lead us into a better understanding of God's Word, give us the assurance of God's care and keeping power, and transform us into Christ's likeness.

This Christmas, let's consider the significance of the Holy Spirit's coming and ask the Lord to help us experience all of His benefits more fully.

Dennis DeHaan

DECEMBER 26

God Promises
Light and Life through Jesus

THE VIEW FROM 400 MILES
JOHN 1:1-14

The true light that gives light to everyone was coming into the world.

John 1:9

"My perspective on Earth changed dramatically the very first time I went into space," says Space Shuttle astronaut Charles Frank Bolden Jr. From four hundred miles above the Earth, all looked peaceful and beautiful to him. Yet Bolden recalled later that as he passed over the Middle East, he was "shaken into reality" when he considered the ongoing conflict there at the time. During an interview with film producer Jared Leto, Bolden spoke of that moment as a time when he saw the Earth with a sense of how it ought to be—and then sensed a challenge to do all he could to make it better.

When Jesus was born in Bethlehem, the world was not the way God intended it. Into this moral and spiritual darkness Jesus came bringing life and light to all (John 1:4). Even though the world didn't recognize Him, "to all who did receive him, to those who believed in his name, he gave the right to become children of God" (v. 12).

When life is not the way it ought to be, we are deeply saddened—when families break up, children go hungry, and the world wages war. But God promises that through faith in Christ anyone can begin to move in a new direction.

The Christmas season reminds us that Jesus, the Savior, gives the gift of life and light to everyone who will receive and follow Him.

David McCasland

God Promises
To Answer Prayer

MOUNTAINS CAN MOVE
MARK 11:20–24

"Have faith in God," Jesus answered.
Mark 11:22

A familiar slogan about prayer is, "Prayer changes things." But prayer doesn't do this—God does. Some people think that prayer itself is the source of power, so they "try prayer," hoping "it will work" for them. In Mark 11, Jesus disclosed one of the secrets behind all true prayer: "Have faith in God." Not faith in faith, not faith in prayer, but "faith in God" (v. 22).

Jesus told His disciples they could command a mountain to be cast into the sea, and if they believed it would happen, it would. Jesus then gave them His meaning behind that astonishing promise. He said, "Whatever you ask for in prayer, believe that you received it, and it will be yours" (v. 24). Jesus was speaking about answered prayer. We can ask and receive answers only if our asking is directed to God in faith and according to His will (1 John 5:14).

I've often wished that I could move mountains by faith. Having once lived in Switzerland, I'd like God to move the Alps into my backyard in England. But He has done something much more important: He has removed mountains of worry, fear, and resentment from my heart and cast them into oblivion through my faith in Him. He is still in the mountain-moving business! Have faith in God and pray!

Joanie Yoder

God Promises
To Help Us When We're Fearful

WHEN YOU ARE AFRAID
PSALM 56

When I am afraid, I put my trust in you.
Psalm 56:3

It was all-out war! The kids I hung around with were battling the kids who lived on the other side of Evanston Avenue. The weapons? Green apples. The stakes? Neighborhood pride and honor.

Then it happened. After an especially bitter green-apple battle, my mother sent me on an errand that would force me to ride my bike right down the street where most of the enemy lived. I was as terrified as a ten-year-old could be. My palms were sweaty. The skin on my back crawled. I was sure I would be discovered and attacked. I was petrified.

Psalm 56 describes how David felt when he was in a similar but far worse situation (1 Samuel 21:10–15). On the run from King Saul, he took refuge in enemy territory. He was in terrible danger and he knew it. But he also knew what to do in times of fear. He said, "When I am afraid, I put my trust in you" (v. 3). Then he wrote, "In God I trust and am not afraid" (v. 4).

David Egner

God Promises

To Calm Your Fear by Being with You

REARVIEW MIRROR REFLECTIONS
PSALM 111

For you make me glad by your deeds, Lord;
I sing for joy at what your hands have done.

Psalm 92:4

I've always thought that you can see the hand of God best in the rearview mirror. Looking back, it's easier to understand why He placed us in the home that He did; why He brought certain people and circumstances into and out of our lives; why He permitted difficulties and pain; why He took us to different places and put us in various jobs and careers.

In my own life, I get a lot of clarity (though not perfect clarity—that's heaven's joy!) about the wise and loving ways of God as I reflect on the ways He has managed my journey "by what [God's] hands have done" (Psalm 92:4). With the psalmist, it makes me glad and strikes a note of joy in my heart to see how often God has assisted, directed, and managed the outcomes so faithfully (Ps. 111).

Looking ahead, though, is not always so clear. Have you ever had that lost feeling when the road ahead seems twisted, foggy, and scary? Before you move into next year, stop and look in the rearview mirror of the year gone by, and joyfully realize that God meant it when He said, "'Never will I leave you; never will I forsake you.' So we say with confidence: 'The Lord is my helper; I will not be afraid'" (Hebrews 13:5–6).

With the promise of God's presence and help in mind, you can move ahead into the new year with utmost confidence.

Joe Stowell

DECEMBER 30

God Promises
His Faithful Care

POINT OF NO RETURN
DEUTERONOMY 11:7–12

*The eyes of the LORD your God are continually on
[the land] from the beginning of the year to its end.*
Deuteronomy 11:12

Longtime California pastor Ray Stedman once told his congregation: "On New Year's Eve we realize more than at any other time in our lives that we can never go back in time. . . . We can look back and remember, but we cannot retrace a single moment of the year that is past."

Stedman then referred to the Israelites as they stood on the edge of a new opportunity. After four decades of desert wanderings by their people, this new generation may have wondered if they had the faith and fortitude to possess the promised land.

Their leader, Moses, reminded them that they had seen "all these great things the LORD has done" (Deuteronomy 11:7) and that their destination was "a land the LORD your God cares for; the eyes of the LORD your God are continually on it from the beginning of the year to its end" (v. 12).

As this year draws to a close, we may fear the future because of events in the past. But we need not remain chained to our old memories, because we can move ahead focused on God. Just as the Lord watched over the land and His people, so His eyes will be upon us.

God's faithful care will extend to every day of the new year. We can count on that promise.

David McCasland

God Promises
Care for Your Year Ahead

NOTHING TO FEAR NEXT YEAR
LAMENTATIONS 3:22–27

*The LORD is good to those whose hope is
in him, to the one who seeks him.*

Lamentations 3:25

God knows it all—every trial, every hardship, every crisis lurking in the new year. Nothing will take Him by surprise. No coup, no pandemic, no threat to world peace will upset His plans for this fragile, strife-ridden planet. His timetable is right on schedule, and He holds the reins of sovereign rule firmly in His mighty hands. How comforting this is as we enter a fresh set of fifty-two weeks!

But there's something else that's reassuring. God has many blessings in store for His creatures. He will make the sun to shine and the rain to fall on both the just and the unjust (Matthew 5:45), even prospering the wicked so that God's goodness may lead them to repentance (Romans 2:4).

One morning I was reminded of this by the sun edging over the eastern horizon. How often since the beginning of time has that occurred? I wondered. Every morning that rising sun reminds us of God's faithfulness. And for the believer specifically? Well, everything—yes, everything—will be stamped with the trademark of His infinite goodness and grace. The writer of Lamentations put it like this: "His compassions never fail. They are new every morning; great is your faithfulness" (3:22–23).

As the new year begins, select one of God's promises in this book as your promise for the year ahead. Memorize it. Repeat it often each day. Trust it. By midyear, if Christ does not return (that would be one of the greatest promise fulfillments), you'll be convinced that we really have nothing to fear this year.

Dennis DeHaan

Our Daily Bread Writers

JAMES BANKS

Pastor of Peace Church in Durham, North Carolina, Dr. James Banks has written several books for Our Daily Bread Publishing, including *Praying Together* and *Prayers for Prodigals*. He and his son Geoffrey wrote *Hope Lies Ahead* about escaping drug addiction. James and his wife, Cari, have two adult children.

HENRY BOSCH (1914–1995)

Henry G. Bosch was the founder of the *Our Daily Bread* devotional and one of its first writers. He was the managing editor of the devotional from 1956 until 1981. Throughout his life, he battled illness but turned his weaknesses into spiritual encouragement for others through his devotional writing.

DAVE BRANON

Former senior editor with Our Daily Bread Publications, Dave has been involved with the booklet *Our Daily Bread* since the 1980s. He has written twenty books, including *Beyond the Valley* and *The Lands of the Bible Today*, both Our Daily Bread Publishing products.

ANNE CETAS

After becoming a Christian in her late teens, Anne was introduced to *Our Daily Bread* right away and began reading it. For many years, she was senior content editor of *Our Daily Bread*.

POH FANG CHIA

Like Anne Cetas, Poh Fang trusted Jesus Christ as Savior as a teenager. She is an editor and a part of the Chinese editorial review committee serving in the Our Daily Bread Ministries Singapore office.

WINN COLLIER

A pastor for twenty-five years, Winn has written a number of books including *Restless Faith*, *Let God*, and *Holy Curiosity*. He and his wife, Miska, have two sons.

BILL CROWDER

A former pastor who is now vice president of ministry content for Our Daily Bread Ministries, Bill has traveled extensively as a Bible conference teacher, sharing God's truths with fellow believers in Malaysia and Singapore and other places where Our Daily Bread Ministries has international offices. His published books include *Windows on Easter*, *God of Surprise*, and *A Deep Dependence*.

LAWRENCE DARMANI

A noted novelist and publisher in Ghana, Lawrence is editor of *Step* magazine and CEO of Step Publishers. He and his family live in Accra, Ghana. His book *Grief Child* earned him the Commonwealth Writers' Prize as best first book by a writer in Africa.

DENNIS DEHAAN (1932–2014)

When *Our Daily Bread*'s original editor Henry Bosch retired, Dennis became the second managing editor of the publication. A former pastor, he loved preaching and teaching the Word of God. Dennis went to be with the Lord in 2014.

MART DEHAAN

The former president of Our Daily Bread Ministries, Mart followed in the footsteps of his grandfather M. R. and his dad Richard in that capacity. Mart, who was associated with *Day of Discovery* as host of the program from Israel for many years, is now senior content advisor for *Our Daily Bread*. He can be heard daily on the radio program *Discover the Word* (discovertheword.org).

M. R. DEHAAN (1891–1965)

Dr. M. R. DeHaan founded this ministry in 1938 when his radio program went out over the air in Detroit, Michigan, and eventually Radio Bible Class was begun. He was president of the ministry in 1956 when *Our Daily Bread* was first published.

RICHARD DEHAAN (1923–2002)

Son of the founder of Our Daily Bread Ministries, Dr. M. R. DeHaan, Richard was responsible for the ministry's entrance into television. Under his leadership, *Day of Discovery* television made its debut in 1968. The program was on the air continuously until 2016.

XOCHITL DIXON

Xochitl (soh-chee) equips and encourages readers to embrace God's grace and grow deeper in their personal relationships with Christ and others. Serving as an author, speaker, and blogger at xedixon.com, she enjoys singing, reading, motherhood, and being married to her best friend, Dr. W. Alan Dixon Sr., a college professor. She has authored *Waiting for God* and her first children's picture book, *Different Like Me*.

DAVID EGNER

A retired Our Daily Bread Ministries editor and longtime *Our Daily Bread* writer, David was also a college professor during his working career. In fact, he was a writing instructor for both Anne Cetas and Julie Ackerman Link at Cornerstone University in Grand Rapids.

DENNIS FISHER

For several years, Dennis was senior research editor at Our Daily Bread Ministries—using his theological training to guarantee biblical accuracy. He is also an expert in C. S. Lewis studies. He and his wife, Jan, a former university professor, have retired to Northern California.

VERNON GROUNDS (1914–2010)

A longtime college president (Denver Seminary) and board member for Our Daily Bread Ministries, Vernon's life story was told in the Our Daily Bread Publishing book *Transformed by Love*. Dr. Grounds died in 2010 at the age of 96.

TIM GUSTAFSON

Tim writes and edits for *Our Daily Bread* and serves as an editor for *Discovery Series*. As the son of missionaries to Ghana, Tim has an unusual perspective on life in the West. He and his wife, Leisa, have one daughter and seven sons.

C. P. HIA

Hia Chek Phang and his wife, Lin Choo, reside in the island nation of Singapore. C. P. came to faith in Jesus Christ at the age of thirteen. During his early years as a believer, he was privileged to learn from excellent Bible teachers who instilled in him a love for God's Word. He is Special Assistant to the President of Our Daily Bread Ministries, and he helps with translating resources for the ministry. He and his wife have a son, daughter-in-law, grandson, and granddaughter.

KIRSTEN HOLMBERG

Kirsten Holmberg surrendered her life to Jesus at age twenty-two. Kirsten married Mike in 1995 in Boulder, Colorado. They have three children and live near Boise, Idaho. Her first *Our Daily Bread* articles appeared in early 2017. When she has the time, she enjoys reading, running, and photography.

ADAM HOLZ

Adam lives in Colorado, where he is the director of Focus on the Family's media review website, *Plugged In*. He has written a Bible study for NavPress called *Beating Busyness*. Adam and his wife, Jennifer, have three children.

ARTHUR JACKSON

After serving as a pastor in Chicago for twenty-eight years, Arthur and his wife, Shirley, returned to his hometown of Kansas City, Kansas. He is Midwest region urban director of PastorServe, an organization that helps provide for the needs of pastors.

CINDY HESS KASPER

A former editor for the Our Daily Bread Ministries publication *Our Daily Journey*, Cindy began writing for *Our Daily Bread* in 2006. She and her husband, Tom, have three children and seven grandchildren.

ALYSON KIEDA

Alyson has been an editor for Our Daily Bread Ministries for over a decade—and has over thirty-five years of editing experience. Alyson has loved writing since she was a child and is thrilled to be writing for *Our Daily Bread*. She is married with three adult children and a growing number of grandchildren.

RANDY KILGORE

Randy spent most of his twenty-plus years in business as a senior human resource manager before returning to seminary. Since finishing his masters of divinity, he has served as a writer and workplace chaplain. A collection of those devotionals appears in the Our Daily Bread Publishing book, *Made to Matter: Devotions for Working Christians*. Randy and his wife, Cheryl, and their two children live in Massachusetts.

LESLIE KOH

Born and raised in Singapore, Leslie spent more than fifteen years as a journalist in the busy newsroom of local newspaper *The Straits Times* before moving to Our Daily Bread Ministries. He's found moving from bad news to good news most rewarding, and he still believes that nothing reaches out to people better than a good, compelling story. He likes traveling, running, editing, and writing.

MONICA LA ROSE

Monica and her husband, Ben, were married in 2019, and they live in St. Charles, Illinois. Monica earned a masters degree from Calvin Seminary before beginning her career as an editor at Our Daily Bread Ministries.

ALBERT LEE

Albert Lee was director of international ministries for Our Daily Bread Ministries for many years, and he lives in Singapore. Albert's passion, vision, and energy expanded the work of the ministry around the world. Albert grew up in Singapore, and served with Singapore Youth for Christ from 1971 to 1999. He and his wife, Catherine, have two children.

JULIE ACKERMAN LINK (1950–2015)

A book editor by profession during her working career, Julie began writing for *Our Daily Bread* in 2000. Her books *Above All, Love*, *A Heart for God*, and *Hope for All Seasons* are available through Our Daily Bread Publishing. Julie lost her long battle with cancer in April 2015.

DAVID MCCASLAND
Living in Colorado, David enjoys the beauty of God's grandeur as displayed in the Rocky Mountains. An accomplished biographer, David has written several books, including the award-winning *Oswald Chambers: Abandoned to God* and *Eric Liddell: Pure Gold*.

ELISA MORGAN
Perhaps best known for her long tenure as CEO of MOPS International, Elisa lives in Colorado with her husband, Evan. Currently, she cohosts the Our Daily Bread Ministries podcast *God Hears Her*. She and Evan have two grown children and two grandchildren. She has written several books, including *When We Pray Like Jesus* and *You Are Not Alone*.

KEILA OCHOA
Keila, who teaches in an international school, also assists with Media Associates International, a group that trains writers around the world to write about faith. She and her husband have two young children.

REMI OYEDELE
Remi's formative years were spent in England and in Kenya. She now lives in Florida with her husband David. Her passion is writing children's literature, and she has a master's degree in writing for children. You can read her blog at wordzpread.com.

AMY BOUCHER PYE
Amy is a writer, editor, and speaker. The author of *Finding Myself in Britain: Our Search for Faith, Home, and True Identity*, she runs the Woman Alive book club in the UK and enjoys life with her family in their English vicarage.

PATRICIA RAYBON
A noted author and journalist, Patricia lives in Colorado with her husband, Dan. Among her books are *I Told the Mountain to Move* and *God's Great Blessings*. You can find out more about Patricia at patriciaraybon.com.

HADDON ROBINSON (1931–2017)

Haddon, a renowned expert on preaching, served many years as a seminary professor. He wrote numerous books and hundreds of magazine articles. For a number of years he was a panelist on Our Daily Bread Ministries' radio program *Discover the Word*. Dr. Robinson went home to his eternal reward in 2017.

DAVID ROPER

David Roper lives in Idaho, where he takes advantage of the natural beauty of his state. He wrote for *Our Daily Bread* for almost twenty years, and he has published several successful books with Our Daily Bread Publishing, including *Out of the Ordinary* and *Teach Us to Number Our Days*.

LISA SAMRA

Equipped with a master of biblical studies degree from Dallas Theological Seminary, Lisa uses her passion for God's Word to facilitate mentoring relationships with women and to develop groups focused on spiritual formation and leadership development. Her husband, Jim, is a pastor in Grand Rapids (at the church founded by the founder of Our Daily Bread Ministries, Dr. M. R. DeHaan), and the couple has four children.

JENNIFER BENSON SCHULDT

Chicagoan Jennifer Schuldt writes from the perspective of a mom of a growing family. She has written for *Our Daily Bread* since 2010, and she also pens articles for another Our Daily Bread Ministries publication: *Our Daily Journey*.

JULIE SCHWAB

Julie is a former assistant editor for the devotional booklet *Our Daily Bread*. She received her master's degree in theological studies from Liberty University. Julie is also an adjunct professor at Cornerstone University.

JOE STOWELL

A popular speaker, former president of Cornerstone University, and a former pastor, Joe has written a number of books over the years, including *Strength for the Journey* and *Jesus Nation*.

HERB VANDER LUGT (1920–2006)

For many years, Herb was senior research editor at Our Daily Bread Ministries, responsible for checking the biblical accuracy of the literature published by the ministry. A World War II veteran, Herb spent several years as a pastor before his tenure with the ministry began. Herb went to be with his Lord and Savior in 2006.

PAUL VAN GORDER (1921–2009)

A writer for *Our Daily Bread* in the 1980s and 1990s, Paul was a noted pastor and Bible teacher—both in the Atlanta area where he lived and through the *Day of Discovery* TV program. Paul's earthly journey ended in 2009.

SHERIDAN VOYSEY

Sheridan is a writer, speaker, and broadcaster based in Oxford, United Kingdom. He is the author of seven books, including Our Daily Bread Publishing titles *Resilient: Your Invitation to a Jesus-Shaped Life* and the award-winning *Unseen Footprints*. You can read his blogs at sheridanvoysey.com.

LINDA WASHINGTON

Equipped with a master's of fine arts from Vermont College of Fine Arts, Linda uses her gift of writing to help people of all ages. She has written for preteens (*God and Me*) and for adults (*The Soul of C. S. Lewis*).

MARVIN WILLIAMS

Marvin's first foray into Our Daily Bread Ministries came as a writer for *Our Daily Journey*. In 2007, he penned his first *Our Daily Bread* article. Marvin is senior teaching pastor at a church in Lansing, Michigan. His Our Daily Bread Publishing devotional compilation book is called *Radical Generosity*.

JOANIE YODER (1934–2004)

For ten years, until her death in 2004, Joanie wrote for *Our Daily Bread*. In addition, she published the book *God Alone* with Our Daily Bread Publishing.